BILL LECKIE

macdonald media publishing

First published in November 2008 by **macdonald** media publishing,
22 Roxburgh Road, Paisley, PA2 0UG.

ISBN 978-0-9553126-2-5
ISBN 0-9553126-2-0

A CIP catalogue record for this book is available from the British
Library.

Photographs courtesy of the Paisley Daily Express, Daily Record and
Norman Macdonald

Design: Cameron Heggie
Sub-editing: David Macdonald

Printed and bound by Bell and Bain Ltd, Glasgow.

For Kenny and Georgia,
my own two Saints.

Stuff That's In This Book..

If What Follows Is A History Of Love Street, Sarah Palin Will Make A Right Good President

FIRST of all, an apology.

This book kind of follows up one called Penthouse & Pavement, which escaped nine years ago. In it, I had at a go at non-football lovers who whine that we make too much fuss about what's really just a bunch of men running around kicking a bag of air.

The line went:

"To say that's like saying when Paul McCartney wrote Yesterday it was just some guy hitting a bit of wood with string on it."

I'm very, very sorry about that. There is no defence.

Because Yesterday is a duff song, so very duff that Homer Simpson could tug back its ring-pull and chug it while he watched telly with his spare hand down his breeks.

Here is a melody and a scribble of lyrics so simplistic they could have been written by a committee of attention-deficit six-year-olds. Moon, June, Spoon to the power n.

Paperback Writer? Norwegian Wood? Within You Without You? Yep, they'd have worked. All wonderful tunes with words that matter. All fitting legacies of the Fab Four's decade of musical omnipotence.

But no, I had to pick the Primary Two class project runner-up.

Still, it's perhaps a decent metaphor for much of the stuff that was in that book and which has run, with frightening predictability, through the three I've written since and all the way into this one.

The message being that there's a point at which you become so big that quality ceases to matter. Just as long as you produce it, people will say it's great.

When tight studio bands become pompous stadium rockers. When Friends got past about Series 6. When people with political consciences are elected as MPs.

And very much like the Premiership.

Back then, I was writing about Monday night games that were all howling wind and Marcus Gayle - and nine years on, the only difference is that the hype that accompanies the mediocrity is even wilder.

This summer, Hull City and Stoke City have been promoted to the self-styled Greatest League In The World. At some point they will have to play each other.

Now, ask yourself. And be honest here. Would you drag yourself away from stripping the paint off your granny's fireplace with a toothpick to watch this game live on the telly?

The answer?

Of course you bloody well would.

Because the growly voiceover and the graphics team's lightning cuts - from goal celly to a close-up of Dean Windass's cheeky wink to a lone fan weeping in the stands - will convince you that this WILL be the greatest 90 minutes of all time.

You'll plan your Monday night around it and you will get in the wife's bad books for dodging bathing the weans or doing the dishes so you can be settled down in front of it with a beer and a sandwich.

And you will be disappointed. Not so much in the game, but in yourself.

For buying into the marketing bollocks. Worse, for never buying out of it again, for sitting through the entire 1-1-thanks-to-scruffy-goals-either side-of-half-time, both-scored-when-you-were-first-putting-the-kettle-on-and-then-having-a-slash guffathon that it will inevitably be.

All because you'd allowed yourself to be convinced that we were forever one second away from seeing the most wonderful goal there ever was.

It's the same with the next Grand Slam Sunday or Huge Enormously Important Tuesday or whatever other tagline they come up with to describe the big Fulham-West Ham/Man City-Middlesbrough double-header.

You'll talk about it for a week, see the trailers more often than you'll see your family. Cancel all appointments, take the phone off the hook, get the mates round, the carry-out in and the wife and saucepans out.

All the while knowing somewhere deep inside that it will be yet

8

another footballing equivalent of the new Madonna album. Promoted to within and inch of its life, but as easily forgotten as ... well, the last Madonna album, I suppose.

Sexy-librarian-stylee Republican hunter-gatherer-cum-Presidential-running-mate (as in, you'd love to take a run and mate with her) Sarah Palin arrived on the big political stage describing herself as a pitbull in lipstick. Democratic candidate Barack Obama, the sharp-cheekboned Tiger Woods figure with potential access to the nuclear codes, immediately came back and said that you can put lipstick on a pig, but it's still a pig.

Though you might throw the lipstick away afterwards.

How does this relate to what we were talking about before? Who knows. I was just sitting here writing when an image of Sarah Palin in a half-unbuttoned blouse and pencil skirt, standing on a little stepladder to put some books back on the top shelf, popped into my head and next thing it was down on paper.

By the time you read this, the same auto-suggestion might well have led tens of millions of Americans to vote her and The World's Oldest Man into the White House.

In which case, may God have mercy on all assholes.

If you sensed a pause in the writing there, it was probably due more to me desperately thinking of a way to link the lipstick-on-a-pig analogy to big-time football than to seeing Sarah Palin bending down in front of me to pick up a copy of the Kama Sutra and her cleavage nearly having someone's eye out.

But the fact is, the analogy doesn't work anyway; because to use it would suggest that football is ugly, which is plainly a million miles from the case. At its finest, it's an art form, a thing of utter, stupendous, spontaneous beauty, like lying in a freshly-mown field with the one you love, having just been caught in a refreshing summer shower and looking up to see a rainbow.

At its worst? It can make you crave that appointment for root canal treatment from a dentist with halitosis who listens to a non-stop loop of Gloria Gaynor singing I Will Sodding Survive.

Here's the thing, though. It's impossible to tell when you're going to get Beauty and when The Beast will raise its Steve Bruce-like head.

That's the fatal flaw in TV's marketing of live games.

If you go to the movies, chances are you've watched a trailer and liked what you saw. If you buy a new album, you've most likely heard a track or two on radio or the web.

You can road-test cars, get 90-day approval on memory-foam

mattresses, even ask the people in Debenhams to take a shirt out of the packet so you can see it in its cotton flesh and not get shouted at.

But football? There are no sneak previews, no tasters leaked to the media.

You turn up and take what you get.

Which means Real Madrid v Barca might ming like Ming The Merciless after a three-week fishing trip. While Albion Rovers v East Stirling might end up 5-4, as indeed it did deep in the winter of 2007.

No money on earth, no amount of marketing genius, no pressure from telly executives or boardroom-stomping sheikhs can guarantee that a football match will be worth watching. That is, at once, the gift and the curse of our magnificent obsession.

For instance. There was a review of Penthouse & Pavement in the magazine When Saturday Comes that reckoned the book didn't know whether it was - and I'm paraphrasing here - a nostalgic romp, a rant against authority or a homage to the team I love.

It was meant as a criticism. I took it as the biggest compliment of all time.

Because anyone who doesn't realise that's exactly how every single 90 minutes of football is...well, they've never had a proper day at the match.

They say that if you don't like the weather in Scotland you should hang around, because it'll change in a minute.

So it is with this game of ours.

NO MATTER who you support - but particularly if it's a club whose existence is based on hope rather than expectation - you'll have been through exactly the scenario I now describe.

It's March 18, 2008. St Mirren at home to St Johnstone in a Scottish Cup quarter-final replay. It may well turn out to be the last-ever knockout tie we play at Love Street before moving to our new stadium come January.

We've drawn 1-1 at Perth in the first game, a great result on a ground where our record's worse than ... well, the 12" Gregorian chant remix of Yesterday by Timmy Mallet and The Wu Tang Clan.

It feels like we've done the hard work. Especially as, after not being able to buy a goal for the first half of the season, we're suddenly on a hot streak.

That is to say, we've drawn two on the bounce.

The only team already through to the semis are Queen of the South,

No, not even all those new concrete boxes masquerading as football stadiums that have sprung up like so many giant lock-up garages.

This, after all, is why this book has come to pass; my beloved St Mirren are moving to raise the money that will pay off our debts and let us start again.

At first glance, our new home looks just like Airdrie's or Scunthorpe's or Wycombe's; four concrete stands with only a street sign and a club crest to distinguish one collection from another.

And to be honest, any number of further glances won't open your eyes to many subtle architectural nuances that set this new construction apart from any other thrown up in the late 20th or early 21st centuries.

Functional? Yes.

Gorgeous? No.

Individual in its design? Definitely not.

Love Street was unique, just as Meadowbank Stadium was unique before Livingston flitted to West Lothian and Airdrie's hostile home at Broomfield was before the bulldozers moved in and caused several millions pounds worth of improvements.

We have a main stand that doesn't go as far as the corner flag at each end, because to extend that way would have meant making it deeper and that would have meant buying up the houses behind the wall on Albion Street and despite talking about it for decades, the club never managed to do it.

Hey, and why should they have? Why should families have been chucked out of their homes just so St Mirren could have an extra couple of thousand seats they couldn't fill once a fortnight?

When I was a kid, we had big old curved, open terraces at each end and the covered shed of the North Bank opposite the tunnel. At the turn of the 80s, the Love Street end was brought in tight behind the goals and in the mid-90s the Caledonia End came down and an impossibly-steep away stand went up.

As the Millennium loomed, they seated the North Bank. Then, in one of those bizarre episodes that characterise the utter stupidity of the people who somehow get to run football, the last of the terraces went.

In 1999-2000, we won the First Division, a triumph described further on. That meant we earned the privilege of playing in the Scottish Premier League, henceforth within these pages to be referred to as the EssPeeEll.

Only one condition. We had to have 10,000 seats.

Didn't matter that we hadn't had a 10,000 gate in donkey's years. Didn't matter that crowds were falling right across the land. Didn't matter that it would cost every last bean we had and then some.

It had to be done. Or we weren't allowed up.

And not only wouldn't we be allowed up, the gits wouldn't even let whoever finished second go up in our place.

So, we did it. Begged and borrowed and put in an outsized Disabled Section so we got maximum grant aid - and got the Paisley Daily Express Stand open in time for it to lie all but deserted throughout the top-flight season that would see us land back where we'd come from once more.

Economic thinking like that makes the guys in charge of Northern Rock look like geniuses.

Still, even idiots can learn from their mistakes.

Can't they?

Not in the case of the EssPeeEll they can't.

In 2006, we won the First Division again. By then, the league had done away with the 10,000 rule. Cheers for that, really made our bank manager feel better.

But they couldn't just let it be, could they? Couldn't just say to the team who'd earned the right to come up: "Well done, welcome in and fun."

No, they had to set some other barbed wire hoop on fire and make us jump through it nudey.

So down came the decision.

We had to put in undersoil heating.

Didn't matter that we were moving from Love Street within a couple of years. Didn't matter that the money we lost from one or two postponed games in the course of a season would be dwarfed by the amount it took to just dig up the turf and put down the electric blanket.

Didn't even bother them that we'd lose a fortune because we wouldn't be able to rip the sodding system up and take it with us.

Rules were rules, no matter how senseless.

Anyway, rant over. The point I set out to make was that our ground is like no other; it looks like no other, feels like no other. Its four stands are a mis-match like no other - and with the best will in the world, this cannot be said of its replacement.

However, that's before fans start clicking through the shiny new turnstiles.

Because that's when any football ground develops its personality. Because football supporters are like fingerprints or snowflakes; all alike to the naked eye, but the microscope tells a different story.

Our supporters are different from your supporters; we may all love the same game and share the same hopes and dreams, but we wear different colours and even if we don't, we have a different design on our badge; an animal instead of a tree, a castle instead of a bridge.

We chant the same tunes, but to our own bastardised words - you know, like Who's The Bastardised In The Black. Those who follow successful clubs will see a 0-0 draw a whole other way from the devotee of a perennial relegation struggler.

So, Mr Reviewer. That, in short, is what this book is about. How the individual fan copes with his or her unique view of football being skewed by the passage of time and the onset of progress.

It was a book that was meant to be delivered to my publisher and one-time Paisley Daily Express news editor, Norman Macdonald, by the start of September. In the end, I got it to him halfway through October, which made him grumpy but left me delighted - because it meant it includes stuff about us winning the last home league meeting with Rangers.

Unless we're very lucky in the few weeks between going to print and moving home, that's likely to be our last great day in the old place. Worth missing a deadline for in anybody's language.

All in all, this isn't a history of Love Street. If it was, I'd give the stadium its Sunday name, but the truth is I've never called it St Mirren Park in my puff.

Neither is it a forensically-researched memoir of great games from down the years; all that stuff's in the Rothman's or on the web if you want to find it.

No, this is about how one piece of land on the edge of a scruffy town centre means to me and to others I have come to know by making it my second home.

In fact, more than that. It's about any football ground that's ever been taken away. It's about anybody being robbed of their childhood.

I owe Love Street. Because had my footballing education not been dished out there, I might not have being doing the job that brings me so much joy.

And even if I was, my attitude to it might be so very different.

This is my chance to say 'Thank You'.

Saying goodbye's a whole lot harder.

Welcome To The FeegieDome

From the Scottish Sun, Friday November 29 2002.

FIRST it's the house you were born in. Then it's your primary school.

And eventually, they decide you're not getting to keep ANY of your childhood.

Because now, Love Street is coming down.

We're selling the family silver to pay the debts and start again. Pretty soon there'll be no North Bank, no Caledonia Stand, no Cairter's Corner. No little patch in the east goalmouth where my Uncle Danny's ashes were scattered.

We can't even hope for some grey-man planning official to knacker the deal, either, because then I'd have no home, no school, no ground AND - pretty soon - no team.

It's a done deal.

So, one day soon, St Mirren Football Club will flit to what was once the roughest, toughest, baddest housing scheme in Europe.

Welcome to the FeegieDome.

Like every fan of Airdrie, St Johnstone, Clydebank, Dumbarton, Meadowbank, Stirling Albion and East Fife, I'd put my fingers in my ears and gone la-la-la-la-la in the hope that the rumours would go away.

Guess what?

They didn't.

So there I was on Sunday at our 125th anniversary dinner and vice-chairman George Campbell's on my left at the top table confirming it IS happening and turning to HIS left to Provost John McDowall asking for all the help we can get.

What could I do but fill an envelope with all the scrap paper I could find, stand up and pass it to the town's political leader in front of 500 witnesses as a sort of ceremonial bung?

Well, if you didn't laugh you'd cry.

Love Street. Every time I see it a shiver goes up my spine. So much of my life has been organised round going there. It's a link between my grandpa and my dad and my big brother and me and my boy and I always hoped he'd take his kid there too.

Instead, my grandchild - he said presumptuously - will grow up walking down past the Sheriff Court, past the Fountain Gardens, past the chippie and see a Tesco loom beyond the tenements.

At firstAn in-store bakery where Hughie Gilshan scored the winner against Rangers in the fog in '68. Yoghurt where Gus McLeod got his fifth in the 7-1 humping of Hamilton in '73. Women's magazine where old Toshie the binman stood slaughtering opponents and linesmen for decades.

Is it just me or is that incredibly sad? Not just from a St Mirren diehard's point of view, but from where ANY lover of the game stands? That football's reached the point where the price of survival is bulldozing our heritage?

That's not a dig at our board. They've tried everything to get us back in the black and it's just not happening. Who knows, maybe this last option might be the dawn of something great.

It just doesn't feel like it right now.

On the morning of my dad's funeral, the tenement where I was born was the last building left standing amidst the demolition of Manor Road, Foxbar.

When we came back, it'd been reduced to rubble.

Spooky.

A couple of years later I came back from living in London to find that Amochrie Primary School, where at eight years old I discovered the headmaster Sam McDougall was a part-time football reporter and immediately got the bug for this job, was gone. Houses were rising in its place.

Hey, nothing lasts forever. You'd just hope the things that mattered would last a little longer than they seem to these days. The house where I was born stood for 41 years, Amochrie Primary less than 30.

You might say that by this yardstick, Love Street's 108-year existence is an eternity. But that's like Trigger saying he's used the same broom since 1972 because it's only had 11 new handles and 14 new heads.

The big, curved Love Street terrace was only replaced by one tight to

17

the goals in 1979. The North Bank was seated a decade ago. The nosebleed-steep Caledonia Stand wasn't there six years ago.

Saddest of all is that the Love Street End was only standified in 2000, that we were forced to cough up so we'd have 10,000 seats and they'd let us into the bloody EssPeeEll where we'd have not a bean left to strengthen the team and we'd come right back down again.

And you know what? That 10,000 capacity was never ONCE tested, not even when the Bigot Brothers invaded. So what was the point of rooking an ambitious club, except to further fuel the ego of Lirrel Roger Mitchell, Lex Gold and all the other numpties who've played at running an elite league?

The waste of all that rebuilding seems obscene, yet our story is far from unique. The Dundee clubs have spent years calling for public money to build a shared stadium even though they've put up FIVE new stands between them in recent times.

How much debt did that create? When was Dens or Tannadice last sold out - and when the hell will a 30,000 capacity be tested if they ever get it?

Kilbowie went from a junior ground in 1965 to Britain's first all-seater senior ground 12 years later. Now it's rubble. Man City are moving out of Maine Road only a few years after building a goliath of a stand.

Football simply can't afford to throw that much cash down the pan, yet we keep doing it. My club hocked itself to the hilt to chase a rainbow and ended up with no money to pay players.

So it's next stop Ferguslie Park.

Still, once we get there at least there's no chance of visiting supporters' buses being stolen.

Not once they're up on bricks...

AND now, as I write this, it's early October in 2008.

For Hughie Gilshan, read Stephen McGinn, who's just scored a wonderful winner against Rangers.

For primary school read secondary, because Camphill High's also been bulldozed and rebuilt where its football pitches used to be.

And for Tesco, read rather cunning chaps. Who bought Love Street on the premise that they'd build a supermarket on it, but who've just announced they're now selling it on again for housing, which pretty much makes it look they only wanted our home so no other supermarket chain could.

The world's giving me a headache.

The clock's giving me a heartache.

St Mirren have just six games left at Love Street, seven if we're drawn at home in the Scottish Cup.

It feels very real now. Very real and very strange.

The other day I spoke to my mate and colleague Gordy Waddell for help with another chapter. He's a Falkirk diehard, so he's been through all this. It's five and a bit years now since their beloved Brockville bit the dust and he and many more like him miss it like they miss one of the family.

In the middle of what was meant to be an interview but which turned into a counselling session, Gordy came out with something that really made me judder.

"I always assumed that when my dad died, we'd scatter his ashes on the Brockville turf," he said. "And to be honest, I'd hoped the family would do the same with mine."

Wow. There's one to pull you up a bit lively.

It wasn't: "Hey, wouldn't it be cool if we scattered dad in the penalty box?"

In his mind, it was a done deal. He'd never given a second thought to his club's home not being there any more. But today, there's a Morrisons superstore where Brockville used to stand.

To some, it might be the greatest retail outlet ever built. They may treasure their loyalty card more than they treasure their own health.

They may live to get up and drive there, to swish into the favourite car parking space, to hunt for the trolley whose handle they've marked with their initials. They may know the staff by name, send them Christmas cards and take them in cakes on birthdays and public holidays.

But when they die, they're unlikely to have made a stipulation in their will that their ashes be thrown all over the deli counter. And even if they did, Morrisons would be unlikely to market Old Bloke's Remains as an exclusive new seasoning.

Plus, if one day Morrisons lets them down, if they find to their horror that there's none of the Hartley's Jam or the Heinz Baby Food they swear by or if a checkout girl's rude to them, they'll just harumph and go somewhere else; some other corporate cave, with all the same stuff under different-coloured Three-For-Two signs.

They'll become Tesco people, with a Tesco Clubcard. Or be tapping their back pockets and winking cheekily at their love of Asda prices. Or going to Lidl, which has a surprisingly good selection of cold meats considering its otherwise sticky-carpet-ish reputation.

Pretty soon, they'll forget Morrisons ever existed. Because that's consumerism.

When you support a club like St Mirren and worship them at a place like Love Street, though, consumerism has nothing to do with it.

If it was, you'd go up the road to Ibrox or Parkhead. Or stay at home and be an armchair Man U fan.

You'd look at our current situation and shrug that it was progress, that we should be delighted at the chance to sell up, pay up our debts and move to somewhere brand new.

Come to think of it, put it that way and it doesn't seem that bad an option.

Until you give yourself a shake and realise it's like swapping your mother for one who's a better cook.

At our level, this level where hope is everything and expectation for other people, the idea of willingly giving up your home is simply unthinkable.

That's what makes football unique.

We buy a telly or a car or a computer and before we're out the shop we see the one we should have got instead. We just get our houses lived-in and cosy just in time to decide it's time to move on.

We say our marriage vows knowing that the odds of keeping them are longer than of the Buds ever winning the Champions League.

Yet in this ultra-disposable world, few ever aspire to getting rid of their favourite football ground and playing somewhere else.

It's the one thing we're happy to see grow old and dog-eared. The one thing we don't need to be better than what our neighbours have - in fact, ask a Falkirk fan or an Airdrie fan and they'll tell you they LOVED the look on the faces of visiting players and fans when they were forced to go there.

One of my favourite days in putting this book together was one spent wandering round Love Street with our groundsman, Tommy Docherty. As you'll read later - presuming you stick with it that long - you'll find that where he saw problems, I saw character.

That's because it's the most aptly-named stadium in football.

Because thousands of us love it and always will.

SO, who's champing at the bit for the big flit?

No one, it seems.

Not our chairman, Stewart Gilmour, nor his joined-at-the-hip sidekick George Campbell. Not their fellow directors. Not manager

Gus MacPherson or his coaching staff. Not the players. Certainly not the fans.

It's just that no one could see another way to get out of the mess we'd found ourselves in.

Here, in October 2008, the world is in economic turmoil. Banks are closing by the day, share prices are plunging. Global recession looms like a gigantic loomy thing.

Millions - clueless punters and financial wizards alike - are paying the price for overspending in the 22 years since financial markets were deregulated and borrowing went from a last resort to a leisure activity.

Looks like St Mirren were simply ahead of their time.

Because for us, the credit crunch came years ago, round about when the Clydesdale Bank said they wanted a £700,000 overdraft repaid - and that if it wasn't, they wanted the stadium sold to settle the debt.

This was where a decade and a half of writing cheques our status couldn't cash had brought us.

In the 80s, we'd done what Thatcher told us to. We got ideas above our station, spent money we didn't have and decided to worry about it later.

Come the mid-90s, we were covering our ears and going la-la-la-la about what a mess we were in.

Then, finally - thankfully - we got a board who took the horrible decisions that needed to be made.

The price we had to pay for them keeping us alive was to have sacred ground whipped away from under our feet.

IN 1980, we'd finished third in the Premier League and marched into Europe for the first time. We were back again in '83, in '85 and then again after winning the Scottish Cup in '87.

The foundations of the most successful decade in our history had been laid by Alex Ferguson, working on a shoestring to mould kids and frees into a team who stormed to the Premier League on crowds that soared 2000 per cent in his four years at the helm between '74 and '78.

Trouble was, we then stopped building. And started buying. Not that we as supporters saw it as trouble at the time; far from it, we loved it.

St Mirren? Selling homegrown kids for £300,000? Buying replacements for £180,000?

Unheard of, yet that's what we got from Liverpool for Frank

McGarvey and that's what we spent on Frank McDougall from Clydebank.

Over the next ten years, we'd do pretty well out of flogging talent.

Tony Fitzpatrick to Bristol City for £200,000. McDougall, Peter Weir, Ian Cameron and Billy Stark to Aberdeen for a combined £1million. Stevie Clarke to Chelsea for £400,000. All building up to a mammoth £800,000 from Rangers for Ian Ferguson, extra-time hero of our Scottish Cup triumph.

Looking back, those fees and plenty other smaller ones should have set us up for decades to come. Replaced the old main stand, built us a training ground, set up as good a youth system as any in the land.

Somehow, though, we ended up neck-deep in debt.

Why?

Because, as chairman Gilmour says elsewhere in this book, we forgot who we were.

THE difference between us and a bank at this time of fiscal fiasco, of course, is simple.

When we hit our credit limit, the bank goes all poker-faced and calls time on their generosity.

But when bankers hit theirs, they put on the big puppy-dog eyes and sweet-talk Downing Street into giving them £500billion of taxpayers' money to make it all better.

Pity the PM of the day supports Raith Rovers and not us, eh? Or he might have managed to siphon off one-fifty-thousandth of that bale-out package to get us out of the mire.

Ten million, 15 tops. That would have done us. Change for the meter in comparison to what the gits in red braces were given.

And it's not as if they were given it out of some secret personal account Gordon Brown had put by for a rainy day. No, it was my money. Your money.

Did he ask us if we minded? Did he bollocks.

Would he have given a a fraction of that £500bn to the football industry if it had come pleading to be saved from meltdown?

I refer you to the previous answer.

It's an odd one. Like the financial sector, football has spent too long living beyond its means. Like finance, it has stuck two fingers up to the basic rules of balance sheets, of spending a penny less than you earn.

Yet when it all comes on top, the politicians stare at the wallpaper and whistle.

Do these politicians love to profess undying affection for their favourite bank? Do they swear that although they've become successful parliamentarians, they'd swap it all for one day behind the counter at the Halifax?

No. They all play the football fan card, all think it makes them more streetwise and electorate-friendly if they can reel off famous players from history.

It should be the law that anyone who stands as a parliamentary candidate has in an electrified Mastermind chair and answer an hour of quick-fire questions about their local team.

Each time they get one wrong, they get 20,000 volts shot through their nipples. If they pass on more than two, they're also barred from the election.

No argument, no appeal.

Sensible policies for a happier Britain.

Anyway, the point is, if these power-hungry buffoons had an ounce of braincell between them, it would seep through that there are way more Brownie points to be had in paying to keep football afloat than in giving banks a second chance.

"But we must keep the financial system afloat," they whinge. "Without it, the economy will collapse."

Yeah?

Well, we'd get over it. We'd just have to start stuffing what spare change we had under the bed instead of putting it in an account and being charged to take it back out of a hole in the wall.

If our football club went down the pan, though?

We'd cry. We'd curl in to a little ball and we'd bawl like babies. We'd set up shrines to the past, even if that past was filled with nothing but abject failure and bitter disappointment.

Because this is a game in which we choose to invest all we have with little chance of any return. This is a game that attaches itself to our very soul in a way no corporate nonsense ever could. Where a rickety old stadium with stinking toilets and lukewarm, over-priced tea-style liquid looks more spectacular to our sentimental eyes than the most incredible, soaring, glass-and-chrome tower.

I mean, did a bank ever get an open-topped parade through the town centre?

Did anyone ever name their kid after a bank manager they idolised?

Can you go to the bank and yell out all the stresses of the week in some kind of primal scream therapy, hurl your half-eaten pie at the teller and call her a blind b******d?

Do we taunt customers of other banks, shout at them to come and have a Gold Card if they think they're hard enough?

No, no, no and a fourth time no.

So, tell me again why the Prime Minister is willing to take a ginormous gamble by handing the last of the nation's saving to a shower of greedy, out-of-touch Yuppies that everyone hates, but would laugh in our faces if we asked that he help people we love with all our hearts?

Oh, it gets me angry, it really does. You might have noticed.

I mean, where are they when Jimmy's Plumbers go under because the bank won't extend his credit line any more? When another Tesco springs up and forces the half a dozen little shops across the road into the grubber?

And in the same way, where were they when Clydebank and Airdrie couldn't get their local councils - people elected to carry out the will of local people - to rubber-stamp new stadiums and save both from the slippery slope to extinction?

Oh look, something fascinating in the wallpaper pattern again...

AND now it's our turn.

Granted, it's also our fault, for all the reasons already stated.

But whose fault is it that Northern Rock went diddies-up? Or Bradford & Bungling? HBaws? That Icelandic mob who half our local authorities seemed to have all their cash tied up in?

No one but their own.

Yet look at the bale-out dosh rain down. A hurricane of help. A tsunami of sympathy.

An unprecedented shitload of wonga.

Now, look at us. Counting the pennies to make sure that the £15million from Tesco - roughly the collective annual bonuses of three top City of London traders - will cover the entire cost of the new ground, pay off what we owe the Clydesdale, settle our other debts and leave enough for a fish supper on the way home.

Feeling miserable about it as every coin passes through our fingers, too.

There's an accepted wisdom about football these days that it's all about money. It's said with such certainty by those who believe it that it's like listening to a Born-Again tell a Muslim that he must accept Jesus as his Lord and saviour.

But answer me this.

Can it possibly be coincidence that it's only since this accepted wisdom came into circulation that almost every club in the business either turned into a foreign-owned megamart or plummeted to the brink of the abyss?

I believe in self-fulfilling prophecies. If you tell someone often enough that they're a good person, they will behave like a good person; but keep dripping into their ear that they're bad and they'll reckon they might as well be bad.

In the same way, if you chant the mantra that It's All About Money for long enough, it'll become all about money, whether it needs to be or not.

And the thing is, not only is it the case that football needn't be about money, basic logic tells you that it can't POSSIBLY be.

Why? Because in the same breath as we're spun the money line, we then hear that it's a results-driven business.

See the teensy-weensy conflict there?

It's just not possible to predict the success and failure of a football club in a budget when in the end everything is dictated by the bounce of a ball. By a cruel deflection. By a referee's inexplicable decision. A missed sitter, a keeper's fumble, a sloppy passback.

This is our real currency; skill, frailty, human error and sheer luck.

If only Stewart Gilmour could have convinced the Clydesdale Bank of that a few years back, eh?

"So, Mr Gilmour - this £700,000 you owe us? Any thoughts?"
"Well, we prepared a 20-page business plan in which we explained our plan to repay every penny within 18 months through swingeing budget cuts, increased admission prices and a fresh issue of shares..."
"Excellent, so if you'd just let me see..."
"...but then we thought, what's the damn point when it could all be screwed by some idiot striker booting the ball over the bar from six yards in the last minute of a cup replay? So we shredded it and decided to base our future finances on the basis that shit happens."
"Yes, thank you. Now if could just leave the keys to the stadium at reception on your way out..."

SO here we are. Moving to the FeegieDome.

A stadium that will do much for the reputation of Ferguslie Park, once the most desirable working class area of Paisley, later to become our equivalent of Fort Apache.

For years, our local council threw thousands of pounds at trying help The Kidz - yoof clubs, trips to the seaside, even a £90,000 BOAT, for God's sake, if memory of a front page from my Paisley Daily Express days serves.

Like undercooked spaghetti hurled at a wall, very little stuck.

But now, years after most of the old scheme has been flattened and thousands scattered to the four winds, weighed down as much by notoriety as possessions, Feegie finally gets something that will change its image throughout the land. It gets St Mirren.

It could be the best thing that ever happened to the area.

What will it give our club in return?

If it's one-tenth of what the old place did, it'll be doing bloody well.

This Is Love Street

The inches we need are all around us.
Al Pacino, from Any Given Sunday.

TWO hours before the beginning of the end and never did that movie quote ring more true for Tommy Docherty.

The day before, he'd been lining the pitch when the pump in his machine packed up. It meant the whitewash was only three inches wide instead of the regulation four.

Tommy didn't sleep that night.

All he could think of was the referee arriving for the first home game of the last season at Love Street, taking one look and calling it off. Months of getting the stadium just right, weeks of pre-season training for the players, thousands heading through the turnstiles.

All of it knackered because a little strip of paint's 25 per cent too little.

It's just before half past one when David Somers and his assistants wander out of the tunnel for a walk on the turf. They check the goalmouth, the nets. Stroll from Caledonia Stand to Love Street end. Come back across to the blaes trackside to chat with chairman Stuart Gilmour and Kilmarnock boss Jim Jefferies.

Tommy watches, waits. Sweats.

But nothing happens. Luckily, St Mirren have landed a whistler more interested in what happens between the white lines than their measurements.

Even then, though, only once the first shrill blast sounded and the first ball was kicked and the crowd roared did Tommy relax.

When everyone else starts getting stuck into the action, his job is done.

For this is the life of a groundsman.

THREE days later and Tommy's red, ride-along mower sits just by the centre circle. The sun's shining over Love Street and the place looks magnificent.

Grass so green it could have been freshly painted. Stands empty and brooding, floodlights watching over it all like giant sentries.

To so many, this is the home of football.

To so many, the very idea of leaving it simply does not compute.

How did we get in such a financial mess? Why can't we find a way to pay the bills and keep our spiritual home? Where else could ever have what this place has?

If Tommy Docherty had grown up from a star-struck kid on the big, curved Caledonia Street terraces to be, say, a joiner or a bank clerk, he might well think that way too.

But he didn't.

He left school on a Friday, started work here on the Monday.

That was 25 years ago.

It's the only job he's ever known, maybe the only one he ever will. He's come to know Love Street the way lovers know each other's bodies, moods, body language. He could close his eyes and take you round it the way a sniper dismantles and assembles his weapon blindfold.

And he, more than anyone, knows that it's time.

The stadium he loves, that he has seen change bit by bit until only the boot room remains as it was a quarter of a century ago, that he cares for like he cares for his own child, has had its day.

When I walk through its gates, I see perfection.

Tommy Docherty sees the flaws. The rust. The cracks.

I wander through the North Bank where dad and I used to stand and my heart fills with nostalgia. Tommy's swells with frustration at the graffiti, the busted seats, leaking gutters and the pigeon crap.

If this was intensive care, the doctor would have a hand on his shoulder, gently asking for permission to turn off the life support.

Tommy would be nodding. Because it's time.

WE crunch down the track towards Cairter's Corner, the shallow, open slab of terrace between the main stand and the Love Street end where fearsome working blokes used to gather and yell and let off the team of a week's hard graft.

When I was a kid, looking directly across the pitch from where dad and I stood on the North Bank, that corner was the Wild West. It was where The Men went. Not that my dad wasn't a man; because for me, there was never a finer one.

But these were hard men; or so at least it appeared to me. Men who liked a bevvy and a swear and the non-stop hurling of abuse at quivering linesmen that would make Irvine Welsh tut-tut. God alone knows what they'd have made of lineswomen. They'd probably have chucked Hoovers.

Cairter's Corner's now long since disused, too awkward a shape to be seated as the ground was developed. It only ever gets a visit when we're live on telly and they build a little hide on stilts for the studio panel to peer out from.

As we stop and stare, it's a clear reminder of what the old place was like when Tommy first swapped his supporter's scarf for working boots. If he's anything like me, he'll be glad this little patch of Love Street has never been tarted up.

It stands as a memorial to past mentalness.

"This is my 25th season," he says. "I came here straight from school as a YTS, did a few months and didn't get offered a job. But six months or so later, someone left and the chairman Willie Todd asked me to come in full-time.

"He took me on a week-to-week basis. And no one's ever told me any different. Seriously. In fact, to this day I don't even have a room of my own at Love Street. There's a little cupboard at one end of the main stand that I keep my bike in along with a few other personal things, the one little bit of my life that I keep here.

"Back when I started there were three of us on the groundstaff, but it's just been me for as long as I can remember. I get some help from the youth players, but most of the time you're on your own.

"I'm here every day - not dawn till dusk, but nine till five Monday to Friday, nine till half six-ish on matchdays and then a few hours on a Sunday.

"The laugh is that people think a groundsman gets three months off when the season finishes, when it's actually your busiest time. That's when the pitch gets renewed, the stands need painted, a million little things have to be done.

"I try and get a week away for a summer holiday, but two weeks is unthinkable. If we have a spell during the season with no home games - an international break, maybe - I might get another few days away, but that's my lot.

"To be honest, it's a relief when the first game of the new season kicks off, because that's the worst of it over for me. In the run-up to the Kilmarnock game I had the chairman down on the pitch every day asking if we were going to be ready in time. Then you've got the manager telling you it doesn't look like the surface will be good enough.

"The last few hours before that first game are a nightmare, so many wee things to do. I was being interviewed by a film crew for a DVD that's being made about the stadium and out of the corner of my eye I saw an advertising board fall off at the front of the Caledonia Stand.

"I couldn't concentrate on what they were asking me - all I wanted to do was get the Black'n'Decker out and fix it before anyone noticed.

"All that and we had that problem over the lines. I doubt if anyone in the place noticed it. But I knew. And it nagged away at me until the game was underway.

"As the season goes on, though, Saturdays should be quiet. Fridays are when I get the lines done, the goals made up and put in the ground, when all the wee odd jobs get tidied up.

"There's always something, though. You never get a lazy day."

LOVE STREET was the classic football ground - a pavilion where the players change with a seated area built on top, semi-circular terraces behind each goal and the long side opposite the tunnel roofed to give some shelter from the elements.

It was this way from long before Tommy Docherty was born and stayed that way almost until the chance came for him to join the payroll. It's only in the final quarter of a century of its life that it has begun to evolve, constantly and noticeably.

As Tommy's got older, the race has been on to make the place look younger. But even Joan Collins knows that cosmetic surgery only disguises the truth for so long.

"When I was a wee boy coming here as a fan, I'd stand up at the back of the Caledonia Street end," Tommy says. "It was big and curved and went miles back from the pitch, a real old-fashioned terracing with one exactly the same at the Love Street end.

"It was just railway sleepers packed with earth all the way round three sides back then. The only seats in the whole place were in the main stand and even then they were old wooden things.

"By the time I came here to work, the Love Street end had been demolished and a new terrace built, squared off behind the goal. It changed the atmosphere of the place overnight.

"Next, me and an old fella who helped out concreted the floor of the enclosure under the main stand. Then we ripped out the wooden seats upstairs and put new plastic ones in.

"After that, the North Bank got concreted - the company who did it gave us the first half dozen steps as a freebie, then we had to pay for the rest."

As he tells me this, he stops by a black plastic seat a few rows from the back. He leans over and touches it, almost like patting a family pet.

"That was my dad Tommy's seat," he said. "He passed away a couple of years back, but I know that every day I can see where he loved to be. It keeps us together."

He gathers himself and strides up the steps again. Then he turns and says: "Want to to see what's underneath here?"

Underneath? I've been coming here all my life and didn't know there WAS an underneath.

But there is. Though to get there, we need to go up the way, up to the back of what used to be open terracing, to where the old wooden shed of a pie stall used to stand. We climb through a barrier that leads behind the back wall, scramble and stumble across a nettle-strewn slope leading down to the spike-topped brick wall that separates the stadium from Springbank Road.

"I try to give this bit a cut every June," he shouts back over his shoulder, "but by the time we're into the season it's growing wild again. It's a never-ending job."

He's done this trip a thousand times, knows where to put his feet so he almost bounds towards a little set of steps 40 yards along the banking. I'm just relieved it's not been raining, or I'd be hanging from the spikes by the seat of my jeans.

Down the steps we go to where once were outdoor toilets whose bricks stunk from decades of being peed on. At the foot, a little door. He jingles a set of keys, swings it open.

Inside is pitch black, with a smell like a damp coal bunker. On the wall to our left, you pick out switch boxes. Ahead, an opening into a dank cavern, with shapes piled against its right-hand wall.

"The switches operate the floodlights and the undersoil heating," he says. "but all there is apart from that are spare seats. I come here to hunt for decent ones when others get broken. That happens a lot - not so much from vandalism, more just from people being careless and the seats not being that strong.

"People climb over them to get out and they break. Some people get angry during games and take a kick at the one in front. And sometimes they just wear out, whether it's the plastic cracking or the metal supports giving way.

"Sometimes we do get games when you know fans will deliberately damage the seats. We had quite a lot after a cup tie with Morton a few years back, that caused a bit of row between the clubs. But while I don't particularly want to pick on the Old Firm, there's no doubt that the bigger the club who come here, the less well their fans take care of the place.

"They don't really bother what damage they leave behind, but luckily some people do have a conscience. I remember once getting a letter from a Dundee United fan apologising for taking his frustration out on a seat and asking how much it would cost to replace it.

"I thought that was brilliant, a really nice touch. But I got the club to write back thanking him for his honesty and telling him not to bother.

"It's a never-ending job, keeping up with the seats. That's why it'll be nice to move into the new place with four stands full of brand-new ones - even if I know I'll soon have to start the process all over again."

We lock the secret cellar again, haul ourselves back up and across the banking, through the railing and along the back walkway of the North Bank. Tommy moans that his efforts to clean felt pen scrawls on the red metal safety barriers hasn't worked, just turned it into inky smudges.

As we walk, he points out more and more seats that need replaced. Shows me the gutter that's beyond repair and gushes water down onto what's now a patch of black blaes on the trackside. Curses the mess left behind by every groundsman's nemesis, the pigeon.

He snarls: "They cause havoc - look, there's twigs and crap everywhere. Luckily, the bit they invade most is the end of the North Bank that's only open a few times a season, like when Rangers and Celtic come, so I don't have to deal with it every day.

"All you can do is get the pressure washer on the seats and the concrete and try to keep it as clean as you can. But there's bugger all you can do about the pigeons themselves - bar shooting them, but that's not very PC, is it?

"Actually, when I think about it, the whole way we deal with pests and weeds has gone full circle. When I started, there weren't really any of today's modern chemicals to help you. Then the market was flooded with them. And now, we're being told not to use them for safety reasons, so you're back to natural methods again.

"It's not just the pigeons that give you grief, though. We had a family of foxes living over in the corner between the North Bank and the Caledonia Stand and they caused havoc - they'd go out after games and scavenge for bits of food, then come down onto pitch, dig holes and hide it.

"You'd come in on a Monday and find bits of sausage, pies, chocolate bars or crisps poking out of the turf. Unless the crows got there first, of course - if they got a whiff of what the foxes were up to, they'd swoop in and dig the food up for themselves.

"And in the days when the goalposts were permanently in the ground, I'd come in on a Sunday to do some work on the pitch after a game, go home happy, then come in the next morning to find punters had sneaked in overnight and had a full-scale game on it!

"So between all that and weeds and the damage that's done by the weather and games, you can see that the pitch is the most important part of my job. The trouble is, there are so many other things to and only me to do them that sometimes it gets neglected.

"To be honest, the pitch has never been the same since we installed undersoil heating. It absolutely knackered the drainage. But it was something that was forced upon us if he wanted to get promotion last time round, even if it seemed crazy seeing as we'd be moving stadium inside a couple of years.

"These are the kind of daft rules the club has to put up with and you feel sorry for the cash they've had to spend on stuff they really didn't need. Apart from anything else, we can't afford to have the heating on all the time during the winter the way a Rangers or a Celtic could, so you might end up losing games anyway.

"Last season we were meant to be playing Rangers in a midweek game, live in Setanta. But the rain was horrendous and no matter what we did we were fighting a losing battle. When it was called off, we got pelters - people were on phone-ins asking why St Mirren's ten groundstaff couldn't get the water off.

"Ten groundstaff? It was me and nine under-16 players! We had no chance!

"I wish they knew the resources we had to work with here. I mean, when it's pouring down it's just you and a fork. But when it's bone dry, we don't have sprinklers, just a 25-metre hose that I need to haul out from over there - (he points to just beside the corner flag between the main and Caledonia stands) and drag across the pitch. It's the bane of my life. I can't wait to get to the new place for that reason alone, because it'll have proper pop-up sprinklers all over the surface.

"So many fans are angry that we're moving to new stadium, but I'd love to take them on a walk around the place the way we're doing. They'd soon see what the problems are, they'd see the massive job we have simply to stop the place falling down. It's a bit like painting the Forth Bridge.

"People say the club is selling the family jewels and that's probably right, but as much as I love this place, the fact is that it had its day.

"To be honest, I preferred Love Street when you could walk around the terraces and pick where you wanted to stand. Now, like at most football grounds, you buy a ticket and sit where you're told. That's not the way it should be."

We come down the North Bank steps and walk across the pitch again. Tommy stops and points down to the far end. He says: "Look at the Love Street end - it's not even really a stand, just a terrace with a roof and some seats. Yet the cost to the club of putting it together was still huge, money they couldn't afford."

Then his eyes fall on the old main stand, an odd construction that in all my years of watching St Mirren has never looked as if it was properly finished. In fact, it was only a few years ago that it was extended at either end to be the size it is today.

A couple of hours before that Kilmarnock game, my colleague Des McKeown had stood looking at it, wondering out loud why we didn't knock it down and start again ten feet nearer the pitch to give us more room behind.

That made so much sense it made me wonder why I'd never thought of it before. But more so, why successive boards hadn't thought of it before. Though maybe they did. Maybe they just never had the money or the support of the council or the will to make it all happen.

Whatever the reasons, though, it has remained a monument to indecision and to lack of funds. And for Tommy Docherty, that's maybe how it should be.

"I like it," he nods. " It's got character, it's different. When you look at it from here, it seems very small - but it's actually a bit of a Tardis, there's loads inside. It's just so full of history and memories that it's the one part of the stadium that will be impossible to replace."

As we walked down the track towards the tunnel, I get the same feeling I always do inside Love Street.

Butterflies.

I can't see it without getting excited, can't walk around it without getting emotional. This place holds so much of my life within it, especially the years I was going up under my dad's wing.

As we stand there, it strikes me for the about the thousandth time how lucky I am just to be able to wander in and out of the place. To be able to chap the dressing room door and go in and see the boys or to pop into the manager's office for a cup of tea.

After I've finished with Tommy, the new physio John McCreadie has agreed to give the once-over to a knee I've knackered running. He doesn't do this in a "well, if I must" way, but because the manager has told him I'm a St Mirren fan and a pal and that's what we do for our own.

As a kid, this kind of intimacy with the club I loved was unimaginable. It's my job that has made it possible. Yet without having this love for Love Street in the first place, I'd never have been doing that job.

Tommy's gone off for a minute to talk to the kitman. Alone on the track, looking round the empty stands, watching youth team players scurry around on errands, I wonder how many Old Firm punters ever get to do this. How many fans of Barcelona or Real Madrid or Man U get to stroll about their stadium, sneaking a cuppa off the kitchen ladies or saying hiya to their heroes?

And they are my heroes, every one of them. Because they play for St Mirren - the one thing in life I would have given anything to do but was never good enough to.

Out on the street, some spotty under-19 right-back could walk past me without his face even registering. Within the gates, though, he becomes something special. That black and white shirt is Superman's cape, Batman's utility belt.

Tommy must be reading my mind. Either that or there are more of us incurables around than I thought. Because as he wanders back across, hands in the pockets of his tracky bottoms, it's clear this break from the grind, this wander through his kingdom, has started the mental videotape running.

Right now, it's whizzing on rewind.

"When you step onto that turf, it hits you what's happened here over more than a century," he sighs. "I can look round and see games from when I was a wee boy or from over the last 25 years of working here. It gives you a wee shiver.

"Sometimes you can almost get a sense of them playing way before you were born, when your dad or his dad was young."

He bends down, strokes a patch of turf. Maybe he's spotted some

35

little flaw that needs fixed, maybe it's just affection.

"The pitch changed a lot over the years," he says, almost to himself. "It used to have a huge camber from the centre to the sides, but when the undersoil heating went in they used lasers at either end to level it. Now there's a different camber on both sides."

There's a couple of seconds of silence. Then he says, in almost a whisper:

"I'm going to miss it."

THE tunnel slopes gently upwards from mouth back to dressing rooms. It has a perspex cover; a recent addition, borne of fears that players might be struck or spat on as they ran out.

Or maybe that they might do the striking and spitting; you never know in football these days.

The mouth is painted black. Inside, it was once bare brick, like walking into a tenement. Now, it's panelled with light wood, the way you'd imagine a stately home's library to be.

Except with a lot less silence.

To the right as you walk in, a cupboard where Tommy keeps bits and bobs of his gear. To the left, a toilet. Ahead of you, staircases on both sides join at the top to create a landing off of which lie hospitality suites, the general office, manager's office, boardroom, hospitality suites and kitchens.

It's hard to fathom how, come matchdays, they get two squads, all their kit, a flock of ballboys, the match officials, two sets of directors, more than 100 corporate diners, all the kitchen staff and all their gear in.

Tommy's right, Tardis really is the perfect description.

But let's not get ahead of ourselves and start the top floor tour, because the beating heart of this old, crumbling pile lies at ground level.

The dressing rooms.

On the right just before you reach the stairs, a door opens into a little square vestibule and then, to your left, another reveals the Inner Sanctum.

The space where Bradford, Findlay and Newbiggin plotted to win the Scottish Cup in 1926, where Walker, Lapsley and Wilson did the same in '59. Where Money, Wilson, Hamilton and the rest of a new generation's unexpected heroes steeled themselves to conquer Hampden in '87.

This is where Fergie chucked a bottle of ginger at the wall in fury

30-odd years ago and where the stain remains, a varnish-coated art installation Damien Hirst could make half a million off.

This is where I have wanted to spend every day of my life, no matter how lucky a hand life has dealt.

Andy Millen - No2 to manager Gus MacPherson - is in his training gear, propped up on an elbow on the treatment table that sits in the middle of the floor. He's talking to one of the youth players. From the shower room, the gabbling of two more kids.

The big communal bath's still through there, but with two individual tubs plumbed into it now. The old days of a dozen guys sharing each others mud and germs and - well, you know - have long gone.

All around Andy's wintergreen-stained chaise longue, outdoor clothes hang on pegs, waiting for their owners to come back and reclaim them. The ones who drew 0-0 with Killie on Saturday are up at Glasgow University today, going through gruelling tests of their lung capacity and muscle strength. For the umpteenth time already in this fledgling season, their skin is pinched to test body fat levels.

Fat is the enemy of the modern football manager, the creeping disease that stops his players fulfilling all their potential. Once, every team had a tubster, the guy forgiven his love of the odd pie and pint or 12 because he could produce the moment of magic that made the crowd ooh and aah.

Now, the slightest gut or a backside bigger than Kiera Knightley's is a hanging offence.

Saturday had been a trial of strength. Both teams tried to get the ball down and play, but once it was clear they were going to cancel each other out that way, it all came down to who had the better staying power. Again, it was a dead heat.

Killie assistant manager Billy Brown summed it up as he wandered towards Gus MacPherson's office for a post-match beer. A shrug and the admission: "You'll see a lot of games like that this season."

MacPherson knows it too. Before and after the game, he talks at length about the science of fitness, about the need for his boys to be able to work constantly at their maximum heart rate. Now, I'm old school about this business. Always believed that there has to be room for a Puskas, the guy whose love handles don't stop him running the show from the centre circle.

The manager looks at me the way Chris Hoy would if you suggested he should train for the Olympics on a diet of fish suppers and Vimto.

"Ability is a big part of being a top footballer," he says. "But it's not the most important part - and before you say anything, even the greatest players will tell you that.

"Think about it. Put the 22 best players on the planet on the same pitch and what will separate them at the end of the day? Which ones can last the pace best, that's what.

"You need tremendous fitness levels this days, plus desire and a willingness to keep improving and if you've got all of that, THEN your ability will come through.

"That's why we're really big on the scientific side here and that's why we decided to go to see a guy called Neil McKenzie at the university. He worked with Scott Harrison when he was on his way to becoming a world boxing champion and he comes highly recommended.

"Spending a couple of hours with him could have huge benefits for us, because we'll find out who's capable of what and can work with them from there.

"With heart-rate monitors and lung-capacity tests, there's no hiding places for the boys. They can't claim to have been working harder than they actually are. It's all there on the computer print-outs. We know who's looking after themselves away from the park and who isn't. It's not enough to be good in the shooting practice or the passing drills, they all need to apply themselves right on the fitness side.

"We've been lucky in our time here. Even in the First Division we had a fit bunch who ate the right things and worked as hard as they could. But we're at a different level now and they know they have to step up again - and to be fair, they are.

"They look lean and sharp after pre-season, but they're not finished yet. They'll keep getting fitter."

BUT science is one thing. Good old-fashioned sweat's another.

A bit later, after I've finished the tour with Tommy, I'll come back into the dressing room and run straight into coach Stuart Balmer as he comes out of the little cubby-hole where the gaffers change.

A 6foot 2in Falkirk boy with the battered nose of a centre-half who's gone in where it hurts ten thousand times for Charlton, Wigan, Oldham, Hamilton and more, he has one of those faces that looks perpetually puzzled. A great guy, a great pro.

Just a bit scary naked at three in the afternoon.

This morning, he's been out at Strathclyde University's playing fields on the outskirts of Glasgow with the ones who didn't play on Saturday.

I ask what he did with them.

"Gave them a f*****g battering," he grinned, evilly.

That means running. Then running. Followed by some running and some running to finish. A pretty comprehensive game of running, you might say.

Not just any old running, though. An even-more-evil grin tells you that.

He nods to his left, at what looks at first like a pile of black bin bags lying in a corner. Then he reaches down and picks up what now appears more like police body armour.

It is, in fact, a vest packed with lead weights to make the game of running that bit more fun.

Put one on and you're carrying an extra ten pounds. But it has room for another ten in a series of little pockets.

The idea's simple enough, to create extra resistance so that when you run without it, you feel more agile. The practice? It must be torture.

"You should see them work in these," he says with a face like a child-catcher. "Wee Craig Dargo's nearly collapsing in the sprints! But it does them good - and they work their balls off, no complaints there."

Thanks for the insight, big man.

Now put some clothes on before you have someone's eye out.

WE climb the carpeted stairs, the walls on either side decorated with framed shirts from the passing seasons.

At the top, the flights merge into a passage leading to the big wooden doors - now locked and barred - that open onto the Good Seats where directors and sponsors sit.

On either side, rooms once used by the board and the management, but now given over to corporate guests. Downstairs, the dining room where the players eat after training is also a matchday money-maker.

This is the kingdom of Campbell Kennedy, the big, ginger-haired, ever-smiling diehard fan who's now Commercial Manager. After Gus, he's one of the most important people at the club - because the income from his hospitality suites and the twice-yearly dinner he organises in local hotels is vital.

Kennedy always seems calm and in control. But goodness knows how, because all week he's hard-selling what is in truth a luxury to people hit by the credit crunch. And once he gets them through the doors at mid-day on a Saturday, the next six hours are mayhem. He never seems to stop, to relax, to think about anything else but keeping this club afloat.

That's why, as much as he loves this place, he too will be glad when the Big Flit arrives.

New stadium, new facilities, see? Built from scratch. Built to order. No shoe-horning as many guests he can into as little space as possible. Room to breath, room to relax. Room to impress and to coin it in.

But here's the thing.

Just as Tam sees the rust where I see the romance, where Campbell sees problems, this fan sees something special.

The atmosphere up here before games is fantastic. The steam coming off the soup tureens and the hostess trolleys stacked with chicken and steaks, spuds and veggies makes your mouth water. The clink of glasses and the roars of laughter from the tables jammed into those twin rooms make you want to be in there with them. Directors rub shoulders with fans, the manager says hello. No jobsworth ever puts up a spoilsport hand and asks to see a pass.

This is a kind of football socialism, all for one and one for all. No red ropes or No Entry signs. It feels like we're all part of the same thing, all fighting for the same cause.

Just before Christmas last season, my old school pal Davie Davidson - now a big success in the pub and restaurant game, the swine - sponsored a game against Killie (Note to readers: We do occasionally play other teams) and asked me along as a guest.

Well, I'd love to tell you all about it. But it's something of a blur. Which tells you how good it was.

I know we had our first small large one at 11 in the Argyll Bar, a Saints-daft boozer he owns two minutes from Love Street. I know we had a great lunch, that it was a duff game (Note to reader: We draw 0-0 with Killie a lot) and that we eventually went back to where we'd started.

The bits in between all that are a tad hazy, though. And the bit when I walked to Gilmour Street Station, got a train to Glasgow Central, walked to Queen Street, caught a train to Falkirk High, bought a Chinese takeaway, got home, went to bed and woke up with the lights and the telly on is a total blank.

Yes, sports fans, a massively successful day at the football.

It's not something me or Mr Liver could do every week. Or month, for that matter. But when we do, it's one of the highlights of the year - and it makes me proud that my wee club's reputation for throwing a right good party extends the length and breadth of the country.

TODAY, though, we're a week away from the next home game, a midweek CIS Cup-tie with Dumbarton. Today's the kind of day the fans and the sponsors and their well-fed-and-watered guests never see.

Just people going about their jobs, the way everyone else does. Answering phones, hoovering carpets, mending fuses, cleaning lavvies.

So why do even they feel different, these folk with mundane titles and workaday lives?

Because of where they do it, that's why.

I don't know how much of a buzz it gives some of them to wake up every morning and go to work for St Mirren. But it means a hell of a lot to me that they do, that every repair they do and surface they dust and match ball sponsor they sign up keeps the club on the right road.

If we ever go to war again, I want these people designated as being in a Reserved Occupation.

PAST the glass hutch of reception, through a connecting door, down the corridor, past Gus's little alcoved office and you find in front of you the Boardroom.

The door's closed. Behind it, chairman Stuart Gilmour and his colleagues are deciding whether or not to give in to the Old Firm's demands for five per cent of every ticket sold to their fans.

Think about that one for a minute folks.

You welcome someone to your home. You make them comfortable, you cook for them. And they want you to pay them.

It's bad enough that it's almost a whole generation since gate money was split evenly between the two competing clubs. To me, that seemed natural - it takes both of them to make a game, so they should both earn out of it. But, of course, that didn't stack up where the Old Firm were concerned.

"Why should some crappy wee mob get half of what came through the gates at Ibrox or Parkhead when no one even cares about them?" they'd whine. "Why should we subsidise them?"

So the wee crappy mobs said: "Well, because without us there's no game - and remember, when you come to ours you get half of our money too."

It fell on deaf ears. And so what had been a crack between the Haves and the Have Nots became a chasm which became a Grand Canyon.

The Old Firm's income from home games doubled overnight. Then, when live TV came on board, they were smart enough to suggest that the away team should get a bigger slice of the dough than the home teams, as they didn't get any of the gate receipts.

Before then making sure that the away team in any given telly game was ... well, generally one of the Old Firm.

Yet STILL that wasn't enough for them, STILL the screw wasn't turned tight enough. So, as season 2008-09 dawned, they called the other ten poor saps who make up the numbers in the EssPeeEll and informed them that from now on, they wanted protection money on top.

For what else can we call it, this addition of 5p in the £1 for every brief sold? The Old Firm come to you and say: "Well, chief, it's up to you - but if you don't pay, we won't encourage our fans to come and then you'll lose money."

So you then go: "OK, we'll sell to your fans through our own club and cut you out."

And they do: "Fine. Just don't come running to us when you end up with a stand full of undesirables who aren't on our official lists."

It's the football equivalent of the Krays sending the boys round to give it: "You just 'ad this pub decorated, old son? Shame..."

The other ten clubs started out by talking tough. Falkirk took Rangers on before they met on the opening day of the season, handling the away ticket sales themselves with a voucher in the local paper and getting the police to vet those who applied.

But from there, others caved one by one. First Dundee United, worried about the loss of income. Then Aberdeen, though with the compromise of putting a £1 surcharge on each ticket to cover the protection money. This was also the road St Mirren would go down.

Behind that closed door, they were hatching a plan to give the Old Firm the five per cent they wanted, but sticking away tickets up from £24 to £25. They'd publicly apologise to Rangers and Celtic fans, but tell them to take it up with their own club bosses. What they'd also have to do, though, was lump the same increase onto their own supporters - but give them a voucher for £1 off at the next home game.

An incredibly complicated procedure that left no one happy, except the already-stinking-rich Bigot Brothers. As ever in Scottish football, everyone was left dancing to their discordant tune - even the very people they claim to be the lifeblood of everything they do, their family of diehards.

The boardroom where the decision was being made is L-shaped, with a lone table as you go in the door, a display cabinet along one wall and a bar tucked round the corner. Plush it isn't, another reason for those who run the club to welcome the move along the road.

WHAT'S striking as Tommy unlocks door after door you've never seen behind is that almost every spare square inch is crammed with ... well, with stuff.

Filing cabinets shoved up against walls, boxes full of stationery, bits of this and parts for that. There's only one cupboard with no clutter, a switchroom that the fire safety people demand easy access to.

So on we go, the man who knows every inch of Love Street showing a fascinated fan what's kept in here and who works in there.

Then it strikes me.

We've been round nine-tenths of the stadium and he's never taken me into his own office.

There's a simple reason for that, of course.

I forgot. He doesn't have one.

"I never have," he sighs, a little smile playing momentarily across his hangdog face. You get the feeling he only gets time to have a laugh once he's home with the family. His daughter Millie started school today and he can't wait to get back and hear tales of her adventures. "There's just never been space. I just come in and wherever I am is my office, the pitch or the stands or the loo.

"Though I do have this..."

Just inside the big gates at the right-hand end of the stand as you look at it from the pitch is yet another door I've never noticed before. It's opposite the tidy switchroom and across the passageway from the ancient, brick toilets into which those climbing the stairs can look down and watch you pee.

He puts the key in the lock, turns - and behold, Tommy Docherty's kingdom.

It's long enough to get a double bed into, but not wide enough. There's a set of rough-and-ready shelves against the wall on the left, filled with what can only be described as odds and sods. There are canisters or this and drums of that on the floor. But it's dominated by two bikes.

"I cycle to work from Erskine every day," he says. "That's my thing. When I get time, I sometimes do 100 miles or more a week. And when there's a spare few minutes in the day, I get the bikes out and give them a clean and a bit of a service.

"Apart from the bikes, I've got a few wee personal things in here. It's the nearest I have to my own office. It's my own little bit of Love Street."

He locks up again and walks over to the toilets.

"I mean, how could they build those stairs and now realise people would be looking down onto other people peeing? It's mental."

The brickwork is black and white, the stench strong on the nostrils despite Tommy's best efforts to keep the place clean.

"I used to paint the walls with bitumen," he says. "That's a smell that always reminds me of Love Street.

"Toilets like these are miles out of date, though, just like the ones in the dressing rooms - come on, I'll show you."

We go back upstairs onto the landing, then down again to the tunnel. Turn right into a little square vestibule with a room for the ballboys, the door to the players' dining room/hospitality suite and the away team changing area.

It's smaller than the home one, with fewer little homely touches. In fact, let's be blunt - it's a hole.

Tommy points into a corner on the right-hand side.

"When I started here at first, the groundsman was an old guy called George Hamilton.

"One Monday morning, I came in and he was sitting there with Tony Fitzpatrick. He was telling Tony what a great game he'd had on the Saturday. The next Monday, I went in and there they were again - George telling Tony what a great game he'd had.

"It became a ritual to start the week. They'd get hot chocolate drinks from the Klix machine in the corridor and George would tell Tony how great he was. Players need that sometimes, they want to hear good things about themselves."

On a bench to the left of the room, a youth team player sits cleaning a bag of training balls. The ones who hadn't played against Killie, the ones who'd had a battering this morning, have their outdoor clothes hanging around the walls.

Tommy leads me through to the showers and toilets. There's no door, just an opening in the wall. What looms on the other side must make the Old Firm's millionaires feel like waiting till their get home to have a wash or a sit down.

"Embarrassing, isn't it?" he says. "On matchdays you've got Rangers or Celtic coming here with all the masses of gear they have and it's piled up in here, next to the showers. Look at the loos, they're knackered. We've even got the washing machine and driers in here. It's a mess.

"And you know what's bound to happen every time a big team's here? A few of their guys get pre-match nerves, go to the loo one after the other - and it blocks. And who has to come in and unblock it? Me.

"To be honest, I find that a bit demeaning, coming in with a plunger while these guys are getting changed for a game. It's not the best part of your week. So sometimes one of the young lads gets the short straw.

"I don't delegate often - not that I often get the chance to. But I do remember one day when I had to out of sheer terror. Fergie was with Aberdeen at the time and when the game ended, I was upstairs for some reason. When I came down, I saw all their players lining up in the corridor and wondered why.

"Then I heard him screaming: 'Where the f***'s the f*****g key for the f*****g door? What the f***'s going on here?'

"I nearly fainted. I'd forgotten to unlock their dressing room and he was going off his nut. I'm ashamed to admit I shoved it into the hand of a young lad who was helping me out at the time and made myself very scarce."

AND still there's more in Tommy's Tardis.

He unlocks a door just inside the white UPVC conservatory that's been stuck on the old main entrance and tells me to watch my step.

A light goes on, but what lies beneath doesn't seem much better illuminated. We go down steep stairs and into a space as hot as a Finnish sauna. Right beneath where the home players change, the boiler room.

Within seconds, you feel your clothes get sticky as heat blasts out from two white, rectangular boilers on the left-hand wall and an old copper water tank opposite the door. The tank's insulation jacket has years of names carved into it, all the youngsters who've run up and down here doing errands.

The boy who's been cleaning the balls comes in at our back. This is where they're kept. Goodness knows how they don't explode.

"When I was younger, we used to come down here for a fly sleep," says Tommy. "It was so comfy, you could drift off in no time.

"Now, there really isn't a minute for luxuries like that."

WE GO back up the wooden steps to daylight and normal temperatures. Back through into the vestibule outside the home dressing room. And into the only part of Love Street's interior that has never changed in Tommy's 25 years.

The boot room.

45

He says: "It's exactly the same as it was when I arrived, only the styles of the boots themselves change. Everything else is identical. The only thing you'll sometimes see here that never used to be is some gear for live Setanta games - they feed cables in through that little window up on the far wall to plug into a monitor that sits on the floor and they put their sponsored backboard up for post-match interviews.

"Sometimes when the cameras are here, I'll come in here and watch the game in peace, away from all the noise. There's definitely something nice about the fact that all the permanent stuff in here is as it always was. I'll be sorry to see this little room go, it means a lot to me.

"I suppose this area here's the heart of everything. Off the home dressing room, where there's an office for the coaches these days, the manager used to have his own bath. When Jimmy Bone was in charge, he used to love to get out, put on his shoes and nothing else and do a wee tap-dance.

"He was a great guy, Jimmy, always good to work with. Alex Smith was the same, a real gentleman who only ever said positive things to you.

"When I came here, Ricky McFarlane was in charge. Then it was Alex Miller, who I got on with well. Long after he'd left and was with Hibs, he'd always come over and talk to you, would remember who you were and what you did.

"That might sound an obvious thing, but you'd be amazed at how many people forget. Some guys are your best pal when they're nobody, but a bit of stardom and suddenly they won't give you the time of day. That disappoints me, there's no need for it.

"I came here as a fan who couldn't believe he was getting to say good morning to his heroes every day and it hurts when one of them turns out not to be the good guy you thought it was. But most of them have been brilliant - and if I had to pick a favourite, it'd be Billy Abercromby.

"The fact that he's the only guy still alive who's captained us to the Scottish Cup makes him a legend for starters. He was just such a good guy too, though. He always had that wee twinkle in his eye, as if he was up to something. Which he usually was.

"He was a bundle of fun and energy, the life and soul of the dressing room. And hard? He'd have kicked his granny. One day we had Rangers here and Graeme Souness was on the bench. Wee Aber was running the show, so Souness sent a sub on with the words: 'Go out there and do that bastard.'

"Five minutes later, the sub's on a stretcher. So a second sub gets

46

warmed up with the same message: 'Do that bastard.'

"You could see the guy going: 'Aye, right, gaffer...'

"It hurt everyone around here that Aber hit hard times through the drink, it was like one of the family being in trouble. But at the turn of this year we heard he was getting better and next thing he was at a game against Falkirk, being introduced to the crowd and getting a fantastic reception.

"The great thing was, for all he looked weaker and his speech was a bit hesitant, that wee twinkle was still there. He'd never lost it."

WE WALK outside one last time, up onto the landing of the iron stairs that look down onto the peeing punters. It's not the prettiest view of Love Street.

To our left, a disused earth banking where the floodlights used to be, some cars parked higgledy-piggledy behind it. Directly beneath us, battered old sliding gates lead into the enclosure, their hinges and runners ready for the scrapheap.

"Around here's going to bits," Tommy sighs. "Those gates are wrecked, for a start. And look down behind you there - see that wee lean-to stuck on the end of the stand? That's the ladies loo. Now, see those bits of clay piping on top? They're all that stops its roof blowing away. There was nothing else I could do to mend it in the end.

"Then look up the way. I've got bits of wire wrapped round the guttering to hold the iron sheeting of the roof down because there's nothing to screw it into any more. Twenty-five years ago, this stand wasn't in very good nick - and all we've done since then to the bricks and mortar is constant running repairs.

"We built the new staircases at either end because health and safety told us to, but that's it. You just do what you can to keep it from falling down.

"I remember one Hogmanay it was really frosty and I came down to check the pitch covers were all still on. Once I was happy with that, I went up to make sure everything was switched off in the stand and found that all the pipes had burst.

"So there I am, the Bells about to go and the town ready for a party, running around turning off stop cocks and finding ways to plug leaks and mop up the water before it froze.

"That's been the way of it more and more over the years, making do and mending. And maybe it's because we know we're moving soon, but over the past six months I've noticed more and more wee things going wrong. It's almost as if the ground itself knows we're leaving it behind and it's self-destructing.

47

"I do as much as possible myself, but for some things you need to bring people in and there's no doubt that as time goes on, small bills are becoming big bills and that's no use for the club. It's not even as though they can ignore problems and say 'who cares, we're moving', because the health and safety people and the fire service come and check the place regularly and if it's sub-standard, there's no game.

"It's amazing to think that the new place is going like a fair just along the road. But I just can't get my head round us being there, not yet, not when there's still so much to do here.

"Our last game here's scheduled for January 3rd against Motherwell and we're due to play Killie (Note to reader: Seriously, we DO play other teams. Honest) on January 31st. But if we get drawn at home in the cup, that'll be the last game, on the 10th.

"So at best, I'll have three weeks to get down to the new place and do a crash course in what it's all about - that'll be a nightmare. It's a totally new pitch, with totally different characteristics. All the controls for the lights and undersoil heating will be different. But I'll have to know the place inside out inside a month.

"I'll think about that later, though. Just now, I can't even contemplate leaving here. The last day will be a nightmare, really horrible, like leaving the house you were born in.

"To think I've been coming here, every day, for 25 years and then - suddenly - no more.

"You know the first job I ever did here? Painting the turnstiles at the Caledonia End. When it was the old, curved terraces they were miles away, right back. Now there's flats there. It just shows how much everything's moved on.

"When I took the brush and the pot round there that day, I thought I'd only be here for a few months and then get a real job. But here I am, 25 years later.

"Who knows, I might still be down the road in another 25. Some thought, eh?"

And with that, he clambers down the stairs, through the stand, down the tunnel. Climbs back onto the big red mower and rides off into the sunset...

Travel Broadens The Mind,
But Narrows The Arteries…

THAT afternoon spent burrowing around the old place really set my mind racing.

Back flew memories of great games, of duff games. Of celebrations and wakes.

But more than that, as Tommy the groundsman spoke of his 25-year journey from yopper to one-man holder-together of a crumbling temple, it make me think back to where Love Street has taken me.

Believe me, it's a loooong way.

From the North Bank to the South Atlantic. From reeking, brick-built, open-air lavvies to an electronically-operated toilet in a Yokohama hotel room.

From dangling my legs over the advertising boards as a kiddie to watch the game almost from pitch level, to the nose-bleed heights of the Nou Camp press gallery.

At eight, my headmaster threw down the chance to write a few paragraphs for a weekly paper that doesn't exist any more. At 46, I'm travelling the world to scribble down thoughts about the greatest players alive.

And it all started here. Every journey in 20 years of foreign reporting, every marathon stint at a major tournament, every shivery wait in the rain to be told to sod off by a player emerging from an angry dressing room in Moldova or Montrose, Killie or Kaunas.

Every dot on the map of my working life leads back to Love Street.

The biggest cliché there is in regard to footballing success is the one where the guy who's hit the jackpot against the odds says: "If you'd tried to tell me at the start of the season that we'd win the

49

league/cup/paternity case, I'd have called for the men in white coats to take you away!"

But I know exactly what he means. Because sometimes, on nights filled with excitement and stress in Sapporo or Seoul or Seville - or sometimes even in places that DON'T begin with S - I get these head-rushes, a ticker-tape flash across the brain going: "What the hell are you doing here? You're a wee boy from Foxbar, behave yourself!"

In those moments, you're almost doing that out-of-body thing, floating up and looking down on a wee freckly fella, all skinny and with a nose yet to be broken in a drunken collision with a telly on a bus back from an 18-30 holiday in Perpignon.

And you're hearing David Byrne singing Once In A Lifetime, but repeating over and over the line: "Well? How did I get here..."

That's not some kind of false modesty. It's just ... well, it's a bit like when you're driving to work and suddenly realise you've been on autopilot for God knows how long. I'm just not sure what happened in between that conversation with the heady and me getting here.

MAYBE that's why I have this recurring nightmare...

ST MIRREN make the Champions League final. Biggest night in our history. The whole of Paisley seems to be there - I can see faces from primary school, from the BB, from standing on the terraces with my dad as a kid. No one wants to miss out.

Dad's there, of course. So's my uncle Sam, who used to drive us to games. His boys too, Richard and Gordon. My old headmaster Sam McDougall's there, sitting beside me in the press box.

(Oh, and Sharron Davies and Rachel Hunter have come along too, in wet swimsuits. Neither are from round our way, you'll understand, but I have a contract with them to make walk-on appearances in all my sub-conscious dramas.)

The team's always a Greatest-Ever XI - Campbell Money, Bobby Reid, Fitzy, Starky, Lexy, Hughie Gilshan, Ian Ferguson, Mark Yardley, all the true heroes.

And in the dugout? Fergie, of course.

So at this point you're thinking: What's the nightmare part?

Your favourite team playing on the ultimate stage? Your favourite manager running the show? Your favourite people watching them?

Your favourite women taking it in turns to give you neck massages to ease the tension?

Doesn't sound too horrible a way to speed through the wee hours towards morning.

But here's the thing.

It's the last minute. We're one-nil down and attacking like crazy, peppering shots in on goal. It's like multi-ball time on a pinball machine.

All around the stadium, punters in black and white are jumping about, screaming, willing the boys to snatch that equaliser.

Me? I'm panicking. Hot and cold at the same time, palms clammy, heart pounding. Hands too shaky for fingers to work.

Because if we score now, it means extra-time. And extra-time means we miss deadline. Which means tomorrow morning, St Mirren's finest hour won't be in the paper.

We always score, of course. And as it's my dream, it's me who scores it. Hanging about the edge of the box, waiting for the scraps from a final, frantic corner. Watching the clearance drop, cushioning it on my right thigh, lobbing left-footed.

Seeing a penalty box full of heads turn and gawp as the ball sails over them all and scrapes in under the bar.

The stadium goes mental. There's only our lot, no opposition punters anywhere. It's pandemonium. Yet I'm sitting there, stock-still. Frozen by panic.

The laptop screen's blank. The gaffer's on the phone, screaming for copy. My fingers are the size of jumbo sausages.

All around me, colleagues are getting the all-clear from their sports desks, but I'm just sitting there, frozen. Crying. Palpitating...

Then I wake up, sweating. Gasping.

You've no idea how many times I've felt like that. And not just when I've been asleep, either.

Because this, sports fans, is what you go through every time you cover a midweek match. This is the tightrope you walk, between the satisfaction of delivering a report you're really happy with - and leaving a giant hole where your words should be.

Time and again, you get there, somehow. But you feel like a Tommy dodging bullets in the trenches, you know that every one that misses only brings the one with your name on it closer.

So you sit there, in the most thrilling arenas in the world, watching the biggest games in the world. Knowing that every other neutral in the world's desperate to see the action go right down to the wire. And to be fair, all you want is a game packed with incident, skills, goals and controversy. As long as it all peters out around the 80-minute mark.

That's just about long enough to take all the stuff you've been typing down, get it in order and top and tail it to sum the whole thing up.

It's not how you should be doing the job. In an ideal world, you'd be sitting back with your arms folded and laptop lid down, soaking up the action with everyone else. You'd have a telly screen showing you all the replays from all the angles. You'd get to listen to the managers and key players talk afterwards.

After which you'd have a good hour to sit and stroke your goatee and compose a work of genius.

If only.

There was a time when sportswriters could do that, when they'd write down snatches of reports and tie them to the legs of homing pigeons. Then, when they'd hand bits of paper to runners who'd go and phone their words of wisdom to the desk. Or, later, when they'd pick up a telephone themselves and dictate it on the hoof while their eyes stayed glue to the pitch.

I've done that last one myself often enough. It's the greatest feeling, like commentating except with a permanent record of it in print the next morning. When you're on song, it just all flows from brain to mouth without hesitation. Throw in a really good copytaker at the other end - one who's done a bit of homework, doesn't have to ask for the spelling of every name, who says 'OK' when they get to the end of the last bit - and it's a joy to do.

So why do we do it on computer, then? Because it's a computer world. Because 1000 words can go from a crumbling stadium in Lithuania to a screen in Glasgow with a single push of a button. And, yes, because the one disadvantage of doing it by phone is that if things change suddenly, you can't see the words you've already dictated.

Cut and paste is a wonderful invention. Control A, control X, control V. Essential keystrokes for the journalist on the move. Highlight the words, make them disappear, move your cursor to where you want them to be, make them re-appear again.

There is, however, no Microsoft Word command for instantly re-writing the whole bloody piece when some selfish git pops up with an 91st minute bolt from the blue that turns a game on its head.

Once upon a time, all they told you to do was leave the 1000 words the way they were and stitch on a last paragraph saying something like ... well, that some selfish git had popped up with an 91st minute bolt from the blue that turns a game on its head.

Then you'd go back in and turn it round and re-file it properly for the next edition.

But those were the days when a newspaper was the first contact most of us had with last night's game. The days before wall-to-wall live TV coverage. Before t'Internet with its message boards and podcasts and mobile phone footage.

Today, we can't kid ourselves on that we're there to tell anyone who scored the winner. Everyone already knows. They've already seen it a squillion times from a zillion angles. They've heard the scorer tell them that he's over the moon.

That means the sportswriter's job has become a reflective one. We have to take the game on a step for the reader, try and explain not what happened but why it happened and what the implications of it all are. Which would be a lot easier if you still weren't doing it on the hoof, as it unfolds.

It's one of the questions you get asked most about this job: "So, when do you write your stuff?"

A few years back I came back in the early hours from watching Hibs lose 5-1 in the Ukrainian ore-smelting beauty spot of Dnipropetrovsk. Got up late morning like a half-shut knife, went out to get the papers and met one of my neighbours in the Co-op.

Now, he has the Scottish Sun under his arm. My byline's on the back page. Yet after he's asked me how the trip was, he says: "So, you away to write your stuff now?"

"Er ... I did it last night," I mumble.

"Really?" he says.

"Yeah," I say. "It's in the paper under your arm."

It takes a second. Then he has one of those light-bulb-above-the-head moments and goes: "Oohhhh, I seeeee..."

Mind you, why should people know - or care? I don't stop to think how food ends up on the supermarket shelves or how telly programmes get onto the box, so what does it matter how words get onto newsprint?

It doesn't.

Unless one day they don't get there.

Which brings us back to that nightmare again.

It's November 21, 2006. Parkhead. Celtic are playing Man U in the Champions League - and being played off the park. United are passing them to death, doing everything but score. As half-time comes, though, and then the hour mark passes, it's still nil-nil. And you're in that state of flux that's no use to man nor beast, that one where nothing continues to happen and the clock's against you.

Yes, you have words. The colour of the occasion, the ebb and flow of attack and counter-attack. The reactions trackside of Sir Furious and his old sparring partner Wee Gordon.

But not the meat. Not the line.

53

By ten minutes from time, the deadlock as intact as a nun's virtue, you're just starting to feel the first faint pangs of panic when - shazzam! - little Shunsuke Nakamura curls in a free-kick and, against all the odds, Celtic are ahead.

Now you do have a line. So you clatter away about how the better team can have all the possession, all the style, all the chances, but it only takes one moment to change everything. Basically, how it's not what you've got that counts, but what you do with it.

You look up at the clock. Two minutes of the 90 left. Tidying it up now, chipping away redundant words, making it as tight as possible. There's a beginning, a middle and an end. It's all flowing nicely.

Job done.

Aye, right.

Suddenly, there's an almighty noise. Your head comes up like someone's lassoed it from ten rows back in the main stand. And the ref's pointing at the spot.

Penalty for United.

The place is in uproar. Celtic, their players, their bench and 58,000 fans are raging. Unfortunately, you're in no position to say if they're right or wrong, because you were writing when the whistle blew.

All you know is that you're as pissed off as they are, but for very different reasons.

If Louis Saha scores, a whole club has to wait another fortnight for the chance to qualify for the last 16 for the first time ever.

If Louis Saha scores, you have roughly two minutes to completely re-write what's just taken the best part of an hour to put together.

I remember sitting there, clenching and unclenching. That's fists and buttocks, by the way. Breathing in hard, blowing out slowly through pursed lips.

Knowing deep inside that wanting the dramatic plot twist not to happen really wasn't in the job description.

Saha steps forward. Shoots low. Artur Boruc dives, parries. The place goes tonto. Yet in the midst of the mayhem as the final whistle blows, you have to compose yourself. Find the right place and the right way to describe the incredible finale you've just witnessed.

Then close the file, create a new email, attach the file, hit send.

Hold your breath until it's gone.

Realise how lucky you've been to get away with it again.

BUT that's the thrill of the job, being at the sharp end on nights like these or when Scott McDonald scored the winner for Celtic against AC Milan and the fan ran on and went for their keeper Dida.

Nights when the glorious uncertainly of football clashes head-on with the absolute need of newspaper production executives to make the presses run on the dot and vans to hit the road not a minute late.

Nights when, as Steve McCroskey put it in Airplane, you realise you picked the wrong time to give up sniffing glue.

Nights that remind you why you wanted to do this for a living in the first place.

No, scrub that. Not for a living - I always just wanted to do this, without ever thinking that it would pay the mortgage.

And when it is done, when the words have gone and the desk give you the all-clear, my mind so often drifts back to where it all started.

Primary Four, Amochrie School. An invitation to go along and write a few paragraphs on a St Mirren game for a weekly newspaper.

Seeing my name in print. Getting hooked.

The Paisley Pictorial is long gone, but it'll always be in my heart. Its St Mirren reporter was known only as Seestu, but someone - who it was is lost in the mists of mistiness - told me it was actually my headmaster, Sam McDougall.

Wow.

He was already someone we all loved, an old bloke who treated every pupil like his own kid. But this elevated him to superstar status in my head.

He used to talk to me because he knew I was good at English, would ask me what I wanted to do. Then one day he asked if I'd like to go to a game with him and do a report to sit next to his in the following Friday's edition.

From that day, there was nothing else on the horizon. It was journalism or it was nothing. To this day, I don't have a clue what I'd have done if it all went pear-shaped.

I have no qualifications to do anything else - and, come to think of it, no qualifications to do this either, having failed all but the shorthand part of my National Council for the Training of Journalists exams at Napier College during a skint and miserable 1980.

Luckily, it's never come to doing anything else. Amazingly, they give me money to go and watch football in the San Siro and the Nou Camp.

Somehow, the work gets done despite having a brain like a sieve that's just been fired on by the Royal Artillery.

SEE, there are four golden rules of covering football abroad.

1. You must be confident.

2. You must keep a cool head in a crisis.

3. You must have an inbuilt ability to exploit your situation to the full.

But most importantly of all,

4. You must be organised.

Some people seem confident but lose the nut when the heat's on. Some are ice-cool but uninspired. Some can rip the pants off any situation but couldn't tell you what time of day it is.

Two out of four won't do. Even three isn't enough. Fact is, until you have all four facets of foreign sports journalism packed away safely in your locker you'll never crack it.

So here's my simple guide for anyone who dreams of breaking into this high-flying, non-stop, whirlwind world of writing about men you've never heard of kicking a ball in cities you've never heard of and are unlikely to be back in again.

1. PREPARATION

It's vital to think of every eventuality. You need to research the weather for the country you're visiting; there's nothing worse than being stuck in a monsoon in a white linen suit.

Or to be stuck anywhere in a white linen suit, to be fair. But you get the drift.

You also need to find out about the stadium you're going to. Is the press box covered? Or are we talking instant electrocution as soon as you hit the laptop's On button?

Does your mobile work where you're going? And if so, have you remembered to tell the wife it doesn't?

2. KEEPING A COOL HEAD

So you're ten seconds from touchdown at Batumi Airport and there's a herd of cows grazing in the aircraft's path. Do you:

a. Panic?

b. Scream and panic?

c. Pooh yourself, scream and panic?

d. Fail to notice because you've been hammering the bevvy since Istanbul?

If you answered d., chances are you were sitting in the section reserved for the press as Celtic hurtled towards death by cattle on September 13, 1995.

56

Superstars shuddered. So did the Celtic players. Chairman Fergus McCann tied his wallet to a lifejacket and hurled it out the window to safety.

The pilot shut his eyes, heaved the joystick and prayed. And someone up there obviously listened, because somehow we avoided splattering the area with Beouf a la Aeroflot.

You'd hope after that fright the worst would be over. But no; welcome to war-torn Georgia and the trip from hell.

As I write this, the country's been in turmoil again. Russia invaded to avenge the death of four of its peace-keepers during skirmishes between Georgian troops and militia in the breakaway state of South Ossetia.

Still, the good news is that it all sounded a bit more ordered than when we were there.

For 30-odd hours as unforgettable as they were unsanitary, the Parkhead party who'd gone to the conflict-shattered former Soviet state for a Cup-Winners' Cup tie were bitten by bedbugs, fleeced by local hoods, intimidated by gun-toting cops, blackmailed by the telephone company and even managed to fit in a football match.

How poor was Batumi? There was a rat in my hotel room and six locals complained to the management that some foreign guy was getting special treatment.

The currency, memorably, was called the Coupon. Each note was little more than a dirty, crumbled piece of used toilet paper and worth slightly less. You were getting roughly one million to the pound - and, yes, they had coins as well.

"Excuse me, chief, you got change for a Coupon? I need to use the phone? Yeah, sixteen thousand ten-blonky bits and the rest in gronkles, that'll be fine. Oh, and you haven't got a wheelbarrow on you..?"

And corrupt? We stayed with the team at the Hotel Sputnik, the place where Yuri Gagarin and his fellow cosmonauts used to stay before being blasted off into space in the early 60s. It sat on a hill overlooking the city and its prime feature was a beautiful open-air amphitheatre where a bunch of us sat and sang in the early hours of matchday.

The acoustics drowned out what Tom Boyd was shouting out of his bedroom window at one point, but I'm pretty sure it wasn't: "Nice harmonies, chaps."

Anyway, we made it through the night, amused ourselves until early afternoon and then it was time to leave for a tea-time kick-off. As we gathered our stuff, though, four or five thick-necked blokes in shades appeared. Nice guys. Very concerned with looking after the Celtic team's welfare.

Well, that's what I took a protection gang to mean.

Basically, the deal was that whatever hotel bill the club had paid, the thick-necks wanted the same again.

Wee Fergus McCann, as you can imagine, was not chuffed. The thick-necks, as you can also imagine, had never heard of wee Fergus and were for sticking his bunnet and his Gregories up his backside if he didn't cough the loot.

And verily, the loot was coughed.

At the stadium, bedlam. Our press seats were right in the middle of Nutter Central and that's all we had when we turned up - seats. No phones, no barrier between us and the mad, mental fans. Sod allski, as they say in downtown Tbilisi.

So we're like, what do we do? Do we need to pay some thick-necks for telecommunications assistance? Or are we simply to be stabbed, skinned and served at the burger stall, with hordes of Batumians denying ever having seen us?

Happily, no. Half an hour before kick-off, engineers turn up and start running in cables and nailing junction boxes everywhere. At their backs, guys in boilersuits arrive carrying iron fencing and oxy-acetylene gear.

And now it's all whoosh, bang, dring-dring, mind yer feet, comrade. They're still at it when the game starts, so we're standing up to see what's happening while they're handing you phones to test and you're brushing stray sparks off your breeks.

Eventually, they're done and we get on with trying to file amidst frenzied noise as Dinamo hurl themselves at Celtic. It's one of those atmospheres that makes our claims to have the most passionate fans in the world seem utterly ridiculous. These people are out of it, off their heads, lost in the all-consuming drug that football has become since every other little pleasure they used to enjoy was taken away in the name of freedom.

Celtic are well delighted to come away with a 3-2 win. I finish sending my report sharpish then fight my way down through the hordes to the tunnel to get quotes off manager Tommy Burns and his players, but end up helping the groundstaff boys load kit onto a van. Everyone's desperate to get the hell away and you can't blame them.

It's been an experience, just not one you'd want to experience again.

Still, an hour or so and we'd be at the airport and settled down for the short flight to Istanbul, where we'd be staying overnight before going home the next afternoon.

We'd reckoned without the thick-necks, though.

Posing this time as BT - Batumi Telecom - they appeared in the departure lounge (well, shed) along with gun-toting cops and demanded payment in cash from the press for use of telephone lines. Not much different from how British Telecom do things, if you ask me, but that's just one man's opinion.

Anyway, we're all outraged and tell them our offices have already paid. But the thick-necks know what they're doing. There are no flights out of Batumi International Airport & Cattle-Grazing Facility after dark, being as how there are no lights on the runway, and as it appears rates back at the hotel seem to have quintupled all of a sudden, we're snookered.

So a couple of us decide bollocks to this and started bullying the others into paying up. Some moan, others keep saying that the office already paid for the phone lines, but they have to be told; this was no time to argue against the immorality of the black economy.

It was time to hit the wide blue yonder before it turned black and we were turned out onto the street. We'd get it back on our expenses, so just get a move on and dig deep. Up we stumped, off we scooshed and once we were in an Istanbul hotel nightclub we laughed about it all.

Plus, it was my 33rd birthday, so that was another good excuse to get howling.

Celtic, of course, complained to UEFA. They got, of course, nowhere.

Georgian president Edvard Schevadnadze complained to Celtic about some Scottish reporter who'd written reports about having a rat in his hotel room and being held to ransom at Batumi International. Some senior members of the press pack, meanwhile, complained that I'd also praised Celtic in my reports for bringing enough food with them not just for the team - they'd shipped out everything from water to cornflakes to whole chickens - but for us as well.

"Ah mean," they whinged, "how the f*** are we meant to fiddle our receipts now?"

3. EXPLOITING THE SITUATION

Still, for every Batumi, there's a Monaco.

And it's my firm belief that when your chance comes to enjoy the flash places, it's a rookie mistake to waste your couple of nights there in some marina-front bar filled with the bored, blonde molls of elderly billionaires or dingy lap-dancing joint where they give out blank receipts like sweeties.

Not when there are once-in-a-lifetime experiences to be had in the privacy of your own hotel room.

Steady, missus.

When Rangers went there back in 1999, they put us in this clifftop pad in Cap Martin, the bit above Monte Carlo where really, really rich people go to look down on those who are merely really rich. It wasn't a spectacularly fantastic building, but the little things made all the difference.

Now, since this trip I've been fortunate enough to stay in some pretty swanky pads. But this was the first, a real unexpected luxury and a total novelty.

So I was lying in bed the first night when I clocked what I thought was one of those old-fashioned radio-and-lights consoles by the bed. Wrong. Well, right, as in you could work the radio and the lights from it. But check this. It also opened the door and the patio windows, lifted the blinds and brought out the sun awning on the balcony.

That'll do for me, mon ami.

I've stuck a breakfast-in-bed order on the door handle, set the alarm and waited for morning like a kid on Christmas Eve. Eventually, 8.30am came.

Frappe, frappe!

"Who is it?"

"Room service, m'sieur."

"One moment, please."

Buzz. Door clicks open.

"Entrez!"

In comes le garcon with le tray and sees me still in le bed.

"Where would you like it, m'sieur?"

"Un moment."

Buzz. Patio slides open. Encore un buzz. Blinds go up.

"On the table outside, please."

"Certainly, m'sieur. And will there be - ahem - anything else."

Les cobblers. Hadn't thought of the tip, so I said non merci and left him cursing the tight Ecossais git. Made up for it next morning, though - when we'd gone through the same electronic routine, I buzzed the awning and when it opened, five one-franc coins I'd left up there the night before fell onto the tray.

Magnifique, if I say so myself.

4. ORGANISATION

But this is the most vital quality of all - because the disorganised roving football reporter is as much use as Graham Norton in a mass brawl with 23 coked-up Hell's Angels outside the Sausage'n'Trumpet.

From the moment your assignment is given to you, it is absolutely crucial to attend to every, last, teensy-weensy detail. Nothing must be left to chance, because there are no second chances.

It is this credo which has stood me in such good stead in destinations from Oslo to Osaka and 100-odd others in between. It's no use being the greatest writer in the world, knowing everything about the climate and the stadium, knowing the opposition's shoe sizes off by heart and lying there the night before the game opening and closing your electric curtains until the remote control gives you RSI if you've forgotten your notebook and pen.

It may seem ridiculous to even consider a true pro coming away from home without such a basic requisite of the job in his luggage, but believe me, it could happen unless every single piece of equipment is checked, double-checked and triple-quadruple-quin-sex-sep-tuple checked before setting off.

I hope this will come as good advice for anyone reading this whose heart is set on a career in sports journalism. There's no room in this game for sloppiness. Only when you've been around as long as I have will it all come as second nature.

7.30am, Tuesday May 28, 2002

SO it's two hours before I fly to Japan for the World Cup, the biggest assignment of my life. I'm in the shower in a hotel room across from Glasgow Airport.

Realising I've forgotten the letter from FIFA that gets me into games.

As the water cascades down the drain, it feels like my life's being washed away with it.

It came to me in a horrible, blinding flash. A moment of clarity, winos call it. A sobering thought that hits you like a bolt from the blue, clears all the other clutter from your muddled brain and brings everything into sudden, pin-sharp perspective.

Except for winos, these moments can often be the beginning of a new life. Right now, at 7.30am in the Holiday Inn, it felt like the end of the world.

Ten minutes till breakfast. Two hours until the flight takes off for Heathrow. Six hours until the plane to Tokyo. Twenty-six hours until I'd arrive at my hotel. Eighty-five hours before kick-off in the opening game of the biggest sporting event in the history of the planet.

An event I - me, small person from up a close in Foxbar - have been handed the onerous responsibility of covering single-handed for the Scottish Sun.

With me in this hotel room is everything needed for carrying out that responsibility. Except the desk from my office back home.

Because that's where the FIFA letter's still lying.

I can see it, waving at me. No, sorry, it's not waving, It's flicking me the Vs.

Bollocks.

No, sorry again, make that triple bollocks. With a size 12 Doc Marten hoofing right into them. And spikes coming out the toecaps. Worn by a tax inspector who's also your mother-in-law.

Seven months I've prepared for this day. Seven bloody months from the morning the gaffer phoned and gave me the most exciting news ever. There hasn't been a single hour of a single day since when I haven't thought about it.

God knows how many hours I've spent working out a schedule of matches to cover, picking hotels, finding out how to get around a huge, strange country.

I've even learned Japanese, for Buddha's sake.

OK, so I couldn't hold a meaningful discussion on the rights and wrongs of organo-phosphate farming and its effect on the Kyoto Protocol, but I know enough to order a beer and buy a train ticket and that's better than a punch in the guts. Which is funny, because I suddenly feel like the tax inspector has got fed up kicking me with his size 12 spiked Docs and given me one.

I'd packed everything days ago. Unpacked it again. Packed it. Unpacked it. Counted it, ticked it off a list - and I never make lists, because lists are for halfwits who can't remember things - then packed it yet again. I had everything. Absolutely everything.

Except the most important thing of the lot.

Honestly, if I'd left home without a stitch of clothing to wear for a month but with my accreditation letter I'd have been happy. I'd happily have stunk in a single pair of pants from Senegal-France through to the final itself just for the privilege of being there.

But no, I had to do it the other way round. I had to stuff the car with gear for every single meteorological eventuality, every possible invite to every conceivable social gathering, a million spare pairs of socks, enough toiletries to keep a wart-hog as fragrant as Jeffrey Archer's wife - and leave the letter on the desk back home.

It's like the time I went to Eindhoven with Rangers and got to the airport before realising I didn't have my passport. Melanie, bless her, went hurtling back 30-odd miles to get it from the suit I'd decided at the last minute not to wear, leapt back in the car and hurtle 30-odd miles back in time for me to just make the flight.

Less than an hour, it took. How she kept her licence is almost as much of a miracle as how I kept my testicles.

Now, however, she's got her hands over little baby Georgia's ears and wondering why she married the monster battering lumps out of the shower cubicle and swearing so hard that wee gink who made Tourette's trendy on Big Brother would have complained to the Broadcasting Standards folk.

Eventually I pull myself together and step out to face the grim reality.

That I am a twat.

"Everything all right, babe?" she smiles.

As I stand before them both, towel wrapped round my waist, I decide this is not the time for losing it. I take a deep breath and explain, very calmly, what I've done. I'm not panicking. It's no big deal. We can get round this.

Who am I kidding?

This is DISASTER.

This is the no-passport-for-Eindhoven fiasco times a squillion with a summons for treason thrown in. This is the end of my life.

Worse still, the end of my career.

I mean, why didn't I remember this last night? I could have got in the car, gone home at my leisure, collected the letter and been back in time to kiss Georgia goodnight. But no, I had to be lying back on the bed with the missus, listening to our daughter snore, watching EastEnders and feeling all relaxed and happy with myself that I hadn't forgotten a single, solitary thing.

Twat, twat, twat.

Still, it could be worse. I could have realised when I got to Japan.

Can you imagine the phone call?

"Gaffer? Yeah, it's about that exty-thousand quid you spent sending me to cover the biggest sporting event of all time. What about it? Well, you'll laugh - but it's all been a complete waste of dosh. Every last yen of it. Why? Because I've left home without the letter that gets me into the stadiums to cover games for you, so I might as well have stayed home and watched it all on the telly. Ah. You're not laughing. What's that? Up my own..? With a..? Certainly, I'll just go and phone for the hotel handyman."

Melanie gives me that look wives give you when they know fine well you're a twat but don't want to put it quite so bluntly.

"Well," she smiles, "I suppose I shouldn't put it past you to forget the letter with your past record, but I thought that for something as big as this you'd surely have remembered something as vital."

I don't know whether that's a compliment or a slap in the kisser, but I say thanks anyway. Then we go through my bags. Everything's scattered across the bed, the floor, Georgia's cot. I have so much stuff it's not true.

Insect repellent? Mosquitoes wouldn't get at me on a particularly clammy day in the middle of the Brazilian jungle. Diarrhoea tablets? I could give a rhino with dysentery the confidence to go commando down the High Street in white hipsters.

We can't move for socks, shirts, reference books, notepads, pens, chargers for every electronic gadget from mobile phones to a portable ECG machine, pictures of my loved ones - plus one of the missus - enough training gear to see me through four sessions a week; or, alternatively, to fill an entire drawer for the duration.

But no FIFA letter.

Tttwwwwaaaaaaatttttttttttttttttttttttttttttt!!!!!!!!!!!!!!!!!!!!!!!!

Melanie's staying chilled. She asks if there's time to ask her grandpa to go to the house, get it and meet me. I say no. She asks if there's any chance FIFA will look up their computer files, see I'm genuine and let me away with it. I say no. She asks if the gaffer will see the funny side. I think I'm going to cry.

Then, being the one in the household who actually possesses all the qualities necessary to be a world-traveller, she comes up with a perfectly simple solution.

She'll drive home, get the letter, drive back to the office, get them to fax it to my hotel and send the original on by courier. Nice and easy does it. No need to freak.

Except there is. Because inside, a little voice is screaming at me that I'm not up to this. I'm kidding myself that because I can say the clarinet of my uncle is on fire in Japanese that I can handle being alone 6000 miles from home with the paper's reputation in my hands.

Oh yeah, they say travel broadens the mind.

But it sure as hell narrows the arteries as well.

BUT on the never-ending flight from London to Tokyo, it hit me. This wasn't incompetence - it was just who I am. This was just the way things would always be.

This tendency to twatism was simply in the genes.

Staying overnight in Glasgow before a trip to Munich, opening my bag in the morning to find one black shoe and one black boot. Having a stand-up barney with a hotel receptionist in Donetsk who I swear has lost my passport, only to go back and apologise sheepishly after finding it on the wardrobe floor.

Leaving bags behind in hotel rooms, laptops in stadiums, mobys on planes. Sleeping in for coaches to airports. It's just a curse that will never be lifted.

For every action, though, there's an equal and opposite reaction. In this case, the fact that no matter how bumbling things might be before and after getting the work done, the bit in the middle always gets done.

That's been the case in Austria, Belarus, Belgium, Bosnia Herzegovina, Canada, the Czech Republic, Croatia, Denmark, Estonia, England, The Falklands Islands, The Faroe Islands, Finland, France, Germany, Greece, Georgia, Holland, Hungary, Italy, Israel, Iceland, Japan, Jordan, Latvia, Lithuania, Macedonia, Moldova, Monaco, Morocco, Northern Ireland, Norway, Poland, Portugal, The Republic of Ireland, Russia, San Marino, Slovakia, Slovenia, South Korea, St Lucia, Spain, Switzerland, Tunisia, Turkey, Ukraine, USA, Wales and counting.

All these places, all those sights. All those stadiums, all those languages. All the knackered power sockets and non-existent phone lines. The gutters leaking on your napper, the loony-tunes fans screaming in your ear. Club officials yelling for you to get on the bus to catch the flight home when you're still trying to write the back page story.

It all becomes as normal as clocking in and clocking out, as catching the 8.15 to Glasgow Central. It's what you do, it's who you are.

Which is why you always, always have to remind yourself of how you got there.

Which in my case was that first Saturday at Love Street as an eight-year-old, not having a Scooby how to write to length or how a newspaper worked or what a deadline was.

I sat at the living room table the next morning, tongue poking out as I scratched thoughts down in pencil, ready to be handed in to headmaster come Monday.

This was the start of a wee boy's dream. Fate plonking you down in a housing scheme whose local primary school happened to have a headmaster who wrote about football for weekend pocket money.

From there to the World Cup Final, to the four corners of the earth, to meeting all those heroes who only ever used to exist in photos and on telly highlights.

In a big cabinet in my office at home are coloured folders holding cuttings all the way back to France '98, the first big tournament a gaffer trusted me to cover. There must be a million words in there.

And all of them, in their own way, are dedicated to Sam McDougall and to the Love Street press box where it all began.

These are seven of my favourite pieces, all from different countries, all splashed with different colours and emotions. There's fear, anger, anticipation. Blind loyalty and uncontrollable violence.

But always, always the same over-riding element.

Passion.

Istanbul, early one Wednesday morning in August 2001.

Potentially the last morning of my life.

EMRAH the taxi driver is lost. I know this because we're freewheeling at 52mph while he waves his arms in the air and makes a noise like a cat coughing a furball.

And because we went hurtling past our turn-off two miles back.

Emrah didn't notice. He was totally focussed on offering me many highly-individual opportunities to die young at no extra cost.

These included him:

a. Ducking under an articulated lorry he decided was moving too slowly.

b. Re-enacting the scene from Men In Black when the car turns on its side to get through a nine-inch space between a traffic jam and a wall.

c. Plain old ramming into something solid at high speed.

And as a special bonus, either of us could have been decapitated at any moment by a shard of glass from a windscreen so badly cracked it was like travelling head-first into a kaleidoscope.

Yep, it's dangerous here all right. Everywhere in this teeming, screaming city of 14 million furball-coughing lunatics all trying to get through the same door at once lurk stubbly blokes with gold teeth, evil glints and deadly weapons.

Not knives or guns, mind - but dying Fiat yellow cabs that they rev so high it wraps your gums behind your ears. This is what being inside a tumble-dryer must feel like.

I flagged Emrah to take me to Fenerbahce's training ground and by the time I'd said "Fe-" I was running along at 30pmh, holding the door and trying to time my leap in like Luke Duke.

For the next 45 minutes I sucked a sweaty leatherette seat up my ever-sweatier backside as he tried to drive through - and I mean THROUGH - one of Istanbul's 24 daily rush-hours, nose pressed so hard to the windscreen it squashed his dung-filled ciggies to his face, one hand constantly on the horn and the other endlessly clashing gears in no particular order.

With each millimetre's-width near-miss and rubber-shredding emergency stop I pleaded more and more desperately to be spared. I told him I had a wife and a baby at home, but he just flashed a 9-carat molar, went ach-ach-aaach and crunched from third to first and back again.

Remember I said he got lost? Eventually he pulls in to the kerb on a dual carriageway and shouts someone over for directions. Loads of arm-waving and acch-ach-ing and we're off again.

Backwards.

Emrah REVERSES through the traffic, notices a parked car at the last second and swerves round it, reverses round a corner into oncoming cars - then turns at right angles ACROSS them, goes straight over both lanes and turns left so we're facing the right way.

And you know what? No one bats an eyelid.

They're all too busy pulling the same stunts.

Turks drive like they talk, at breakneck speed and over the top of each other. Eighteen floors below me as I write, the streets are a porridge of metal and exhaust fumes. All you can see are thousands of tiny clenched fists poking out of thousands of Dinky toy windows.

I was wakened at 6.47am yesterday by the last dregs of the previous evening's jam parping at each other to move. Where? Who cares, just ach-ach-aching move! They love to parp here. Parping's the law. They have signs saying: "Parping Obligatory, Particularly During Hours of Darkness".

As I watched, an ambulance tried to get through the morass, giving it big Nee-Naws. Twenty minutes and four yards later, it was whining something like Aw-Naw. No one gave a monkey's for its mission of mercy. So the driver parped.

Emrah parped a lot.

Me too, come to think of it.

He'd go over bumps that shot you up into the roof, then dive into potholes while you were on your way down so the seat wasn't there when you arrived. Outside was one giant mushroom cloud of smoking tyres and exhaust fumes. Inside was an impenetrable fug from his fags.

But all of it, all the madness, is worth it - because Istanbul is wonderful. It is a truly awesome sight - and size. This one city has a population nearly three times that of Scotland.

You can see for miles from the roof bar of our hotel, but Istanbul never seems to end. And you never want it to, because it's unbelievably energetic and exciting.

It's a far-out place, a mass - a mess, even - of history, of bazaars and the bizarre. Seventh century palaces, crumbling walls from hundreds of years earlier, endless Mosques whose minarets rise into the skies like nuclear warheads. Though I'm fairly confident they're not.

Even the money's huge. You get TWO MILLION lire to the pound, so you have a sandwich and a coffee and they hand you a bill for 12,000,000 and you almost faint. Emrah's meter looked like the national debt of Nigeria.

The greatest thing of all about Istanbul, though, is that it spans two continents. Fight through the traffic on the massive bridge over the slow, sludgy Bosphorus and the sign reads: Welcome To Asia.

Hey, let's have breakfast then leave Europe for an hour.

An American lady taking the air outside the hotel's rooftop bar the other night was wiped out by this. Two whole continents separated by a mile of water? Two different continents to our left and our right?

"Gee," she breathed. "What's a continent?"

JAPAN turned out fantastic in the end. A couple of tear-streaked emails to FIFA, a courier job from the magnificent Susan back in the office that made sure my accreditation made the hotel before I did and we were sorted.

Just over 100,000 words later, it was over. The most amazing of adventures, six weeks in the Far East, a whole new culture and a whole new ball game.

Twenty-two games in a month-long tournament, tiredness that left me ill at home for a fortnight afterwards. But the shivers and the headaches were well worth it for the utter thrill of being part of one of the most exotic, exuberant sporting occasions of all time.

It all started with this...

Early June 2002

From our You-Couldn't-Make-It-Up Department.

AN Ing-er-lund fan books a hotel room in Sapporo for the Argentina game and gets this e-mail back:

"Thank you for your reservation. Two Argentinians will be staying here the same day as you. Please try not to have a fight with them."

Absolutely true. And absolute proof of why their knucklescrapers get into so many barneys abroad.

They simply forget not to.

"Cor blimey, Darren, wozn't there sumfink we 'ad t'rememba t'do?"

"Dunno, Wayne, it rings a bell - but wot was it?"

"Lumme, that's annoyin'. It's doin' me 'ead in!"

"That's it! 'Ead in! We 'ad t'rememba' not t'kick any Argies 'eads in!"

"Yaay! Now let's finish kickin' this Argie's 'ead in and go for a celebratory pint..."

Trouble is, so many of them are just SOOO forgetful. Marseille, Charleroi, Luxembourg, Dusseldorf, Rome, Brussels, Cagliari, Oslo, Glasgow, Dublin - you name the place, they've had that pesky mental blank about not getting into scraps.

I was there at France '98 when they had a mass night of forgetfulness. They were charging up and down the boulevards, trying to remember what it was, bumping into French guys, knocking them down and tramping over the top of them in their absent-minded frenzy.

Turns out they'd actually written what it was they had to remember on their hands, but they hadn't brought the guy who learned to read. He'd forgotten not to get into a fight before they left Dover and was at that very moment in the pokey.

Of course, we have to give the guy with the Sapporo hotel room the benefit of the doubt and suppose that he won't fight with the Argentinians.

But the very fact that the Japanese have to ASK him not to is a timely reminder of how nervous their whole nation is about the arrival of the people they know as the Igirisujin.

It's such a different culture over there, so much more ordered and self-conscious. They're simply not prepared for the arrival of Prehistoric Man In Union Jack Beanie Hat.

See, they don't like people who laugh too loud. They don't like people being right up in their faces. They need space in bars. They generally only get aggressive when they've had a drink, but they drink a lot to relieve the stresses of their ultra-disciplined working lives.

They disapprove of people who take their shirts off in public. They loathe tattoos. And if they disapprove of you, they let you know by hissing loudly through clenched teeth.

Oh dear.

It's going to be hard enough for our neighbours to remember not to fight Argentinians - well, it woz 20 years after the Falklands, so 'ee woz askin' for it, wunnee? - without all that other stuff being thrown in.

I fear the worst for them in as different a civilisation as Japan.

You can see Darren and Wayne swaggering into the Osaka Arms, bare chested, St George and the Dragon tattooed on one arm and a naked lady on the other, guffawing their heads off as they go nose-to-nose with the barman and bawl: "A'wight, mate?"

The poor guy would get halfway through his first hiss before his clenched teeth were tinkling onto the floor.

Then there's rail travel. If you've ever seen football fans on a platform, it's like rush-hour in Karachi. Twelve hundred of them all trying to squeeze in one door at the same time then all use the bog and the snack trolley at the same time.

Not in Japan, old boy. The deal there is that you stand on the platform EXACTLY at the spot designated for the carriage noted on your ticket, the train swishes in at precisely the right time and stops precisely where it's meant to and you sit where you're meant to and nowhere else.

Japanese travellers wouldn't even think about moving to another seat because someone else was in it. You can see the potential for Wayne/Darren/ticket inspector's head hilarity.

Still, one good thing is that the Japanese don't like eye contact, so they're not likely to hear those dreaded words "Oo You Lookin' At?"

And, of course, there are some local traits that'll come as second nature to some Ing-er-lund fans.

For instance, a Japanese man who wants to show courtesy to a new acquaintance will automatically hand them a small card - or meishi - with his name on it.

Without these he is deemed to have no personality, no status in society. He'd no longer leave home without bundles of the things than he would his trousers.

So when he comes across some knucklescrapers, he can pass round endless meishi reading: "Greetings! I am Yoshiri Yakomoto!"

Then when he regains consciousness he can read theirs.

"A'wight? You've just met the Chelsea Headhunters..."

AND although Ronaldo would steal the show and Ollie Kahn would sell the shirts come the final, for me it all came to a shuddering crescendo the night South Korea's bid for glory final stuttered to a halt.

I'd first flown across to the co-host nation for the opening game, Senegal's fairytale win over former colonial master France. True to form, I turned up at Seoul airport with my visa lying in the hotel room safe. Thank goodness for the world's most understanding immigration staff.

A week later, I made the 14-hour trip by train and plane from Sapporo - on the northernmost tip of Japan - down to the glorious island of Jeju off Korea's south-west coast for a spectacular Saturday night watching Brazil beat China 4-0 in a stadium in the shape of a fishing boat, sitting in the shadow of a volcano.

A few days after that it was back over the sea again, to Daegu for a terrific game between the Koreans and the USA.

Then, this.

Not a great game as great games go. But as an occasion? Hopefully this at least scratches the surface...

June 2002. South Korea have just lost their semi-final to Germany

COMING up for midnight on Deoksugong Street and my taxi is stuck in a jam.

A great, big strawberry jam.

Red to the left of us, red to the right. And red, red, red, in front as far as the headlights can see.

We've come this far from the stadium, but we can go no further. There's just no more Seoul left to drive through. They've taken up the tarmac and rolled out one giant red carpet.

I'd wondered how they'd react once their country went out of the World Cup, if they'd maybe turn ugly when all that nationalism suddenly had no happy focus.

I underestimated them. Yes, they were sad. But no, they weren't angry. How could they be? Their unknown, unfancied team had come a single kick from the final itself.

And they were going to celebrate it, by God they were.

The pictures of the sea of people crowding city centres for every Korea came at this tournament have become as familiar to TV billions as the players themselves. At City Hall Plaza here in the capital, in central Daegu, downtown Gwanjon, Busan, all points from the border with the mysterious north to the tropical islands of the south, just people, people, people.

And with each game, as excitement and expectation has got higher, the crowds have got bigger. And noisier. And a little crazier.

71

Last night was the biggest, the noisiest, the craziest of them all. I swear it was the most incredible mass of humanity I have ever seen. Me in a little black Crown taxi, with maybe THREE MILLION of them outside.

Thank the stars they didn't get angry. They'd have picked us up by the bumpers, carried us away and we'd never have been seen or heard from again.

But they didn't. They just swarmed around us, kept trying to move somewhere, anywhere. You wondered who the ones at the front were, how early they'd had to be there. Maybe they just never went home from Saturday's quarter-final with Spain. And if they were first in, they'd be last out, so when would they get home from this one?

Just in time for Monday and the last big party, they'd hope.

President Kim Dae Jung has declared the day after the World Cup ends as a National Holiday. All business, shops, banks, the lot, all closed. All down the boozer, because they do like a booze here.

And especially Dutch booze.

Since Guus Hiddink became such a monster hit as coach of the team, sales of Heineken have gone through the roof. Thousands upon thousands of cases walk off supermarket shelves each week. It's now the biggest-selling foreign beer in all Korean bars.

Hiddink should think about bringing out his own brand-name lager. Or a range of clothes. Or a political party. He'd be a billionaire running the country in no time.

They gave him a $1million dollar bonus just for winning their group. They've cut through forests of red tape to grant him Korean citizenship. He and his players - none of whom now have to go through the rigours of national military service - will all be granted the country's highest civil medal, the equivalent of the George Cross.

On the gorgeous island of Jeju, a Dutch explorer was captured and imprisoned hundreds of years ago. Now they want to make up for that slight by building a statue of Hiddink on a hill - and giving him a luxury beach house to look out at it from.

The latest call going up in parliament is for Seoul's World Cup Stadium to be re-named Hiddink Stadium. The man can do no wrong. If he'd asked the thronging millions to lie down and let him walk across them in hob-nailed boots they'd have hit the floor like a shot.

I wish he'd been around just after midnight on Deoksugong Street. I'd have asked him to part the red sea and let me get back to my hotel for some kip.

But no, there was no way through, not even with 33,000 police on duty. The main square and every main drag leading to it, every side street leading to the main drags, every alleyway between the side streets, was jammed. The boy started to reverse, but now there were people behind.

So, with a shrug, he pulled in to the kerb and motioned me to get out. Across the road - and only 5000 or so red shirts away - was an underground station. Take it to as near your billet as you can and trudge, matey.

And guess what? Every platform, every carriage of every train was packed with red, like so much tomato sauce in big glass tubes. As I write this, I've just made it home to watch the re-runs of the night the World Cup fairytale finally ended for little Korea.

Then I'll sleep. Oh boy, will I sleep.

You can take that as red.

AND this?

This is the punishment for all that glamour and excitement. The yin and yang of football reporting balancing itself out.

Or as well as anyone of anything could balance itself when half-cut and halfway up the side of a Faroese mountain in a kilt and Adidas Sambas...

Saturday September 7, 2002

A very confused night in Toftir

YOU'VE spent the last two nights in a converted shed on a windswept hillside, sleeping on a fold-down bed with a bloke who snores like a buzzsaw.

You've stepped off a sick-bucket of a ferry at ten to three, looked up and realised the game's taking place on top of a cliff.

So you run up the stairs, scramble a quarter of a mile up a grass bank, twist your ankle along a pot-holed path, go round an astroturf pitch and up even more stairs. And they haven't even held up kick-off for you.

Eight hundred knackered fans get to their seats just in time to find out they're uncovered and thirty seconds before the rain starts sweeping down.

Then the Faroes score and the day really starts to ming.

By the time it's 2-0, you're in some horrible nightmare where their teachers and truck drivers have turned into Brazil and your overpaid superstars into Ally Brazil.

73

Our lot get so bad that at one point Paul Dickov passes to no one and out for a shy and you realise he was aiming for Stevie Crawford. Who's a subbie and was only out for a stretch along the touchline.

It's truly hellish. And it keeps getting worse.

In the mile-long queue for the bogs at half-time, a drunken Faroese bloke who hasn't washed his hands pokes you in the chest and slurs: "You're going to lose, loser!"

That's when you know you've finally hit rock bottom as a Scotland punter.

You go behind their goals for the second half and pray for something to turn it all around, try to ignore the locals passing whisky bottles to each other, unable to believe their luck at having come out of the hat against opposition so pigging awful.

Even when we score they're laughing, partly because they're so blootered, but mostly because it's a joke goal. It goes in off six backsides and someone's left ear. They don't even particularly care if their team hangs on now. They've had an absolute ball.

We're just bawling our lungs out in sheer frustration, anger and misery. We've gone beyond the days of glorious defeat, beyond being brave losers, beyond We'll Support You Evermore.

When the equaliser goes in, we barely even cheer.

Because to cheer this result would be like boasting that you're no longer the village idiot.

While a handful of our players acknowledged the half-hearted applause afforded them at the end, the rest looked down at their boots and slunk away in shame. Anyway, by this time most of the Tartan Army were only clapping their hands to keep them warm.

They reserved the real ovation for the Faroese players who'd already gone on a mini lap of honour in front of their booze-sodden supporters. This collection of guys who kick a ball for fun were the only ones who deserved any credit at all from this farce of a match.

International class? Sure, it was a game between two nations - but there was absolutely no class out there.

As we'd stood on the slopes, drenched and freezing and staring defeat in the face, there were only two options. Laugh or cry.

In the end, most of us laughed, if only at the sheer absurdity of what we'd come all this way to see. Because it was simply bizarre.

I mean, what about that 14-man scramble in our penalty box as we desperately tried to hang on at 2-2? If you'd seen it in a primary school game while you were out walking the dog, you'd have split your sides. Yet there it was, happening in the frantic dying minutes of a hugely-important, UEFA-sanctioned glamour clash.

It was hard to get your head round the fact that the last game we'd played in this competition had been at Wembley, the night the Tartan Tigers ravaged the Three Lions in front of 70,000 screaming punters.

Now, less than three years on, we were roping ourselves together to do a Chris Bonnington just so we could reach what you can only describe as Cliftonhill transplanted onto the peak of Arthur's Seat. And for what? To see 14 guys all trying and failing to kick the same ball at the same time.

You can almost excuse the Faroese for their part in it, because they had played to their best and often beyond it in unquenchable desire to rack up an unforgettable victory.

We had no such excuses.

As I stood among the rest of our poor, baying supporters, though, doing my bit to achieve a Guinness Book of Records attempt at the most cases of pneumonia in the one place, the only thing that even threatened to stop us shivering was our blood boiling.

Scotland couldn't pass, couldn't tackle. Paul Lambert spent more time sliding on his backside than he did on his feet, didn't know where to run and couldn't have shot a tin can off a wall from two feet with an air pistol.

Talk me through how Kevin Kyle managed not only to miss unmarked from four yards in the second half but also managed to do it by shooting into the ground and up over the bar. You have to be some kind of special plonker to achieve that.

Talk me through how no matter where any dangerous Faroese player was, our defenders managed to be somewhere else. It was like we were deliberately avoiding contact with the enemy. Talk me through how long the Tartan Army will put up with it.

Not much bloody longer, if the conversation on the ferry back to slightly drier land was anything to go by.

Stevie Crawford's was the only name used in any kind of positive way. The general consensus was that the Dunfermline striker changed the game when he came on at half-time and that's pretty much bang on.

No one else comes out with pass marks, from a ponderous keeper through to our giant, wooden centre forward.

Although that's probably unfair on Kyle. It's not his fault that he's not up to it at this level. What is his fault, however, is his inability to trap a sack of puffin poo or jump without flattening an opponent.

Yet what could you do but laugh as his performance - and those of far better players around him - got so ineffective?

We still had to get back down that hill and through the driving rain to the ferry. We had to amuse ourselves in a one-horse town until three in the morning, when we'd start the seven-hour trek by ferry, bus, plane and train to get ourselves home.

The only way - the Scottish way - to look at it was that a dreadful football match had got in the way of a few days on the ran-dan.

Unfortunately, that's the way more and more have to look at it in order to put up with watching Scotland.

The guy I admired most through it all was a bear who stood right behind the goals in just a kilt, a pair of boots and a furry Cossack hat.

On his right shoulder, a tattoo: "Stranraer till I die."

Presumably it'll be from hypothermia.

Two minutes after the ferry pulled out of the harbour, he collapsed across a bench with his kilt around his waist and his tackle on full view to hordes of passengers.

No one made an attempt to hide his shame.

After all, what was one more monumental balls-up after a day like this?

SEVILLE. What more do you need to say?

A legendary trip, a pilgrimage that 70,000 Celtic fans undertook and 200,000 more claim to have. A city that turned green overnight and turned the other half of the Old Firm blue with envy.

Along with photographer Keith Campbell, my Seville began nine days before the UEFA Cup Final against Porto. From the moment the very first fans stumbled into town, right through to the hours it took tens of thousands to trudge six miles back from the stadium after the organisers kindly omitted to lay on transport, we were there.

The tsunami of support for Martin O'Neill's team was unforgettable. Yet the moment in time that sticks most firmly in the mind was before 99 per cent of them had even got on a plane.

Sunday May 18, 2003

The Last day of Sevill-isation

SUNDAY night in Seville will forever be branded on my memory as something wonderful.

A night of mouthwatering aromas, of the hum of conversation and laughter from locals at peace with life, of a whole community coming together as the searing sun went down.

As shadows lengthened and colours changed from white to pastel, the Gothic monster that is their 600-year-old cathedral never looked more stunning.

As you strolled, alleys you never knew existed introduced you to their friends, all of them welcoming you with the promise of a drink or a meal.

Then, drifting on the breeze as gentle on the skin as a masseuse's fingers, the very sound of Spain itself. Flamenco.

As the last alley opened out into the Plaza Santa Bianca, sultry senoritas clumped out the Morse code of passion with their heels; eyes tight shut, a singer wailed accompaniment while a guitarist's fingers flew and a third, silk-shirted senor turned his own hands into musical instruments by clapping to the beat.

In an unforgettable city, an unforgettable night. The last night of civilisation as we know it.

As you breathed in the sheer gentility of Seville's unique atmosphere, your heart bled for these people. It's been said so many times this past week, but it's worth repeating - they really DON'T know what's about to hit them. Within 24 hours, their favourite restaurants and bars, their secret alleyways and communal square would no longer be their own.

Seville would once more be under foreign rule.

I can't make me mind up whether these lovely people deserve 70,000 mad mental football fans less than 70,000 mad mental football fans deserve these lovely people.

But whichever is the case, as I wondered through a living work of art, it hit me that I've been wrong all along about the venue for this UEFA Cup Final.

Ever since touching down last Monday, I'd been convinced it was a wonderful place for Celtic to meet Porto. I no longer believe that; not because the two sets of fans will come to cause trouble or with an in-built disrespect for local life and culture.

It's just that football fans come on these jaunts like already-hyper kids hooked up to Kia-Ora drips and then let loose in a toy shop. The excitement drives them tonto, strips them of reason.

Put it this way. It was only when heads turned at a score of pavement cafe tables to glare at a young guy yelling down the street to attract his pal's attention that it hit me - I hadn't heard a single raise voiced in six nights here.

And this guy was a reporter with a Scottish paper who'd run around all week in his Celtic strip.

This is no downer on football fans. I'm the same when I travel with the Tartan Army - we all think we're charming and quaint and there's no doubt that in terms of damage and violence we're excellently behaved. But we take over town centres and force regulars out of bars and bawl off-key until Dark O'Clock and beyond.

That's why these games should be restricted to your Warsaws, Moscows and Birminghams, bland sprawls where a bit of singing and dancing can only help enhance the grim existence of the huddled masses.

Seville's political leaders were desperate to have this game because they need to raise the profile of their white-elephant Stadio Olimpico. Their plan of convincing bitter rivals Sevilla and Betis to quit their city centre homes and share out on the Isla Cartuja have flopped. Their dreams of hosting the 2012 Olympics seem doomed. So Wednesday night is massive for their battered self-esteem.

You just wonder what price the taxpayers will have to stump up in return for the privilege of being the hub of European football these next few days.

The stadium is miles out of town. That's not where the 70,000 mad mental will be tomorrow night. They'll stick to the heart of the action.

But here's the thing. For all that this is a big city, the heart of the action is tiny, an old town quarter where dozens of those little alleys snake out from the cathedral.

That's where the best pubs and eating houses are. And they fill up fast.

On this special Sunday night, with only the locals around, there was barely a seat to be had or a space at a bar to squeeze into.

As darkness fell, you could still count the Celtic shirts in dozens. Today, it will soon become hundreds. Tomorrow, thousands. By matchday? Pick a number and treble it.

The more I wander, the more I wonder where the hell they're all going to go.

But I knew where I'd be going if I was a local. Off to the seaside until Saturday...

FIVE years later, give or take a week, it was the turn of Rangers. An ultra-ordinary team galvanised by an amazing manager into extraordinary achievements.

In a later chapter, I'll explain why I stopped watching them away from home in Europe. The neddery and the threats just weren't worth it.

But when they made a European final, 36 years on from their last, the exile had to end. And so, I got off the plane from a weekend in Spain with the boys, got in the car and drove south overnight.

Manchester, anybody?

That had been their slogan ever since beating Fiorentina to make it through to face Zenit St Petersburg. It was a smart little phrase, delivered with a wink and a twinkling grin. It was laced with a humour that would soon disappear under a hail of hate.

There were four of us down to report on it - myself, Roger Hannah, Robert Grieve and Andy Devlin. Our excitement at covering a Scottish team on this big a stage would also soon evaporate.

The first fears of what was to come arrived when we were wakened on matchday by the sound of Orange band music blaring from a hotel window across the lane. They cranked up a few notches when we brought the car out of our underground car park, straight into an immovable wall of red, white and blue crammed between that hotel and a dingy old pub at the other end of the alley.

Our only way out was to physically nudge the bumper against legs and hope the owners were bright enough to move and sober enough not to try and overturn us. Most were. But at the end of the land, where it opened onto a one-way street where we were meant to go left, there was simply no way through.

So we had to drive the wrong way, out and onto a busy road to make an illegal right turn and pray the cops weren't watching.

We shouldn't have bothered.

They were already too busy going after that fleets of hire-vans that were pulling up at every kerb, throwing open their back doors and flogging bevvy by the case-load.

We were at the City of Manchester Stadium by half past one. For a quarter to eight kick-off.

That's the effect an invasion twice the size of Seville had on everyone who wasn't in the Bluenose Brigade. It soon hit home that the best thing to do was stay the hell out of their way and hope they went home again without causing too much hassle.

It was to prove a vain hope.

Thursday May 15, 2008
The morning after the nightmare before
WEDNESDAY morning and you strolled through the city to the soundtrack of Follow, Follow.

Twenty-four hours later and the only sound is the crunch of glass under your feet.

In hotel rooms, on sofas, in doorways and in police cells, they wake. And through the fog, the thought begins to form in thousands upon thousands of heads.

"What the hell have we done..?"

Well, chaps, here's what you've done.

You've let yourselves down. You've let your club down. You've let your country down.

You came as a conquering army, you left as a hated mob.

And it has to be asked where you will ever be welcomed again.

That's not the fault of every Rangers fan. Nine out of ten who swarmed all over Manchester will be as disgusted as everyone else about the carnage that occurred during and after the UEFA Cup Final.

But enough of their number caused that carnage to tar the whole lot with the same, stinking brush.

It's still hard to get my head round how it all unfolded. My colleagues and I had been in the stadium, writing about a football match and reporting on the outstanding support 30,000 Bluenoses had given their team.

We know now, of course, that a Zenit fan was stabbed there and that is appalling. But from where we sat, what we could hear and what we could see was awesome - and this from someone who has been the fiercest critic of a support tarnished by decades of sectarianism and aggressive behaviour.

So to emerge late at night after interviews with winners and losers to hear of baton charges and overturned cars, of bottles being hurled and heads kicked, of windows smashed and shops looted, was utterly appalling. To drive back into the centre and see the aftermath of it all was like an electric shock to the system.

The atmosphere gone midnight was horrible, a mixture in the foetid air of menace and fear. It was for all the world like those TV pictures of the riots in Brixton and Toxteth.

After we parked the car under the digs, a couple of the boys nipped out to try and get us some food. They got about three feet outside the front door and turned back. It was that threatening, that unpleasant.

So we sat in a strange apartment, eating crisps out of a vending machine and cursing the fact that here we were, covering a Scottish team in a European final yet locked up behind closed doors for our own safety.

God alone knows how the masses of decent Rangers supporters must have felt at that moment.

Cheated? Angry? Devastated?

Yeah, and then some.

Last time their club had made a game this big, it had all been tarnished by fights with Spanish police. That earned a two-year ban, later cut in half.

This time, it seems impossible that Rangers themselves could be held responsible for what went on in Piccadilly. If that was the case, England would never have been allowed to play in a major tournament for the last 30 years.

The damage, though, will be take a long time for David Murray and his cohorts to repair.

They came here knowing the world was watching - Celtic more than anyone, after their Fair Play Award-winning performance in Seville - yet they were let down badly by people wearing their colours and bawling their name.

Their attempts to turn themselves into a more acceptable, family-friendly club have been set back years.

It wasn't just the violence, either. The mess the fans left behind was quite revolting - rivers of pee, vomit slicks, a carpet of broken bottles and mangled cans. Boarded-up shops, graffiti-ed walls.

Thanks for your hospitality, Manchester.

Here, take this boot in the bollocks as a tip.

There's no doubt the sheer scale of the invasion left this city simply unable to cope. It went from an estimated 80,000 to more than 100,000 to an eventual total put nearer 200,000.

Only an idiot would believe that, even if Rangers had won, there wouldn't have been enough neds within that 200,000 to get blootered and cause trouble - just as only an idiot believes the myth that Celtic fans in Seville were all helping old senoritas across the road.

Difference was, the authorities there controlled the situation. They understood what drink does and watched the bigger picture. They made sure the lid stayed on.

Here, the police and council chiefs seemed to think that selling booze from 10am on a scorching hot day when a big game didn't kick off for another ten hours was a good plan.

Plus, it seems they bought their big screens for a tenner off some geezer in a pub.

That's your combination right there. A right good bevvy and a right duff telly.

You go all that way without a brief, the least you expect is to see the game in a square with your muckers. Then, five minutes in, it goes blank - and all you can think is: Have we scored? Will we miss the greatest moment of our lives?

That frustration doesn't excuse what came next. There IS no excuse for bottle-throwing, cop-baiting or stranger-knifing. But Manchester itself surely has to hold up its hands and admit it DIDN'T do enough to keep the lid on.

It was a bedraggled, crestfallen Rangers support who hauled itself up for breakfast yesterday. They looked at the front pages, shook their heads, barely tasted the food.

One or two sneered that the press would be loving it. Many more wore a look that growled: If we could get hold of the swines who did this...

Most of all, they all wished they could turn the clock back.

To see their team do a little more on the park. And the neds do a lot less off it.

It's too late, though. Way too late.

The cup has gone. Their reputation with it.

Manchester, anybody?

No thanks...

BUT the night where it all came together, the night where the privilege of doing this job melded with the joy of being a fan and was electrified by the terror of a squeaky-bun deadline was ... Paris.

What an occasion. What a buzz. What a team effort - players, manager, punters, media.

We got back from beating the French in the early hours. It was about half eight when the phone went and through the fog of weariness I hear our editor, David Dinsmore, asking if I'd come in and write an eight-page pull-out on one of Scotland's greatest nights.

It ran as a real-time account, from the start of the week until the last player disappeared into the darkness outside Glasgow Airport. It's too big to reprint in full here. But this is the bit that makes me quiver when I think back, the part from 75 minutes into the game until about 20 minutes after.

We came in with the nightmare of not being able to file on the big occasion. Well, this was as close as it's come to happening.

Thursday September 13, 2007
The morning after the dream before
WITH 15 minutes left, Faddy got the personal ovation he deserved.

Up went the board with 9 on it and, as one, the Tartan Army rose.

Like the pro he is, he'd gone as far away from the bench as humanly possible to waste as many precious seconds as he could trudging off.

Garry O'Connor, tattoos poking out above his shirt collar, bounced nervously as he waited for the goal scorer to finally reach the touchline, then sprinted into the action.

Faddy didn't look like he had the legs to make it ten feet to the dugout.

They all came to shake his hand, ruffle his hair, pat his back. All around us, his name rang out amidst wild applause.

At this stage of a big midweek match, it all becomes a blur from where I'm sitting. You're trying to watch and write and take phone calls from the office all at once, one eye on the clock to make sure you're ready to file a report the moment the final whistle sounds.

Ten minutes to go. Please don't let them score - this stuff's too far gone to be rewritten now.

Five to go. For God's sake call a halt, ref.

One to go. The fourth official holds up the board to show us three extra minutes are being added on.

Fifty-nine seconds into the first of them, my laptop crashes.

The screen went blue. Followed by the air. Then the little chip-driven git wizard powered down, sat there sneering for about 30 seconds - and switched itself back on.

With 90 seconds until the Send button had to be pressed, I sat there wondering if 900 words had been lost. It was a Basil Fawlty moment, you were looking around for a big branch to batter the swine with.

The fact that every letter was still where I'd left it was final, conclusive proof that this was a night when nothing could go wrong.

What happened after that's all a bit hazy.

The ball was in our box, someone hoofed it for miles, the wee Austrian ref turned to face the centre circle, raised both arms high above his balding head.

Blew his whistle once, twice, three times.

And, again, we had that split-second of disbelief. Before we leapt again, propelled by this roar coming up from the soles of our feet, a nuclear outpouring of every emotion you can mention.

There's no shame in admitting that I went to bits. The lip wobbled, tears came, the head went down on the desk. Then I realised that beside me, Andy Devlin, sports writer with the Scottish Sun was the same. Across to our left, Radio Scotland frontman Richard Gordon was standing with his jaw gaping, like a kid who's just got up on

Christmas morning to find a new bike. With Jennifer Aniston sitting on it. Naked and smeared in honey.

The players didn't have far to run to be with each other. Most of them had been back in their own area, standing up to the desperate blue tide.

Paul Hartley stood stock still, arms aloft, a living statue of triumph. Barry Ferguson, Scott Brown, Graham Alexander and Stephen Pearson were in a little mini-huddle, arms clamped around each other's shoulders. Craig Gordon went up to Faddy and they pressed their foreheads together, exchanging words of mutual admiration.

Alex McLeish was hugging his staff, then turning to salute the supporters whose devotion he'd vowed to reward with a historic result.

When you looked back up, most of the French fans had already shot le crow. Which was when you realised just how massive the Tartan Army presence was in that place.

Two local journalists stopped to shake our hands and one said: "Look at them - you have more people here than we have. It is your home game, not ours."

The other gave one of those Gallic shrugs that makes their heads tortoise down into their shirts and sighed: "The difference between your supporters and ours is that ours want to support when we are winning. They had no response when we were losing. Yours sang and cheered however the game was going."

IN THE tunnel, French faces glared, steaming with disappointment and resentment. The Scots puffed out their chests and grinned.

Barry Ferguson was one of the last into the dressing room. He expected to be plunged into a zoo, a riot of noise and nonsense.

Instead, silence.

He stared at the faces of team-mates sitting on benches, starting to peel off sweat-soaked gear, just milling around in a daze.

His eyes met those of Paul Hartley, his childhood pal and now midfield mucker. For a second, they communicated almost by telepathy, a lifetime of desire for success suddenly worth every bruise, every defeat, every manager who ever bollocked them to within an inch of their lives.

And then, the pair of them started to laugh. Uncontrollably.

The guffaws spread round the room, a release of tension coupled with the same feeling the rest of the nation was transfixed by: "How the hell did we do THAT?"

It was then that the enormity of what they'd achieved began to sink home. As each turned his mobile phone back on, the beeping was like a geiger counter in a blast zone.

Ferguson had 73 texts. McLeish had 162 - which, yesterday, he was trying manfully to answer all of. Craig Gordon's pals were telling him how much of a knees-up they were going to have. Mums, dads, lovers, mates - they all queued up to wish them well, to idolise.

The power of the text is immense. During the game, my phone went non-stop with them as pals kicked every ball back home. When it was over, everyone wanted to say something about what they'd seen, to feel even the tiniest bit a part of it.

That's teamwork.

IT DOESN'T get much better than that night. Not as a fan, not as a sportswriter.

Never before was I more glad at having stuck in and believed in what I wanted to do and to be. Never before have I had more reason to look to the skies and thank Sam McDougall.

If the new stadium inspires some other wee boy to go on and do the same, to follow his dream and find himself floating above himself, wondering how it all happened, it will be able to call itself a true home of football.

Let's wait and hope...

This Isn't Love Street

MATT KERR hears the whole town talking about a football stadium in Ferguslie Park and wonders what all the fuss is all about.

After all, there was one there when he was a kid.

Right there, the very same site that St Mirren have built on.

Except that the terraces on all four sides were bustling tenements and the pitch a patchwork of back greens, crowded with weans dribbling in and out of the clothes poles, blasting muddy balls into their mammy's clean sheets.

Matt's home was at 5 Ferguslie Park Avenue.

Now better known as the bit of the FeegieDome's away end nearest the main stand.

He grew up Saints-daft and still can't believe he managed to spend 12 years working for the club, doing everything from scouting players to running a fitness centre to helping coach the side who won the First Division in 2000.

Today, Matt can't quite get his head around the fact that the club he adores has put up a stadium where the posters on his bedroom wall used to be...

"IF you've grown up going to Love Street, that will always be home. You might go to the new place and enjoy your football, but it won't be the same.

I drive past it and all I can think is that it's boxy. It's grey.

It's hard to imagine walking through the front doors one day and getting the same feeling as I still get going in the main entrance at Love Street.

My Uncle Paddy was involved with the Pools they used to run at Saints and he was the one who first took me in that main door. I can hardly describe what that meant to me.

I've heard reporters talked about as fans with typewriters. Well, when I got a job at St Mirren, I became a fan with the key to the front door. You just imagined then the place would be there forever. Yet now, not only isn't that the case, but they've built right on top of my old house.

That's bizarre - especially as it was our arena back then, too. That was where we imagined that we were playing for St Mirren - and now that's where they'll be playing for years and years to come. It kind of blows you away.

There were tenements going round in a square - Greenhill Road, Drums Avenue, Logan Drive, Ferguslie Park Avenue. And in the middle of them all, the back greens where we played.

If we weren't playing on the greens, we'd go up a couple of hundred yards to a patch of waste ground at Craigielea and have some brilliant games. If clubs had scouted properly, they could have plucked out a team of world-beaters. You had kids with unbelievable skills, older guys playing in their stocking feet. Sometimes we used a proper ball, sometimes a burst ball, a tin can, anything.

They had old-fashioned lamp-posts on Logan Drive with big hexagonal bases. We used to paint them white and they were our goalposts; not two of them eight feet apart, but just one. We'd play with a tennis ball and you scored if you hit it off that base.

It sounds like I'm an old man here, but football really was all we had. It was the classic story of kicking a ball before school, at playtime, at lunchtime, coming home and going straight back out to play till your tea was ready, wolfing it down and playing some more till it got dark and you got shouted in.

Yet very few boys every got picked up, because in those days there was no real youth system. Most senior clubs got their players from the juniors. If Ferguslie today was the way it was then, St Mirren could throw a net over the back greens and fill the squad.

But the tenements are long gone. The families we grew up with are long gone. It's a changed place, maybe not for the better."

Sunday, September 14.

FAMOUS birthdays on this day.
- Billy Abercromby, last St Mirren captain to lift the Scottish Cup;
- Ray Wilkins, nicest man in the world and former England captain;
- Ivan Pavlov, scientist of dogs fame;
- Amy Winehouse, dog of pharmaceutical fame.

Birthdays nobody but his mammy cares about?

Mine.

Forty-six today. Another year older and deeper in debt.

Though maybe it's true that with age comes at least a tiny bit of wisdom. Because here I am, standing on the steps at St James's Station, looking across at the new stadium.

And finally, it dawns.

After seven months of watching a muddy mess sprout a giant's Meccano set, of seeing one concrete box go up after another, of watching the grass grow and the floodlights rise, the fogs suddenly clears and the something-or-other that's been rumbling round my head like cotton wool becomes something definite.

One of those moment of clarity things.

I don't like this place.

No point dancing round it any more, no use hiding from it. No need for me to pretend just so I don't hurt the feelings of the Board or the architects or the builders.

Love Street might be fraying at the edges. The bills to stop it unravelling altogether might be crippling. Selling up to your friendly neighbourhood SuperHyerMegaGiganta-Store and moving here might be the only way to keep us from going under.

But that doesn't mean we have to be happy about the alternative.

Even if we were flitting to a cross between Noo Wembley and the Nou Camp, with heated leather armchairs for every fan, green velvet shag pile instead of grass and our own private weather system so it never rains during games and the wind only blows the other team's shots away from our net, it wouldn't be right.

Because it wouldn't be Love Street.

Because there will never be another.

Just like no house will ever match the little two-bedroom tenement flat I was born and brought up in, just like no one will ever go to a school like Amochrie Primary, there will never be a football ground like the one we're leaving behind.

And how do I know this to be true?

Because everyone else who loved any other ground it happened to says exactly the same.

Muirton Park, Perth. Biggest playing surface in Scotland, big covered shed, main stand where when Alex Smith was Stirling Albion manager he once took a wrong turning coming down the tunnel and fell into the coal cellar.

Replaced by four concrete boxes on a farmer's field.

Broomfield, Airdrie. Choc-a-block with mentalists, from Section B neds to old spunkers in the the main stand, wearing two hats and spitting boiled sweeties at the back of the away manager's head.

Replaced, eventually, by four concrete boxes in the middle of a dodgy housing scheme.

Meadowbank Stadium, Edinburgh. Home for two decades to Meadowbank Thistle, the electronics firm work team who came within a point of making the Premier League before eventually becoming Livingston and moving to West Lothian.

Still standing, but under sentence of death.

Kilbowie Park, Clydebank. First all-seater ground in Scotland, first ground I ever covered a game at as an employed reporter. Social club behind one goal, press box right outside the home dressing room, which meant you missed the last ten minutes because of the steam from them running the big bath.

Abandoned, abused by vandals, torn down, forgotten.

Bayview, home of East Fife. It seemed to have about 17 different little shoe-box stands, a place where no two bits hung in the same direction, but which had atmosphere oozing out of every sweaty pore.

Replaced by new Bayview, possibly the coldest place on earth not actually inhabited by polar bears buying parkas on eBay.

Boghead, Dumbarton. I loved the big, covered terraces behind each goal; that and this little stand they used to have opposite the main one, where the press box had old-stylee phone kiosks that you had to miss the game to use.

Replaced by The Strathclyde Homes Stadium. One stand, built down at the famous Dumbarton Rock. But somehow, ridiculously, built facing away from it.

Annfield, Stirling. Where players used to change in a mansion house and where before they built a stand, fans used to watch from the back of the club chairman's coal lorry.

Replaced by Forthbank Stadium. Two Lego stands, two four-row terraces.

Then there's Telford Street in Inverness, replaced by Caledonian Stadium, now home to the city's hugely-successful young senior club. Recreation Park, Peterhead, which they quit to move to the excellent Balmoor when their chance of SFL football arrived.

Over the past 20 years or so, I've been to the final game at many of the above and wished I'd been at all the others. From personal experience and from anecdotal evidence, I can safely say that never once has the atmosphere at closing time been one of excitement.

Only of sadness, of nostalgia, of bitterness and regret.

No one ever sees it as an adventure, as an opportunity. They don't see doors opening, only closing.

Take Gordy Waddell, 40 years old and steeped in Falkirk Football Club.

His dad, Ken, edited the local newspaper and has followed the club from the 1930s. His brother, Bruce, started covering their games as a teenager before going on to edit the Daily Record.

Gordy himself has loved them as a fan and written about them as a journalist for the Daily Record and Sunday Mail for 30-odd years.

Today, he refuses to shop in the Morrisons superstore that stands where Brockville Park used to. Nothing against the company; he just can't get his head round the fish counter being where his favourite haddies used to play...

"THE WEEK before we played our first game at the new place, I wrote a piece in which I tried to say that it shouldn't matter where a football team plays, that it's all just so much bricks and mortar.

I now know that I was wrong.

Yes, some fans whose clubs have moved to shiny new grounds might be happier that they have a nice plastic seat all of their own and that they don't have to queue in the rain for a pie and a Bovril. They might like the idea of not even having pie and Bovril, but a slice of pizza and a cappuccino instead.

But I'm willing to bet that for every one like that, you'll find another ten swear it's just not the same. I'm one of that ten.

Your home ground should be an asset - not a financial asset, but one that helps the team do their job. Brockville was that for us. Other teams and their fans hated coming to us, couldn't wait to get out again.

They called it a shithole and they were bang on. But it was OUR shithole.

And I have no doubt it was that shithole that won us countless games down the years because the opposition got intimidated by the crowd or simply didn't fancy the facilities.

No one gets intimidated at the new Falkirk Stadium. Everyone raves about the facilities. It's not our 12th man.

Brockville had amazing atmosphere. Falkirk Stadium has very

little and not just because it's a breeze-block job, but because it's only HALF a breeze-block job. Two stands and two open sides do not a stadium make.

As for atmosphere? For me, all-seated grounds are killing it. Unless you and your family or mates all buy your season tickets at the same time, you end up scattered around the place. When you are all together, you all let yourself go more, you all react off each other. When you're kept apart, you're much more likely to keep your feelings pushed down. My dad, who's in his 70s, still likes a shout, but I see people turning round and looking at him like he's got two heads.

So if all around the place you have groups of fans who used to stand together and shout and sing together all being separated and quietened down, it's no wonder the atmosphere dies.

They call it progress, or change in the name of safety after the Taylor Report, but all they've done is make football more anodyne. Clinical. Plasticky. No one will convince me there's not a place at every level of football for properly controlled terraces.

There were guys who stood near me on the old Hope Street End whose names I never knew, but who I saw every two weeks and who always said hello and I said hello back to. They were fixtures in my life. Now? I couldn't tell you where most of them go at the game, if they go at all."

FOR GORDY, this change of atmosphere, this erosion of cameraderie, began on May 13, 2003, when Brockville closed its doors to football for the last time.

Falkirk had won the First Division, but their lack of 10,000 seats meant the EssPeeEll elite denied them the promotion they'd earned as of right.

There was no arguing that if they wanted to progress in league terms, they had to flit. And so, after years of back and forth with the local council, they finally won permission to build on waste ground a mile or so out of the town centre at Westfield.

But before they could go there, they had to endure a day of raw emotions when Inverness Caley Thistle came calling to bring down the curtain...

"HUGH DALLAS. He's one of my abiding memories of that day. All season we'd gone unbeaten at home and it meant so much to us to finish the job against Caley, but at 2-2 with about eight minutes left they went forward, a ball got cut back when it was clearly over the by-line and Charlie Christie scored the winner.

Right in front of the Hope Street it was, too. What a boot in the stones, the last goal ever scored at Brockville and it wasn't by a Bairns player.

Though to be fair, the game was pretty much a so-what in the midst of everything else that was going on, all the festivities beforehand and the sadness after.

When I walked out of my door that lunchtime, it really hit me. This was it, the last time I'd ever make this walk. Two or three minutes that had been one of the biggest parts of my entire life.

I'd grown up in Arnothill Gardens and now, as a married man, I was back living right next door to where I'd grown up. How many times did I make that walk, then? God alone knows. Hundreds.

Out the door, left down the street, left again, through the underpass, up Cockburn Street, down onto Hope Street, in the turnstiles, up the steps. Usual spot, never taken by anyone else. Everyone had their own favourite place.

I could have done that journey blindfolded. And that day I nearly had to, because with every step another tear formed.

They had a marquee up round the back of the main stand, with loads of old players and other well-known locals invited. My dad was there and Bruce and I were too. That was when it struck me how much it must have meant to dad, a guy who'd been coming here for close on 70 years, whose whole life was invested in it.

How could he get excited about some new-build site, out of town and with no history, no stories, no ghosts.

He watched John White at Brockville. Alex Parker. Saw the 1957 cup-winning team. He was there in crowds of 20,000-odd, when the ground was no different from when it came down. We had 7000-and-a-bit against Caley Thistle and you wondered where they'd have put twice that number again. The biggest I was ever in was about 16,000 and you couldn't move.

There was a spell not long before Brockville went when dad and Bruce and Bruce's wee boy would all sit together in the stand. Three generations, all loving the same thing. That was fantastic to see.

And one day, I suppose, there will be another generation who couldn't tell you where Brockville was, never mind what it was like to be at a game there.

I just wonder if they'll feel the same affinity with the Falkirk Stadium as we did with what we've lost."

It would be a year before the new stadium was ready, which meant a season sharing with near-neighbours Stenhousemuir at Ochilview.

92

A campaign Gordy describes as "a slog to survive ... nothing more than that."

Falkirk Football Club were marking time...

"IT WAS a rotten season. No one wanted to be there, not the fans or the team, nobody. It was great of Stenny taking us in and all that, but it just felt like we were going nowhere.

That showed in our home form. From winning 15, drawing two and losing just that last one in the final Brockville season, we only won eight at Stenny and finished well off the pace. It wasn't much fun.

Honestly? If we'd been there another year I'm not sure how many fans we'd have lost. Look at what happened to the likes of Airdrie, Clyde, Hamilton and Clydebank.

But it was all a means to an end. And that's where I came in, with that article when I tried to claim that the bricks and mortar didn't matter.

Of course they did. Or why would we have been queuing up to BUY that bricks and mortar?

Around the start of the Ochilview season, they auctioned off loads of stuff from around Brockville. My mate Peary got the boardroom door - he had to take off the hinges himself - and paid a fiver for the urinal from the ref's dressing room.

Some guy bought the pie stall from the Hope Street End. They were bidding for turnstiles, seats, crush barriers, everything that could be ripped out and flogged.

I wanted the Hope Street sign that was on the wall behind the terracing and was willing to go to £800, but some other guy went to £900. Funny thing is, about a week later he phoned me and said that once he'd got the sign home, his mates admitted they'd been down at dead of night before the auction and nicked the real one from the wall - he'd paid nearly a grand for a replacement!

Anyway, I got one of the signs from over the turnstiles with the gate prices on it. But what I really wanted was the nameplate off the Press Lounge door.

The auctioneer was down in front of the main stand and punters were sitting all the way back. I was right up the top, in the press box itself. When the nameplate came up, I started the bidding at a tenner and thought that'd be it. But next thing, down in the front row, a hand went up and offered twenty.

I thought bollocks. But OK, I'd go to £30, that'd do it. Then up went a hand: Forty.

Double bollocks. And on it went, me to £50, this other punter to £60.

Eventually, I was at £90 when someone from the club steps in. Turns out it's some woman who just wanted something, anything, to remind her of Brockville. Which was fine. But this was something I really, REALLY wanted.

Luckily, the guy from the club realises this and says to her that my dad and my brother Bruce and I had spent most of our lives in this press box and the Press Room and she should really let it go.

So she goes: 'Oh, if I'd known that, I'd never have bid in the first place...'

Pity she didn't realise till it had cost me an extra £80!

Anyway, a week after that I go back with my wife, Susan to pick up my stuff. There were maybe a dozen other people in doing the same thing and they were all in a daze. They were just hanging around, taking it in one last time.

I went into the home dressing room and there was a guy sitting in the big, empty bath. He must always have wondered what it felt like and now this was his chance.

So while we were there we took one last walk round to the spot at Hope Street where I'd always stood as a fan.

I had tears in my eyes then and I have tears in my eyes now just thinking about it.

This was the end, the last time I'd ever be there. They were coming to tear down MY step, MY barriers, MY terracing - MY football ground.

As a fan and as a journalist, I'd been on sunlit Saturdays and rain-lashed Tuesdays, seen us beat Hearts 6-0 in Joe Jordan's last game as their manager and seen us lose 6-0 to with Roddy Manley scoring two own goals.

I'd laughed there, cried there, celebrated and commiserated there. It'd been a huge part of my life and a focal point of my town.

Once you lose that, you never get it back..."

IT was February 20 when I first set eyes on the FeegieDome.

Mum was in hospital, getting a replacement knee. See? Even she wasn't happy with what she had.

The new one wouldn't be the same. Nothing ever is.

Anyway, after visiting time I went up to the Broomlands Street lights, down the new link road to the foot of Well Street, round the roundabout, then left onto Greenhill Road.

And there it was. Shrouded in misty rain, still nine-tenths mud. Our new pad.

I drove right round it, down Ferguslie Park Avenue, then back along to what would be the main entrance.

Then I parked up and wandered across to the steps of St James's Station, the one place where you could get a slightly higher vantage point of what was going on.

It was the first time I'd stood on those steps for close on 30 years. Never had any need to get on or off a train there since. It's a desolate place now, the stairs overgrown with weeds, not somewhere you want to be alone on the platform when it's dark.

But back then, when we were schoolkids and Fergie was teaching us all what football was about, St James's was a place that made us feel special.

It's about five minutes walk from The Racecourse, the sprawl of pitches where schools and Boys Brigade leagues, youth clubs and juveniles and hard-bitten amateurs went at it hammer and tongs every weekend.

For me, it was the BB. The 16th Paisley. Played for them there scores of times from 12 to 18. And when the game was over and we'd showered and changed, we'd come out of the steam-filled dressing room block and down the path and out the gate, over the dual carriageway and onto Greenhill Road.

We'd stop at the little paper shop for a hot pie or a bacon roll. Then go and act like stars.

Well, when you're 13, that's how travelling with the team by train makes you feel.

It took about two minutes back to Gilmour Street, plenty long enough to top off your morning, especially if we'd won. From there, it was round to Smithhills for the bus to Foxbar, off at the swing park, up the 59 steps, turn right and along to 25 Ivanhoe Road.

Dad would have the Heinz Beans and Pork Sausages on, the rolls buttered, the tea masking. We'd eat, watch Football Focus, then my Uncle Sam would pick us up and we'd head for Love Street.

All these places, all these little things, that on every other day of the week meant nothing. All stuff you took totally for granted - until match day.

All these years on, I always have tins of beans and pork sausages in the cupboard. And I still can't drive past St James's Station without remembering the part it played in my Saturday ritual.

Matt Kerr sees the boxes rise from the ground and, like me, his mind floods with thoughts of his relationship with the area and with his folks...

"MY MUM Patsy grew up in No3 Ferguslie Park Avenue, then actually sold a house she had to move back to No5. That's how much people wanted to live in the area back then.

My cousin Ricky McLaughlin lived at what's now the other end of that stand. He grew up to play for St Mirren in the early 70s and won under-23 caps for Scotland.

And round where the main entrance to the stadium is where Totty Beck stayed. He was a really big name when I was wee, an Icelandic player who'd come from Rangers to St Mirren. All the weans used to hang about and try to see him.

I moved to No5 from round the corner in Well Street when I was three and stayed for 27 years. It was a good place to live, full of good people. Feegie got a really bad reputation, but you had to live there to know what it was really like.

My dad Willie had a fruit and veg van that went round the streets. Everyone knew him. Not everyone paid their bills on time, but everyone fed their weans. Nobody went short.

And right across the road from our house, Stewart Gilmour's dad had a wee shop, a grocer and off licence. My mum worked in there for years. It's the only thing still standing now that all the houses have been flattened.

Mum and dad also worked in the Slumberland mattress factory just at the other end of where the stadium is now. It's also long gone, it's now a car park.

These days I work with vulnerable kids in a project based up at Castlehead High School in the centre of the town and it strikes me how different their upbringing is from how mine was. We didn't have any of the stuff they have now, the Playstations or iPods, but what most of us had were solid families and the prospect of a job.

As well as Slumberland, the town had Kellogg's, Tudor Crisps, Robertson's Jam, BMK carpets, the two giant thread mills, Chrysler, Watson's paper mill - all gone now, all of them. Thousands of jobs wiped out, thousands of families changed forever,

Then they blame the people for the way the town is."

SO I'M watching the shiny, grey metal growing from the ploughed land like some mutant crop.

First thought?

It's too small.

They've put up the back girders of the main stand and bolted onto them at either end are the end supports for what will be the rows of seats. They look so shallow, way more so than the North Bank or even the MFI stand at the Love Street end.

OK, so we're cutting our cloth, both in terms of what we can afford and what the club think our gates will be. They're maybe not daft; after all, what's the use of spending extra millions on extra thousands of seats that will never have bums on them?

But even so ... oh, I don't know. Looking down from those steps, it just seems such a sad reflection of the position we've got ourselves into, the position the whole of football has got itself into.

We play in a ground with a record crowd of more than 47,000. Where as recently as the late 70s we had more than 20,000 for Old Firm visits and the centenary game against Liverpool. Where year by year, crowds fell as prices rose out of all proportion with the entertainment on offer - and wages soared out of proportion with both.

Where bit by bit, we put in more seats and took away more choice over where you watched the game from. Where capacity was reduced and reduced until it was set at 10,800.

And now, that's 2000-odd more than the new place will have.

You can look at this two ways. The majority view will be the same as the Board's, that this is just where the game's at now, that this is our market. That the days of cramming in shoulder-to-shoulder are gone forever.

What if that's short-sighted nonsense, though? What if the good times return, if it turns out telly and computer games give you cancer and shopping goes back to being a necessity rather than a leisure activity and the ordinary punters remembers how much fun an afternoon on the terracing can be?

What if we turn up another Fergie, who goes round the streets in his hover-car, hollering through a bullhorn about how fantastic his club is and Pied Piper-ing a whole town along in his wake?

Where would they all go this time, those born-agains and new recruits who bought into his dream back when I'd just become a teenager?

Mystic Meg couldn't have seen the upsurge in interest coming when we were losing 5-0 at home to Queen of the South in front of 1400 in the austere autumn of '74.

Can anyone put hand on heart and swear we'll never see the like again?

I mean, it's only a generation ago that they shut all the cinemas because they said no one could be bothered with them any more - and look at the industry now, a multiplex in every town, popcorn sellers doing better than some US banks.

It's my dream that football gets that kind of lift again one day.

If it comes true, get down to our new stadium early to avoid disappointment.

BY THE first week in March, you could see where the front entrance of the FeegieDome would be.

As the frame for the main stand went up on Greenhill Road - right on the pavement, no driving through a car park or up a walkway - a box jutted out halfway along.

Gazing across from the station steps, seeing metal girders on three sides now, it was starting to look like what it would one day be.

The following month saw the frame of the fourth stand go up. The main side had its roof girders on. Concrete flooring had started going in. As the miserable, endless winter finally relented, the builders were given a fighting chance to deliver on time.

Now, you could count the rows. Fourteen.

Just 14.

Too small.

And, although I'm no expert in geometry, you got the feeling it meant if the rake of the stand was that shallow, the space beneath it would be reduced. Which would take away from the facilities inside.

If you were Gus MacPherson or his players or Tommy the groundsman, you'd have dreamed of giant dressing rooms and oceans of storage space. Somehow, looking across on the latest of my regular pilgrimages, that just didn't seem physically possible.

At the start of May, I flew to Spain, meaning a crack-of-dawn start when the car got dumped at an off-airport parking centre round the corner from the new stadium.

Seeing the place in the dark was spooky. It loomed, brooding, like some stranger hunched against the early morning chill. It was big enough for even the non-fan to realise what they were looking at; but not big enough to make them go Wow.

Suppose that's what I'd hoped, that it'd make us go Wow.

But the new ones never do...

IAIN MACFARLANE'S a lifelong Airdrie fan who's made his name as a sportswriter with the Daily Star and Daily Express.

He started going to Broomfield in the late 70s with the grandpa and still can't believe he got to see them play a Cup-Winners' Cup tie there before it was bulldozed.

So he knows what every St Mirren fan is going through. And he wouldn't wish it on anyone...

"WHEN they were building our new stadium, I went along to do a feature with Sandy Stewart, who'd been in with the bricks in Broomfield's final years.

The place was still a building site, a bit of a mess, but you could see the shape of what was coming. You could tell it was a football stadium.

But as we looked at each other, we were both thinking the same thing. It wasn't OUR football stadium.

We knew all the arguments for moving out of the old place. Safeway wanted the site, we were hanging on until we got permission for a new ground, Monklands District Council messed the club about for years and eventually the supermarket told us to either take the money or it was off the table.

So the board gambled on selling up and getting a deal done for a ground and it didn't pay off. We ended up having to move to share with Clyde at Broadwood and the arrangement ended up lasting three years, by which time we'd lost so much in terms of support and belief.

Of course we were delighted to get the news that we were moving back home. And it's a perfectly nice stadium - to be fair, they actually spent a fair bit making the frontage and the foyer really smart.

But as I stood there with Sandy that day, the phrase that springs to mind is non-plussed. I was neither here nor there about it.

I thought then what I think now - and I'm sure every St Mirren fan will understand this. It just wasn't Broomfield.

That place was unique, just like Love Street's unique. It had that daft little doll's house pavilion at one end, a real tardis of a building that held the dressing room, the boardroom, tearoom and God knows what else.

There was talk about it being taken down brick by brick and rebuilt at the new ground and I'm not sure if that would have been right or wrong. But one thing's for sure, it was utter sacrilege for it to be ploughed flat by a wrecking ball."

Broomfield staged its final match on Saturday May 7, 1994, a First Division game against Dunfermline. I was there and it was a fantastic occasion. Back then, Iain was editing the match programme.

"THERE was a kind of symmetry about the timing of Broomfield coming down, because it had been staging senior football for exactly 100 years.

We knew all season the end was coming, so there were a lot of "last ever" games along the way. The last ever time we'd play this team or that team. The last ever Scottish Cup tie, a 0-0 draw with Dundee United.

And then, it was the last ever game. I still remember it really clearly, from first to last. One major thing is that as well as doing the programme, I was with Radio Clyde and was due to be working on the Scoreboard show that day. David Tanner, who's now with Sky Sports, was in charge and I told him there was no way I could work that day.

Fair play, he knew how much it meant to me and that if he said no, I just wouldn't turn up, so I got his blessing. But come hell or high water, I'd have been at Broomfield.

Still, at least when St Mirren get ready for their last day, they know the new stadium is built and ready to go. We didn't have one and that made the Dunfermline game all the weirder.

The over-riding emotion from that day is still sadness. My grandpa had died a couple of years earlier and it seemed wrong that he wasn't there. My gran was there, though ,as was my dad and my wife Tracey.

We went to Sharelle Dalziel's coffee shop for bacon rolls, then walked up the High Street, went in our usual turnstile behind the goals at the pavilion end, walked round to our usual place about ten yards short of halfway under the shed roof.

When I was wee, there was no segregation fence, so we'd change ends at half-time. If there was a penalty at the far end, all the kids would run round behind the goals to see it. At the pavilion end, there was one of those old scoreboards that had letters on it instead of team names, so you had to buy a programme to get match them to the fixtures.

People would be going: "I see game F's two-each". And someone else would go: "Aye, what's F? Anyone got a programme..?"

The match ball was delivered by parachute that day. Old managers and players were introduced to the crowd. After all that, the game was almost an irrelevance - though even then, there was a disappointment, because although we won, we did it with an own goal.

It just doesn't feel right that the last-ever goal on the last-ever day at Broomfield was scored for us by Neale Cooper of Dunfermline.

As soon as the goal went in, police and stewards ringed the place to stop us getting on the pitch, but they had no chance. When the final whistle went, thousands went on, grabbing anything they could rip up.

I got a lump of turf. My dad climbed into the main stand and tore out my grandpa's old season ticket seat. Everybody wanted something, anything to remember the place by.

After that? I suppose everyone just milled around holding their souvenirs, not quite sure what to do with themselves. It was like: "What happens now?"

I remember standing on the pitch, feeling a pang of regret that I never got to play on it. My grandpa and my dad had both been in Airdrie Schools finals there, but my folks were uncaring enough to move to Lanark when I was five and that was my chance gone.

The other memory was of my first-ever pitch invasion - it was a Lanarkshire Cup Final against Hamilton Accies, an amazing night when we had to start with our centre-half George Anderson starting in goals because John Martin was on a miners' strike picket line!

We were 2-0 down in about 20 minutes, but then we saw big John Martin running round the track and everything changed. We ended up winning 3-2 and everyone went on the park to celebrate.

My first riot was when I was about seven, a Motherwell game in '79 when we beat them to win promotion to the Premier League. It all kicked off big time just round from the corner flag at the pavilion end.

Some of their fans must have sneaked in and next thing there were bottles flying and people scattering all over the shop, people getting carried away bleeding. And I'm this wee boy standing there going: 'What the..?'

As for seeing us play in Europe? That still seems utterly surreal.

We'd lost to Rangers in the cup final, but they won the league, so we got into the Cup-Winners' Cup as runners-up. We drew Sparta Prague and it's a night that will stay with thousands of us forever.

I got the train in and as I got off the sky was black, a real dirty night. I walked the 500 yards or so up the hill, the ground loomed into view - and there it was, the UEFA flag flying over Broomfield. All I could think was: 'Hang on, this isn't right.'

We lost that night and went out after the second leg, but it didn't matter in the big scheme of things. We'd been there, which my dad and his dad could never have imagined ever happening."

And then, the odd little stadium that bound their lives together was gone. A trolley park where the doll's house once stood, the cheese aisle over the halfway line.

They shacked up at Broadwood; home of Clyde, themselves turfed out of Glasgow by progress and long-term nomads before settling in this windswept, concrete box on the edge of Cumbernauld new town.

Home was never a word Airdrie or their fans used to describe the place...

"WE HAD about 9000 in for the final game with Dunfermline. Of them, maybe 3500 would have called themselves hard-core fans. By the time we left Broomfield to move back to our own town in '98, we were down to 1500 or less - and that was to watch a team sitting in the top half of the First Division.

The team actually did not bad in the Broadwood years. They even made the Scottish Cup Final again in '95, losing 1-0 to Celtic. But we still lost fans and we've never really got them back.

Why's that? I think community and a football club's place within it has a lot to do with it. Broomfield was like most 19th century grounds, built in the town centre, within spitting distance of the railway and bus stations and surrounded with pubs.

Broadwood? It was only a few miles over the A73, but so inaccessible it might as well have been on the dark side of the moon.

You couldn't get a train to it from Airdrie, there was no scheduled bus service. In short, unless you had a car, you were screwed.

When we had Broomfield, you could sit in the Double A pub across the road till ten to three, drain your pint and stroll in. Now, people had decisions to make; they'd look out the pub door at two o'clock, see the drizzle, look back into the pub and ... well, you know the rest.

Even the ones who did go didn't like it as much. In an all-seated ground, you can't choose to wander over and see your pals. Your choice is restricted, your movement restricted. It all adds up."

The club Ian supported was actually called Airdrieonians. Today, they are no more, forced out of business by financial collapse in 2002.

A new board, led by accountant Jim Ballantyne, formed Airdrie United. They tried to get into the Third Division, but were pipped by Gretna.

Then, when Clydebank folded, Ballantyne took them over and used their league membership to keep Airdrie's name alive. The best Ian can say of the move is that it was a means to an end...

"I FULLY accept the original Airdrie board's reasons for selling Broomfield. My problem with them is that they didn't do more to get us somewhere to move to there and then.

I also don't have a problem with what Jim Ballantyne did - at least there's still football in Airdrie and we still play in the famous diamond shirts.

But there's no doubt in my mind that while some clubs have moved from their long-term home seamlessly, we came apart at ours.

If I'm honest, my heart's not in it with the new club the way it was with the old one. I'm still a supporter, I still want us to win, but I don't feel as bad any more when we lose.

My job has something to do with that; you detach yourself a bit when you're watching different teams every week, you're not right in there with your pals on a Saturday. But I'm sure I'm one of many, many who thought they'd be Airdrie till they died, but who were left watching the club pass away instead and who haven't got over it.

My favourite time to be a fan remains the spell from about '86 until Broomfield went. We got Gordon McQueen in as manager at the start of that period - imagine, us with someone famous in charge! - then Jimmy Bone won us promotion to the Premier league before leaving in the summer and being followed in by Alex Macdonald.

Under him and John McVeigh, we had that amazing spell of the two finals and European football with a team full of characters, or real men who our fans loved and everyone else's hated.

My favourite memory of Broomfield? Any game when we attacked the pavilion end in the second half. No matter the game, no matter the score, you always felt like there was some magical power in that old doll's house, sucking the ball towards the net.

Broomfield was a fixture in my family life. So much so that when my grandpa had a heart attack, he chose to have it in the main stand.

It was a game with Alloa - and to be honest, there was nothing happening out there to make your heart stop. But he took ill and next thing I'm shouting for ambulance men and they're hauling him out and we're heading for Monklands Hospital.

He told me not to tell my gran, though when he didn't come home at five o'clock she soon found out.

That was our ground for you, though. Good memories, bad memories. Even memories of something as serious as that make you smile..."

THE thing that amazes me about building projects is how they get the straight lines straight.

Think about a motorway. How do they start with one digger

ploughing one yard of soil and end up with 50 miles of perfectly undulating, six-lane road?

It's all very well having computer-generated plans and those wee tripod-y things they look through to heck they're going where they're meant to, but what if Johnny JCB goes all skew-whiff or Tommy Tarmac's got a hangover?

For me, it's a miracle the M8 from Glasgow to Edinburgh didn't end up taking you via Fort William.

Maybe it's just because I draw less straight than a cross-eyed cowboy. But even Tommy Doc lining the pitch baffles me. How does he get everything at right angles?

As the final season at Love Street kicked off, the FeegieDome was a stadium in all but fans and action. It had four sides, a white-panelled roof, floodlights.

Most importantly of all, it had a pitch. The one thing the game of football cannot do without.

Without it, we could build an 80-seat perspex-roofed arena with electric recliners and hot and cold running dancing girls and it would not be a stadium.

With it, we don't need stands, we don't need corporate boxes, we don't need turnstiles.

It is the game's one constant. It is the game's heart.

One of the great privileges of my job is the access it gives you to parts of grounds you could never enjoy as a paying punter. Cup of tea in the boardroom, chat in the manager's office. Wander in the tunnel without being pulled up, chat with the players out on the track.

There are, however, two things I will not do before a game.

1. Go into the dressing room.

2. Walk on the pitch.

Both are sacrosanct. Outsiders have no place in either place; and by outsiders, I mean anyone but players, gaffers and match officials.

That's where Matt Kerr's a lucky man:

"IT WAS 1992 when Saints took me on as a scout and youth coach. I became under-18s coach under Jimmy Bone and Kenny McDowall, then when they opened the fitness centre in the new Caledonian Stand, I got taken on as manager.

Jimmy left, Tony Fitzpatrick took over and he made me community coach. When Tony went and Tom Hendrie came in, I moved to become reserve team coach and chief scout.

I suppose what that all shows you is that at a club like St Mirren, everybody pretty much does a bit of everything.

Just turning up for work at the place every day was a joy, but there's no doubt the 2000 title-winning season was the highlight for me. I was working with the first team on matchdays, so to be that close to what was happening was a dream come true.

It was a season that started really badly for our family, because my dad died of cancer in the August, the same weekend as the young left-back Chris Kerr got his knee wrecked at home to Caley Thistle. It was a terrible time, but I'll always be grateful to the club for the way they treated my dad so well in his final months.

There was a game against Morton when they fixed him up with tickets for the good seats right in the front of the main stand. That was such a big thing for him, because all his life he'd been a terracing man - his favourite place in Love Street was right at the old floodlights, between the stand and the Caledonia Street end, where the ground came up into a mound.

We beat Morton 3-0 that day and I just remember looking up from the dugout at the end of the game and seeing his face beaming, his fist clenched in triumph. That's a memory that will never leave me.

The day of his funeral, we were all settled down when we heard movement at the back of the church. When we turned round, Tom was leading the whole squad in, all wearing their club suits. My mum said they looked like an army on the march. That gesture still means so much to us.

So as that season went on and we were right up their fighting for the championship, I thought about my dad more and more. It felt with every win that we were kind of doing it for him.

We had some great wins, too - 6-0 away to Raith, a fantastic 4-1 at Morton, 8-0 at home to Clydebank. By the time it came down to the last few weeks it was just tremendous to be part of.

And then, on the second-last Saturday, it was all about beating Raith at home to win the league and to go up.

What a day. Everybody seemed to have a black and white flag, it was party time. But everyone was nervy, too, and we struggled right through the first half. The thing about that time, though, was that we just kept going and kept attacking and once we got one goal we got two and then three and the place went mental.

The release of happiness at the end was frightening, everyone was just overjoyed. Eventually, we got back in the dressing room and players started drifting off to get changed, Tom went off to do interviews and there were only a couple of us left.

I looked at the trophy sitting there. Thought about it for a second. Then I picked it up and walked out the dressing room, down the tunnel, onto the pitch and into the centre circle.

Then I held it up to my dad and we had a wee chat. It was a lovely, private moment between us.

Or at least I thought it was private...

It was only when I got back inside that Shug Murray and Steven McGarry said to me: 'Was that you?'

I've gone: 'Was that me what?'

'On the radio?'

Turns out a Radio Clyde microphone had picked up every word, it had gone out on air and Hugh Keevins and Derek Johnstone were discussing this daft guy having a conversation with his dead dad!

The following week, Hugh actually apologised because his wife had pulled him up and said it was wrong for them to intrude on my privacy. But the truth is that my mum was thrilled that it had gone out live and that it was then reported in the Scottish Sun on the Monday.

For her, having her husband become part of such a special day meant the world. She still keeps the cutting from the paper with her.

The next day, we had an open-topped bus ride through Paisley, finishing with us on the balcony of the Town Hall. My wee boy David called it the best day of his life and it's not far off mine, either.

Mind you, if I had to pick my other greatest moment with St Mirren, it would be one that had a totally different meaning from winning a title - the day we won at Stirling to make sure we didn't get relegated from the First Division.

It was 97-98 and the club was under huge financial pressure. A guy called Reg Brealey was trying to buy his way and most of us were convinced that would be really bad news. I'll never forget how Tony Fitzpatrick came out publicly against Brealey and backed Stewart Gilmour's plan to take over instead. Tony could have kept his head down and protected his own back, but the club meant more to him.

Anyway, with a couple of weeks to go we could still have gone down. It was going to be us or Albion, so we went to Forthbank desperate for three points.

When Shug Murray popped up with the goal late on, you could taste the relief. We celebrated at the end as if we HAD won something - and then I remember me, Tony and the other coach Joe Hughes going back out onto the track, hugging each other and bursting into tears with the sheer emotion of it.

We didn't even notice that there were still about 300 Saints fans in the stand opposite us, all partying and singing. Those fans deserved better than they got that season, which was why I couldn't have been happier for every one of them when we won the title so soon after.

To hear them still singing when we were 5-0 down at Inverness on the final day, the flag already in the bag, was incredible. In the end, Tom had to go into the main stand and shout down to them: "Go to the pub - have a night out!"

MY greatest dream was always to play at Love Street. If not as an actual player, then in a BB cup final or even in some Old Fat Blokes charity game.

The chance has passed me by.

Played at Hampden, twice. Cappielow, where I took a pee in the home dressing room sink and it came out the bottom of the pipe and went all over my socks. Brockville, three times. The wind tunnel that is Gayfield, Arbroath.

On the rock-hard, first-generation astro at Stirling Albion's old Annfield, I smashed a left-foot volley into the top corner and my pal Tim Harper - now sadly taken from us - called it the best goal he'd ever seen scored by someone as bad as me.

I had half an hour for the Scottish press against the English press at Parkhead, the night before the Euro 2000 play-off game. They had me man-marking Peter Beardsley. I might as well have tried to teach him to recite Shakespeare in Italian.

But the call never came to run out of the Love Street tunnel. And I suppose now it never will.

Why am I standing here thinking all this?

Dunno. Maybe because I don't want to entertain what my mind wants to think. That what I'm looking at isn't the start of something new.

That it's the end of all I've ever known.

First it's the house you were born, then it's your primary school. And eventually, they decide you're not getting to keep ANY of your childhood. Because now, Love Street is coming down...

AND here's the real kicker.

As mentioned right back at the start of the book, it's not even about making way for a SuperHyerMegaGigantaStore any more.

Turns out Tesco were never actually going to build one in the first place, the little scamps. All they really wanted was the right to build one, but with the option to build one somewhere else instead.

That somewhere else is about a mile down the road at Wallneuk, just off the Renfrew Road where there's currently a ten-pin bowling alley, a lorry park and a faintly sinister-looking boozer.

Tesco's plan now is to sell Love Street for housing; which presumably means they'll make a loss, as St Mirren's whole argument with the local council was always that the site was worth about half to a property developer as it was to a supermarket chain.

Which, if my tiny brain's keeping up with it all, suggests that there will soon be a whole whack of smart new homes springing up where our beloved team used to play. But nowhere for the smart new householders to buy a loaf.

Well, except for the wee ethnic minority shop on the corner of Albion Street, whose owner will now be forgetting his own beliefs and singing What A Friend We Have In Jesus.

Because it looks like he'll be having Christmas every day.

Whit Ur Ye Really?

HE'S a diamond, is wee Matt Kerr. Forty-two carat, Del Boy would call him - honest, kind, 100 per cent committed to everything he does.

But more than anything else, he is what he is. No side, no airs and graces. No pretence.

And that goes for his love of St Mirren more than anything else I know about him.

Now, for viewers outside Scotland, that last statement might be a bit of a So What? Job. It might never have occurred to you that anyone could doubt that if you say you're an Exeter fan or a Sheffield Wednesday fan or a Hartlepool fan, that's what you are.

This side of Hadrian's unfinished patio, though, we know different.

Because this is a country where even if you walk down the street wearing a St Mirren shirt, a St Mirren scarf, a St Mirren woolly hat, St Mirren gloves your mammy knitted for you with the name of a player on each finger (then realise that's only ten players and decide to get the name of the 11th tattooed onto an actual finger), even if your socks and underpants read I LOVE ST MIRREN AND ABSOLUTELY NO ONE ELSE, even if you change your name by deed poll from Arthur McDonald to Saint Love Street O'Buddies Mirren, there will be halfwitted people who will look you in the eye and say:

"Aye, but whit ur ye really?"

These people are known as Old Firm fans.

A breed - not two tribes, because colours apart they are one and the same - who cannot accept that anyone outwith their nasty, bigotry-and-suspicion-fuelled little world might choose to devote their support, their energy, their money and their loyalty to anyone who isn't Rangers or Celtic.

They are, they have always been, they most probably always will be, the bane of my life/

Sunday, August 10, 2008.
IT'S the week before that Kilmarnock game when the pitch-lining machine packed up.

Love Street is empty.

But it's not silent.

No, it's growling from its foundations to the top of the stripey North Bank roof. It's an angry old sod. Because when one of us is hurting, we all hurt.

And boy, are we hurting.

Another away day taking on one of the Bigot Brothers. Another trip home wondering why we bother our arses trying.

A better whitewash job than any groundsman could ever manage.

Down to the bare bones through injury, up against the EssPeeEll champions and their 60,000 punters, we're having a blinder. Knocking it about like WE'RE the ones heading for Europe. Denied the lead by the width of a post. Stifling the McGeadys and the Robsons and the McDonalds as comfy as you like.

Until the 61st minute.

Then, Lee Naylor lumps another hopeful ball forward. John Potter misjudges the flight and it flicks off the back of his head. The mistake wrong-foots Will Haining, who lets it through his legs and is turned by Jan Vennegoor of Hesselink.

Then .. well, what happens then is a microcosm of the eternal, unwinnable struggle between the Haves and the Have Nots of the beautiful game.

It's St Mirren away to Celtic. But it could be Kilmarnock at Ibrox, Wigan at Old Trafford, some La Liga struggler in the Bernabeu or Serie A relegation fodder in the San Siro.

The big team's striker knows he's not getting his shot off properly. So down he goes. Up go the 60,000.

Into the ref's mouth goes the whistle.

Down the pan goes all the wee team's hard graft.

Which would be hard enough to take in itself without the knowledge that it simply wasn't a penalty, all day long. All night long. And all the way through the next month of Sundays.

Here's what referee Eddie Smith saw.

Jan Vennegoo ... cobblers, call him The Dutchman ... gets away from Haining, who panics, grabs him and hauls him to the deck. Stick-on spot-kick and therefore a straight red card.

Now, here's what actually happened.

The Dutchman sees his chance, puts himself between Haining and the ball, puts his left arm out behind him and grabs the front of the defender's shirt. Tries to get his shot off, slices it wide of the right-hand post. Falls over.

From behind, you see Haining put his left hand on The Dutchman's wrist, the way you do instinctively when someone grabs you. His right arm's spread wide. He's done absolutely nothing to make the striker go down.

Yet he's off. We're a man down. They have a penalty.

What makes it worse is that when Barry Robson takes it, our keeper Mark Howard gets his legs to it, takes the power off, but just can't get back in time to scoop it off the line.

Goal down, ten men. Game over.

I was off work that day and sitting watching it on the box. When it all happened, I picked up the phone to ring my colleague Robert Grieve at the game. Rewound the Sky+, watched it another couple of times to make sure bias wasn't clouding my judgement and told him what the script was.

Robert's a St Mirren man too. He was raging. I was raging. Poor Will Haining was raging. The ten guys he left behind were raging. On the bench, manager Gus MacPherson, his coaches, the subs, the kitman, the physio and the doc were raging.

And, yes, I like to believe that Love Street itself was raging.

That's the relationship we have with our football ground. It's not just bricks and mortar, it's way more than a rectangle of grass with concrete steps on all four sides.

In fact, if the smug gits who make those Marks & Spencer ads were marketing a football ground, they'd have some honey-throated sort breathing:

"TURNSTILES, smooth as nyloned legs crossing. Stairwells feeling like new-mown grass beneath your feet. The first glimpse of the arena, like dawn in the pink-walled Jordanian city of Petra.

Bovril that plays with the tastebuds like '67 Chablis. Gourmet pies. Wagon Wheels the size of manhole covers.

Premium seats that make those Audi ones in the Man U dugout look like a splintered park bench. Match programmes handwritten in fountain pen and placed on your lap by Sharron Davies in a wet swimsuit.

Constant sunshine, but never in your eyes. No wind, except when their goalkeeper tries to take a bye-kick. Every goal celebrated by the scorer coming straight over and thanking you personally for your support.

This isn't just any football ground.

This is SMFC's football ground..."

Anyway, the reason for sharing all this is that on occasions such as these, the full extent of how lucky I am to be in this job hits home. Because it allows me to be one of the very few to have somewhere positive to channel my rage through.

One hour later, one column written. A demand for refs who can't tell a foul from a fair challenge to be suspended and sent back to school until they see the error of their ways.

After all, this wasn't Smith's first offence. Not even in fixtures between these two sides.

Six months earlier, three minutes from the end of our game with Celtic at Love Street, Gary Mason tracks back with Shunsuke Nakamura. It's 0-0, we're working our tails off to keep it that way.

Mason gets himself between man and ball, cutting off any chance of a shot. Nakamura goes down.

Smith gives a free-kick.

Nakamura puts it in the pokey.

The ref swears to this day he got the decision right and that he would make it again. In other words, take your dumps and shut up, little team. You can't fight The Man.

That was the basic premise of the next morning's column - that not only did Eddie Smith need to learn the rules, he needs to stop assuming that because the big team player goes down, it must be a foul.

However, here's the twist. Here's the jaw-dropper.

Here's why the Old Firm are the bane of my bloody existence.

See, to Celtic fans, this was not a journalist with St Mirren leanings ranting about his team getting the rough end of it against the same team from the same ref for the second time in two meetings.

This was an anti-Celtic, anti-Catholic journalist ranting because Rangers were in the middle of a crisis.

Mental? Of course it is.

But you know what? If I'd written exactly the same article except about us being robbed at Ibrox, THEIR fans would have come out with allegations about anti-Rangers, anti-Protestant journalism with an agenda to help our pals at Parkhead.

For this, my friends, is the lot of the non-Old Firm supporter.

The constant frustration at their utter inability to accept that anything happens outside their horrible little bubble.

The persistent argument they put up that everyone cares one way or another about them.

The question that never goes away:

Whit Ur Ye Really?

A bizarre inquiry if put by, say, an Ayr United fan to a Stirling Albion fan, a Scunthorpe fan to a Rotherham fan.

In Bigot Brothers world, though, perfectly pertinent. If not absolutely essential.

See, they exist by a credo that everyone is either One Thing or The Other. By which they mean Protestant or Catholic.

And therefore, by their bitter little definition, Rangers or Celtic.

It doesn't sink in that someone might be a devout follower of their given faith without it impinging upon what team they follow. Doesn't compute. Blows their chips big time.

Chips away at my patience every time they spin their stupid, narrow-minded theories.

Which is often.

Email No1 the morning after the Haining sending off:

"STRANGE to see that you want Eddie Smith sacked as a referee, whilst not calling for the same punishment for other referees who make glaring mistakes.

Why do you not want Mike McCurry banned from refereeing, for two incredulous decisions that benefited Rangers against Dundee Utd last season? Two mistakes in one game, both that denied Dundee Utd goal scoring opportunities and could have influenced the outcome of the SPL title?

That's right, it's only the few supposed Catholic referees that you want banned ...isn't it?

Let's all allow McCurry (Baptist minister ...wonder who he supports, eh?) the freedom of Glasgow ....and let's castigate Eddie Smith. Yeah, sounds about right for the Scottish media."

Now, point one. Who ARE Baptists supposed to support?

And point two, I never mentioned Smith's religion. Neither know nor care what it is. Yet that's what it gets turned into.

113

Which brings us to e-mail No 2 of the day:

"MY seat is right behind that goal, it looked a stonewall penalty when Big Jan ran through with Will Haining behind him. With benefit of countless replays, you can see it's not a penalty and that Eddie Smith was conned by a top player.

It doesn't suit someone like yourself to be balanced though. Think Helicopter Thursday and Kaunas have gotten to you a bit.

Let go of that hate, eh? It's only a football match."

Helicopter Thursday, for the uninitiated, was the final night of the previous season, when the EssPeeEll trophy was on a chopper waiting to see if Celtic clinched the title at Tannadice or Rangers snatched it at Pittodrie.

Celtic won it. And their gloating carried on into August, when Rangers were then knocked out in the Champions League qualifiers by a tinpot Lithuanian outfit.

What's all that got to do with a St Mirren player being sent off?

Hee-haw.

But these people have a magnificent talent for shoe-horning their own petty grievances into any completely unrelated scenario.

HERE'S how it works.

Whenever Rangers win an Old Firm game and I happen to write that they played well, I know what's coming next.

Floods of Celtic fans labelling me an Orange bastard.

Whenever Celtic win an Old Firm game and I happen to write that they played well, I know there will always be an equal and opposite reaction.

Floods of Rangers fans labelling me a Fenian bastard.

And even when an Old Firm game ends in a breathless, frantic, titanic 3-3 draw packed with every physical and emotional element from wonderful football to limited nuclear skirmishes and I write that the result was just about spot on, I still know what's coming next.

Floods of Rangers and Celtic fans calling me a dirty Fenian Orange Mickey Tarrier Pope-Loving Queen-adoring Masonic Knight of St Columba Bead-rattling Big-drum-battering Bastard.

Got it? Good, I'll be asking questions later.

Like: Why don't they sod off and get a life?

Answer: Because they truly believe they already have one and that it's better than yours and mine.

114

These are people so one-eyed they make Cyclops look like Buddy Holly, whose minds are so narrow their brain-cells walk in single file. Not that three brain cells in a line hold the traffic up for long.

They have this thing going on inside their heads that if you criticise their half of the Bigot Brothers then you must be a full-paid-up fan of the other one. Even if their half is having the season from heaven and you've written a million words of praise, stick in one half-hearted jibe and they're straight on to you.

"Ye just cannae see us daein' well, can ye? Ye're just so sick that YOUR lot urnae winnin', eh? Eh?"

"In what way?"

"Well, in the 26th paragraph of your report on Saturday's game, you mention that one of our players hit a poor pass. Ye've just been sittin' there, waitin' tae pick holes. Ye're lovin' it!"

"Look, sorry to split hairs here, but didn't you read the previous 25 paragraphs and the ten after that in which I called your team's performance the finest since Brazil won the 1970 World Cup?"

"Naw."

"So all you read was one line that wasn't even criticism, but simply a comment on the fact that one of your guys DID play a poor pass?"

"Aye. Ye've always had it in for us."

Then you get the calls after their team have taken a real humping.

"You really are in yer element, eh?"

"Sorry?"

"Ye couldnae wait tae put the boot in, could ye? Aye, go on - gie us a slatin' just because we got beat."

"Well, it was 4-0. At home. To Albion Rovers."

"Aye?"

"And Rovers did get three men sent off in the first half."

"So?"

"And the ref did give you six penalties, none of which your guys even got on target."

"And yer point is?"

"My point is that a packed stadium booed your team off at the end, thousands of scarves were thrown onto the track, season tickets were ripped up and the manager and players needed police protection."

"So? That's not unusual!"

"From their own families?"

"Aye, well…"

"Aye, well, the point is this - I take it you're a regular. In which case

115

there's every chance you booed them off along with all the rest?"

"Aye, as a matter o' fact, Ah did."

"So what's the problem?"

"The problem is that it's OK for us to boo them - they're our team. But you're well out o' order, because they're no' your team."

It's not just the fans, either. The clubs themselves, right up to the top bananas, live by the belief that you're either with them or against them.

If you're against them, you might as well be dead. But even if you're for them - something that can be applied to a lot of guys in my game - it's no guarantee of a warm welcome.

If anything, it can be harder for reporters who are also Old Firm fans, because once the fans know they're reading something written by one of their own they expect the same blind loyalty they themselves show. Anyone who doesn't comply is even worse in their eyes than the likes of me.

Neither club, neither set of fans, ever genuinely welcomes you. They merely tolerate you - and that tolerance diminishes in direct relation to how badly they've performed, because in Bigot Brothers Bizarroworld, the worse they do, the more they believe your enjoyment increases.

And you know what? The more they tell you that's how you feel, the harder it is not to feel like it.

The more barriers they put up against you, the more they distrust you, the more they treat you like an outsider - an enemy - the more you have to resist getting off on them doing badly. Even though every cell in your body is screaming YEEHAH when they fail, the same way you'd react against anyone who makes your life a misery.

SEE, had Oscar Wilde been a football fan, he would surely have observed that the only thing worse than an Old Firm diehard whose team has just lost is an Old Firm diehard whose team has just won and is sticking it right up your every orifice.

Take Celtic. For years they won nothing and their paranoia at the perceived conspiracy being mounted by everyone non-Celtic-minded (© former chief executive Jock Brown) to make sure they continued to win nothing was hysterical both in its frenzy and its laughability.

Then, once Martin O'Neill arrived at the turn of the millennium and they started winning stuff again, they got all paranoid that everyone non-Celtic-minded couldn't wait to see them lose.

Yet here's the thing. Rangers - the club as a whole and the fans as individuals and a unit - react exactly the same in both victory and defeat as their arch-rivals do.

So you have to wonder why the pair of them have never sat down and thought for a second that for this paranoia to be justified would mean the outside world wanting both of them to win the league, which simply isn't possible.

We're in single-file brain cell territory again...

What is possible, of course, is for the outside world to want neither of them to win the league. Or anything else, for that matter.

The only problem is trying to get them to believe it. Because there hasn't been an Old Firm diehard born who believes for a nano-moment that it's possible for any non-Old Firm diehard not to have a preference for one or the other of them.

So here we go.

The grilling.

A pair of them - could be from either side of their invisible barrier - sidle up with that self-satisfied look that comes with too little respect for too much success. And it begins.

"St Mirren fan, eh?"

"Yep."

"Good for you."

"Thanks."

"No problem."

"Well, that's nice, then."

Pause...

Aaaand...

"OK, so who d'ye really support?"

"Er ... St Mirren?"

"Aye, but, really really."

"Like I said, St Mirren."

"Aye, but who's yer Old Firm team? Ah mean-"

And this is the crux of the whole thing...

"-whit ur ye really?"

"Listen, let's stop this nonsense before it starts. I don't have an Old Firm team. What I am really is a St Mirren supporter."

"Sure, sure, they a' say that. You an' Chick Young anyhow. But we a' know what he is, so what are you? Forget for a minute that ye need tae keep yer cover as a neutral. It's me ye're talkin' tae."

"Doesn't matter if I'm talking to the 17th Annual Convention of Namibian Washing Machine Repairmen. I'd still tell the truth, that

117

I'm a Paisley man who supports St Mirren and nobody else."

There's now another pause while they prepare to change tack as tactlessly as a tack salesman spilling tacks on a racetrack.

"Soooo...Paisley man, eh? Nice town, Paisley. Nice people. Lovely streets. Idyllic scenery. Good, er, schools, eh?"

"S'pose."

"So..."

"So...what?"

"So which of these aforementioned good schools did ye go tae?"

Bingo.

Time to make their combined brain cell collection - six - run round screaming like a drunk woman on a hen night who's just seen a mouse at the very moment her knickers caught fire.

"Eyal Berkovic Academy."

You give them a few seconds. Then, deep among the cobwebs, something begins to compute. They go into a little confab. And you hear one whisper to the other: "Eyal Berkovic? Whit was he, then?"

"He was Jewish, wasn't he?"

"Aye, course he was - but was he Proddy Jewish or Catholic Jewish..."

You see this as your chance to make a sharp exit. But they're like dogs with a bone now, they're on you.

"Aye, right, smart-arse - funny wan. But listen, see when ye cover an Old Firm game, right?"

"Riiiiight..."

"Whit wan wid ye prefer tae win?"

"Neither."

"So ye always want a draw?"

"No, I always want them both to lose."

"Ye cannae."

"Well, whaddya know? I do."

"No' possible."

"Is."

"Isnae."

"Look, if this debate's going to get all intellectual, we might as well agree to disagree."

"OK, OK, but if somebody held a knife tae yer throat-"

At this point you start hoping the conversation remains on a hypothetical plain.

"-an' says ye must pick a winner or die, what's yer choice?"

"I'd take the cut throat."

"Bollocks. Everybody supports wan or the other."

"No they don't."

"Aye they dae."

"No they DON'T."

"Aye they d-."

"Again, the level of argument's making my head spin, so if we could move on…"

"OK, so who'd ye tip tae win the last Old Firm gemme?"

"Rangers."

"Ah! So ye're really a Rangers man!"

"No, I thought they'd win. And, by the way, they lost."

"So ye were takin' the piss, then? Ye're a Cellic man really?"

It can go on like this for hours. I remember one year at the Daily Record when Rangers were going for 146 In A Row or something and I was the only one on the sports desk to tip Celtic to stop them.

Guess what? Come Monday morning the phones are going mental with Rangers fans calling me a Fenian bastard. Apparently I'd offended their sensibilities, the sensibilities of their entire families, of their local Free Church minister, of John Knox's ghost, of Her Majesty Queen Elizabeth II and all her Commonwealth and of Bomber Brown and Durranty.

Then, after about an hour of abuse, this guy comes on.

"Hello, Bill Leckie speaking."

"Izzat Bill Leckie?"

"An astute observation, whatever gave me away?"

"Well, ye said: 'Hello Bill Lec-.'"

Irony. Close cousin of goldy and bronzey in this gentleman's vocab.

"Never mind. How may I help you this fine morning?"

"By admittin' ye're a dirty Orange bastard."

Now, even by the standards of the most ingrained Old Firm halfwit, this one came right out of left field.

"What? An Or-? How do-? I mean, where did-? Listen chief, what you on about?"

"That keech in the paper on Saturday."

"Would that be the keech where I was the only sportswriter on the paper to tip Celtic for the league?"

"Aye."

"Which by definition made me the only sportswriter on the paper not to tip Rangers for the league?"

"Aye."

"Not to mention just about the only sportswriter on any paper not to tip Rangers for the league?"

"Aye."

"Notwithstanding the fact that there are as yet undiscovered tribes in the darkest recesses of the Amazonian rainforests who sent smoke signals to William Hill putting all the beads they possess on Rangers for the league?"

"Aye."

"And that makes me a dirty Orange bastard how exactly?"

"Because ye were just bein' sarcastic..."

And he meant it. He really spat the word sarcastic, especially the sar- bit, like I'd personally coughed on him and given him incurable Hong Kong flu.

You can't win with people whose minds are set this way. If you tell them to beat it, slam the phone down, walk away from them in the street or the boozer, they turn back to their mates and say: "See? Tosser!"

If you don't take their calls in the first place or blank them when they shout your name, they think you're Charlie Big-Spuds.

But if you give them all the time in the world, you just get your ears battered and there's less chance of you getting a result than of both the Old Firm meeting in Champions League final in the same season as Holyrood forces through a Bill making the singing of sectarian songs within football grounds punishable by life imprisonment.

So it's back to our Dynamic Duo. And on it goes.

"So come oan, whit ur ye really? Who's yer team."

Sigh.

"For the umpteenth time, St Mirren."

"Well, Ah thought as much. Ye look the type."

"What type?"

"Ach, they were always a big Tim team, eh? Whit aboot the five-nothin' gemme, last day o' the season in '86. Lay doon oan the Pope's orders that time, nae sweat."

"Sure. The fact that Hearts chucked the league away by losing 2-0 at Dundee the same day had nothing to do with it. And neither did us having ex-Rangers star Alex Miller as manager and Jim Stewart on loan from Rangers in goals. And remember, we had ex-Rangers boss Alex Ferguson as manager before and Rangers-daft Ian Ferguson once scored the winner for us in the Scottish Cup Final."

"Aha! So ye know for a fact that they're a' Huns, then?"

"That's right, you got me. I cracked their secret codes."

"Anyway, Ah'm still no' clear about what ye are really. So-"

Rearrange the words camel, back and straw into a well know phrase or saying.

"No, not so. No more so. End of so, take your so and stick it where the sun doesn't shine, Poirot. Then listen to this carefully, pal, because it's not going to be repeated. I hate the Old Firm. Both halves. Equally. I loathe Old Firm games. I think they should both be deducted points just for playing them."

"Well that's a bit mu-."

"Shut it. I also hate Old Firm fans like you. I despise your bigotry. I hate the way you wangle tickets for the home ends at away games and treat the place like they own it. I abhor the platitudes both boardrooms spew out every so often to make it sound like they want rid of sectarianism rather than be honest and admit it's their greatest marketing tool."

"Naw, come oan. It's only a minority who-."

"Bollocks it is. And anyway, I said shut it. I wish Glasgow City Council had the guts to close Ibrox and Parkhead on the grounds that both are used as breeding grounds for the support of terrorism. I wish the rest of Scottish football had the guts to refuse to let Old Firm fans into their grounds - in fact, better still, not to play the gits ever again. The Premiership? Europe? Jupiter? I don't give a monkey's where they go and play, I just want them to GO - in fact, I'll drive the train, sail the ship or pilot the bloody rocket that takes them there? But better still, let's not have them playing anywhere. Let's shut them down. Bankrupt them. Jail them. Nab them, grab them, jab them, stab them - crush them, grind their horrible faces right into the dirt. Exterminate the bloody pair of them! OK? Get the drift? I'M A ST MIRREN FAN AND I DESPISE THE VERY EARTH BOTH RANGERS AND CELTIC WALK UPON? RIGHT?"

And as I catch my breath and feel the veins in my neck throb, there's a short silence and then they put their palms up in a fair enough gesture.

"OK, pal, OK. Don't chuck the teddy oot the pram. Ah get it, ye're a genuine St Mirren fan who has no preference for either of the Old Firm and who, moreover, loathes and despises them both and wants nothing more nor less than to see them exterminated. Point taken."

"Good, glad that's sorted."

"Right then."

"Excellent."

"Ah'll go then."

"Fine. Have a nice day."

"Ah'm offski."

"Right, nice talking to you."

"You an' all."

"Love to the kids, we'll do lunch."

"Sweet."

"Your people can talk to my people, eh?"

"Sure. Oh, but just wan last thing, though…"

"What?"

"Ye know how ye want Rangers and Celtic exterminated?"

"Yeeeessss…"

"Which wan dae ye want exterminated just a tiny bit less than the other wan..?"

MAYBE I bring it on myself by giving them both so much stick. But their reaction to criticism only proves just how small and insecure they are despite their size and on-paper wealth.

They should be so big that one guy writing one column in one corner of one paper should be like a flea bite on an elephant. It's not, though. Every word really gets to them. They hate it. Which to me means they know most of what I'm writing - be it about the underachievement of their millionaire idols, the overspending of directors who lose all business sense at the first glimpse of a floodlight, or the way they themselves cling to sectarianism like a Linus blanket - is nearer the truth than they'd ever dare admit.

The upside of it all is that other fans of non-Old Firm clubs, people without the platform of a national paper to express their feelings on, come up and say thanks for saying what they'd love the chance to.

The downside is going to beautiful cities across Europe and having to keep your head below the parapet instead of taking in the sights like any other tourist.

In Valencia or Turin, Lisbon or Istanbul, you'll be walking down a street, soaking up a new culture, when you see them coming the other way. Five or six strong maybe, all in their wash-and-re-wear replica tops or club polo shirts, scarfed up, club-shop-blinged up. Swaggering.

Oh, oh.

Now you've got a dilemma. Do you:

d. Keep walking and ignore them?

e. Acknowledge them and get a mouthful of abuse? Or;

f. Cross the road, probably get a mouthful of abuse anyway and look like a wimp?

So you're across the road looking intently into an ironmonger's window and you hear it: "Aye, you, ya dirty Fenian/Orange bastard! Ye write a loada shite!"

(Note: Few fans actually call me a Fenian/Orange bastard. It's rarely a grey area with them, although I did once have a nasty run-in with East Stirling's infamous Agnostic Casuals.)

Still, it says a lot about the kind of people who shout this stuff that:

1. They usually wait until they're ten yards past before shouting it;

2. Their patter's usually as unfunny as an MP's joke during Prime Minister's Questions.

And that's fine. If a few cowardy-custard jibes is where it all ends. But the more the years have gone on, the nastier these people have got.

The first iffy moment was in Kaunas with Rangers back in 2000. Just after time up, with their team safely through, three beer-bellied, 40-ish, drunkish Rangers fans walked into the press box - it's down at ground level, right in with the punters - and started giving me dog's abuse.

"Aye, you, ya Fenian etc etc."

"Ye write some loada etc etc."

"Yeah - and on top of those criticisms of your work, we also feel ye could do with shedding a couple of excess pounds!"

Then one of them decides I haven't paid enough attention to this riveting banter, so he comes over to me, right up close and paranoid, nose-to-bulbous-nose. And stares. Just stares, so hard that he goes cross-eyed. Or maybe they were close together to start with. I look away. He tries to follow my eyes.

My colleagues suddenly find something very interesting to look at under their desktops.

Eventually, the guy gets bored and walks away, but about five minutes later he comes up again while I'm on the mobile to the office. Again, he gets up close and personal and stares, breathing stale beer in my coupon.

I keep talking.

He keeps staring.

Then, fed up with his failing attempt at intimidation, he walks off, muttering words such as "fat", "Fenian" and "bastard".

In Vigo with Celtic a couple of years later, we were leaving the hotel to walk 400 yards to the stadium and had to pass a gang of fans crowded round the bar.

One of them blocks my path.

"Leckie?"

"Guilty."

"Ah know what room you're in. And Ah'm gonnae set your bed on fire."

"Fine, we've just checked out."

Inside, though, you're a bit shaky. You always see those signs up in the Post Office and in shops, warning customers that staff have the right to go about their business without being threatened. Raise your voice to some call centre drone whose firm have failed to deliver the goods and they'll hang up on you.

But in this job, you stand there and take it. Especially in these days of camera phones and website gossip - as I found out in Milan with Celtic at the tail end of 2007. We're having a beer in a bar next door to the hotel, eight or nine of us. The place is full of Celtic fans, all happy that they've just made the last 16 of the Champions League. We're having a real laugh with them - a cracking night.

Except that, sitting at a table in the far corner, there's a group of half a dozen young guys. Giving us the eye. Every time one of them goes to the loo, he has to pass us - and makes sure he brushes against me.

Eventually, they make to leave. As they do, they stop, turn and start chanting about ... well, about me and some one-in-a-bed sex romps. One of our lot notices one of their lot filming it on the mobile, so we keep our mouths shut.

Then, as the bar staff shepherd them out, one turns back and says something that I hope he woke and regretted. I certainly regretted trying to get at him and having to be held back.

Next morning, the whole thing was on YouTube.

Still, that wasn't as nasty as a night in the Polish town of Wronki in October 2004.

On the way into the ground, I met an old school pal, Tom Donaldson. Huge Rangers man, good guy. We had a laugh, caught up, wished each other good luck.

An hour later, I'm sitting in the press box, wondering if I'm going to get out in one piece.

I was sitting second from the end of the row, with Gordy Waddell nearest the iron railing that divides us from a 20-foot drop down to a gangway. On the other side, there's a new stretch of terracing. The official Rangers support - maybe 600 of them - are in a section in front of us, but directly to my right are a gang of around 50 who've obviously travelled on their jack and picked up tickets on the night.

They do not look like they've just come from cuddling sick puppies.

They give it away ten seconds after kick-off. And then one pipes up.

"Leckie, ya Fenian bastard!"

That's fine, keep the head down.

"Aye, you, ya wanker!"

Yes, I'm aware of to whom you're referring.

Then it's two of them at the same time.

"Ya prick!"

"Tosser!"

Their patter's magic, I'll give them that.

It's a classic situation where any reaction and they'll be right on your case. But no reaction will only make them try harder to get one. By the time 20 minutes have gone, they've still not had one, though I'm noticing that many colleagues seem to have edged away to the other end of the row.

Away at the far left, six appear to be in the same seat.

Unfortunately for the guys covering the game for Radio Five Live, they can't move. A point brought home to them when from across the gap flies a crusty roll that misses me by inches but whacks the commentator square on the napper.

I mouth apologies to the guy, shrug and nod my head towards the drongos. He nods his understanding.

Now, at this point, it would be nice if a steward or a cop moved in and told them to calm down or they're out. No such luck, though. In fact, they do the opposite of calming down - there's now three of them right up at the railings on their side, gripping them like monkeys at the zoo and screaming non-stop abuse.

Between then and half-time, I get the full bigoted megamix - You're A Papish Tosser (U-huh, U-huh) - and it starts to grate. These clowns don't know you, have never spoken to you, have never been personally mentioned in anything you've written. Yet they hate you and it shows in every spit-flecked insult.

Two in particular - a lanky, thin-faced fella in a woolly hat and a wee podgy one with a permanent, malevolent sneer - have barely watched a kick of the ball. All they care about is yelling at some journalist they've never met. And the longer they go on, the more others who started out having nothing to do with them decide it'll be fun to join in.

All the while, by the way, I'm sitting there with my laptop actually on my lap - there's no desk to put it on - writing about what's happening on the park. No problems with nail-biting finishes here, for once, because Rangers were coasting from early doors. No, the only worry was how to keep focussed on work when the No Surrender brigade are giving you dog's.

Soon, the catcalls are coming from all over the Rangers section, all religiously-motivated. All fairly disgusting. And all, as it happens, inaccurate. Though one manages to make me laugh to this day.

"Haw, Leckie," came a voice from in among the Brains Trust, "you've a cheek callin' yersel' William!"

Where do you start, friends, where do you start? You feel like calling him over, sitting him down and going: "Mate, I don't call myself William. It is true that my mum and dad had me christened William, but my part in the creative process was less than minimal. It's also true that my family refer to me as Billy, but I've long since dropped the 'y' for several reasons.

"The first is a simple linguistic one - Billy Leckie just runs together too much like I come from Stranraer. The second is that Bill sounds more growed-up. And the third is because if I stayed as Billy, then people very much like you - but totally opposite, if you see what I mean - would give me the very same pelters that you and your pals are at this present time. Yes, even though the guy who once lifted the European Cup for their team was also called Billy. Now, sod off and let me get on with being abused in peace..."

Instead, I just smiled inside and shook my head. And the lanky, thin-faced once shouted: "Whit the f*** you shakin' yer heid at?"

Then something bounced off my shoulder and whacked into the temple of the Five Live commentator. It was a coin. This was as far removed from fun as it is possible to get without actually being in the same room as the cast of Keeping Up Appearances.

Fair enough, they took a break at half-time, had a fag and a beer and discussed tactics for when it all got going again. But then they were off and howling again.

Won't bore you with the whole second half repertoire, but it included some hugely unpleasant songs about my wife, children and mother. Let's just say their depravity was matched only by their capacity for invention.

Yet with the increase in intensity of the verbal carnage came the need for an equal and opposite likelihood of reaction. In other words, the louder and nastier they get, the calmer and more detached you need to try to be.

I managed well enough. In fact, with ten minutes to go they were almost tuned out of my head as I clattered away on the keyboard.

Until a big grog landed on the back of my jacket.

It felt like someone else was standing up, turning to face them and shouting that they were dirty bastards. Sadly, though, it was me. And they loved it.

They're hanging onto the railings now, faces purple, fingers pointing. They're signalling that they'll be waiting outside for me - and the fact is, we have to walk past their exit to get back to the bus.

No point hiding it, I was trembling. Only Munro the Cleaners will ever know how much they shook me up. It was a nightmare situation to find yourself in any time, but right there and then it felt like no one else cared. No one was stepping in to stop them. Even the ones who'd think of themselves as decent Rangers fans looked like they were enjoying it.

Earlier in the game, I'd phoned club PR officer Carol Patton - sitting in another stand with the directors - and told her the situation. I'd hoped they'd maybe send someone over to have a word with them, but it never happened. But a couple of minutes from time up, the podgy one with the sneer shouted:

"Leckie - you're getting' slashed when this is done!"

That was that for me. I phoned Carol again and asked her to get someone across pronto. She sent their security guy, all blazered-up and ready to run the gauntlet.

The final whistle went. The drongos hung about at the top of the terracing, watching. My colleagues got their stuff together and disappeared as quickly as possible - all except, to their eternal credit, Gordy and Daily Record man Davie McCarthy, two guys who'd never see a pal stuck.

All I had to do now was send the copy. But would the phone line work? Would it hell. One try. Two tries. Three tries. Now, I've got the office on shouting about deadlines and the drongos bawling about violence.

Home seems a long, long way away. Suddenly, the idea of this being a dream job feels like a sick joke.

I do what all computer whizzes do. Shut down, unplug, take the battery out, put it back in and boot it up again. It seems to take hours.

I hook up the mobile to the machine by its little cable. Do the keystrokes that tell it to send.

We wait. The drongos wait.

Never will I ever be happier to see the word: SENT.

Then out we went, me in the middle of the other three, the security guy at the front. None of the drongos carries out their threats.

Back to the main stand, straight into interviews with Dick Advocaat and his players. More copy to file. As I hang on the phone, waiting to speak to my gaffer, it strikes me that I'm still shaking.

Only once we were back on the bus did I tell him what had happened. He promised to take it up with Rangers. The club promised to do something about it. Nothing happened, of course. It never does.

Go to Ibrox or Parkhead as an away fan and stand up to complain about a dodgy decision and the stewards will have you out on the cobbles before you can say The Ref's A Homer.

Yet thousands upon thousands of home supporters get to spew out the kind of stuff I got in Wronki throughout every game and it all gets rubber-eared. What happened to me that night is only the same as happens to the away dugout all the time, to opposing players from the moment they step off the bus to when they take throw-ins and corners to when they head back to the bus again.

That's not to say that fans of EVERY club don't dish out abuse, because there's no doubt that over the years a day at the game has become more about slagging off the other lot than it is about supporting your own heroes.

There's no doubt, though, that Rangers and Celtic have more nasties, louder nasties and nasties with nastier agendas than anyone else.

When I came into newspapers, nights in foreign countries reporting on our biggest teams were what all the hard graft was for. They were the goal, the grail.

Yet in the wake of Wronki, I barred myself from going abroad with Rangers again until the club could guarantee safe passage.

In fact, it would be another 43 months before I went to see them anywhere outside Scotland. And after Manchester, another 43 months without following them would be about 4000 too soon.

OH, and I got an actual death threat once. Landed on my desk three days after a piece digging Rangers up for not disciplining Paul Gascoigne after he beat up his missus.

We were right in the middle of all that Zero Tolerance stuff, yet they were more concerned with the fact that he'd been red-carded in a Champions League game away to Ajax.

Anyway, the article's in on the Monday. The death threat comes on Thursday, by fax. A fax sent from the threatener's place of work, a factory in East Kilbride. I know this because the name, address and fax number are at the top of the page.

BRIGHT BOY WANTED:
Apply within

So I phone the number and ask for personnel, explain the situation and they're horrified. I fax them it over, they check the handwriting against staff records and bingo, there he is. The man who says he's going to kill me.

Turns out he's 50-odd, a husband and father, a faithful employee with a blemish-free disciplinary record. Yet he reads something in a newspaper that makes him so angry that three whole days later he risks everything he's worked for by telling the guy who wrote it he's for the malky.

They hauled him in, suspended him pending an enquiry, asked me if I wanted to press charges or have him sacked. But why do that to his family? I told them to give him a fright and let it be. In the end he wrote me a letter of apology, but I never read it.

And he hasn't killed me yet, so that's nice.

The Gascoigne wife-beating thing really did open my eyes, which isn't something you can say for poor Sheryl. You wouldn't believe - or maybe you would, maybe I'm just naïve - the number of blokes who phoned or wrote saying: "Aye, right - so you're sayin' ye've never gie'd her a slap for steppin' out o' line? What ur ye? A saint or somethin'?"

That shook me as much as all the abuse that's spewed in down the years.

Loads and loads of them send emails and letters, maybe 100 a week. And they're never, ever about football. They never want to talk about how this one's playing or why that one should be dropped. It's always some spin on bigotry, division and hatred.

You get regulars, ones you end up playing tig with. It can actually be quite fun, these little sparring sessions. Sometimes they have the class to drop a quick line when something you write actually impresses them, though usually the best you can ask for is that they appreciate the fact that you've bothered to reply at all.

But then there was this one bloke. A real trumpet. A Rangers fan whose sheer horrible-ness stood out like Sharron Davies in a cold snap, who bombarded me with bile about the fact that I'm not dead yet, how when I go it should preferably be in a horrible motorway pile-up, how I'm a traitor to everyone who ever fought for the right to be Presbyterian and how my Auntie Sadie's an astronaut.

You know, constructive stuff.

He called me Jill Specky, a hilarious nickname first used in a Rangers fanzine. If you don't get its Izzard-esque subtlety, try rhyming it with my real name.

Take your time, take your time.

Got it?

Bet you're glad now you wore the extra-strength girdle today.

Used to get about one a week from him. Never answered them, yet he kept on churning them out. Sometimes I used to think he had half a dozen templates for them set up on his PC and just sat there going:

"OK, time to abuse that twat again - but which one to choose? What mood am I in?

"Do I wanted him mutilated by an oncoming juggernaut? Or burned at the stake for not being a good enough Protestant? Let's see - eeny, meeny, miney, Mo - no, not Mo, he was that Fenian who played for Her Glorious Imperial Majesty's Sons of William FC and forever sullied the colours - no, come on, catch a grip, more important things to think about here. (But note to self: Send abusive e-mail to M. Johnson soonest.) Anyway, which one for Jill Specky today? Ah, there it is:

"Dear Heretic,

You still breathing? Shame. Isn't it time you fell off a charging horse, tumbled into an electrified fence, rolled over it, plummeted 120 feet down a sheer cliff on the other side, just missed a massive pile of mattresses and came down head first into a mantrap? No, that would be too good for you, ya dirty (continues in this vein of insanity for another 2546 words)..."

Still, it comes with the territory, a small price to pay for the privilege of being paid to travel the world getting into football games free and writing about them.

He said through gritted teeth.

One thing I always insist on, though. Whenever I've been abroad, I always like my next game to be as - how do I put this? - homespun as humanly possible. So if it's Munich on the Wednesday, it's Montrose on the Saturday. I came back from a Tuesday game in Eindhoven once and went to Dingwall the next night. It's a kind of detox, it reminds me what football's all about.

(Who's ghost-writing this stuff? Tom Hanks?)

Same goes when there's an Old Firm game on a Sunday. On the Saturday, I'll try to go somewhere with three or four hundred punters who don't feel the need to bring their intolerances with them to the game like a foul-smelling packed lunch.

In among that hardy 300 might be Protestants so bitter the Rev. Ian Paisley would ask who the uptight fella was. Catholics so paranoid about being repressed by the evil Establishment that the Holy Father himself might pass them a spliff.

But somehow, with incredible force of will, they manage to forget all that and just shout at the referee for being blind or at the right-back for having two left feet.

The hardcore among the tens of thousands who follow the Bigot Brothers - which by my reckoning is in the nines of thousands - will tell you all they're doing is expressing their social beliefs through the medium of sport.

Wur Culture, they call it. Even if as culture goes, it's down there with the stuff that grows between a tramp's toes.

Yet between them, their clubs have won something like 200 major trophies. One has a European Cup in the cabinet, the other the Cup-Winners' Cup. Both have been in UEFA Cup Finals since. They've been thrilled by Jinky Johnstone, Davie Cooper, Ally McCoist, Henrik Larsson, Alan Morton, Danny McGrain and scores more wonderful players.

Yet what do they ding about? Irish potato famines, 17th Century battles and the paramilitary struggle over British rule in Ulster.

Well, tell a lie. Celtic fans did come up with one about the great stars of their past, the chorus starting:

"And he gave us James McGrory and Paul McStay..."

But even then they couldn't resist adding in: "...and the IRA."

Which I'm sure would have made both men sooooo proud.

Then there were the Rangers lot with their anthem Simply The Best and the bit Tiny Turner never sang:

"Call when I need you, my heart's on fire,

F*** the Pope and the IRA..."

They are a truly bizarre breed, your lesser-spotted Old Firm supporter. So arrogant and yet so insecure. So much to be happy about, yet so obsessed with anger.

We should envy them the easy life of following teams who nearly always win.

Instead, we almost end up pitying them.

If only one day we could be rid of them.

Now that WOULD be simply the best...

FINALLY, a footnote on where we came in.

St Mirren appealed against the red card, the SFA threw it out, Will Haining served his ban.

Eddie Smith was shown the video evidence of the diddy team player not fouling the superstar. But still said he was quite content with the decision he'd made.

Not really much more to add, is there?

But Never Mind Me,
Whit's HE Really..?

CHICK YOUNG finished interviewing the Rangers manager, put down his headphones and walked across to where Alex Rowan used to sit.

He said a few words to an empty seat about St Mirren's 1-0 win over the Glasgow giants. Had a little laugh to himself. Then went downstairs to meet Jimmy Rowan in the corporate lounge next door to the away dressing room.

Jimmy's a diehard Bluenose. He's also Chick's brother.

As Radio Scotland's main man walked through the door, every head turned to see him grinning all over his face.

And Jimmy shouted: "Ye see that? Surely NOW you believe who he supports..."

But most never will. Chick knows it and we all know he knows it.

Does he care?

Does he bollocks.

BIZARRE, isn't it? That what team some football reporter supports can have become the subject of such heated argument for so many years.

Everyone wants to know who Chick Young really supports. It's sparked more mass debates than Kim Basinger's performance in Nine-And-A-Half Weeks.

Johnny Watson, the mimic who made him a legend on the Only An Excuse radio and telly shows, has him pegged as the guy with the best eyesight in Scotland - he can follow St Mirren from the upper deck of the Copland Road Stand.

Everywhere I go and the whit-ur-ye-really thing comes up, you say you support the Buds and somebody in the company goes: "Aye - like wee Chick."

Sigh.

But that's the baggage that comes with the kind of fame Chick's earned over the years.

If you live outside Scotland and don't know who we're talking about here, this is the potted version. He's a balding, smiling, wise-cracking writer, broadcaster, after-dinner speaker and frustrated midfield genius with an eye for the ladies, a taste for a nice glass of vino, two mobiles that never stop ringing and a diary that overflows with offers of work.

If you didn't know him, you'd meet him for the first time and reckon he was all front. But beneath the bravado, he has the kindest of hearts. Not to mention one that's been broken more than once.

He manages to graft non-stop but still have a frantic social life. To constantly sniff out stories yet stay close with those he unearths them about. A city boy who's rarely happier than when messing about on his boat in blissful silence.

A mass of contradictions. Bit like his footballing loves, really.

In the 30-odd years since he started out as a cub sportswriter, he's become way more than a name at the top of a match report or a voice coming out of your wireless.

For two decades now, he's straddled the line between the media and the celebrities it creates, feeds off and ultimately destroys. One minute he's putting his microphone under the chin of a star everyone's talking about, the next he's being talked about himself.

His private life has become public property. His mannerisms have been charicatured to the point that if it was him v Watson for a Chick Young Soundalike contest, he'd be lucky to come second.

Yet of all he's done - and sometimes hasn't done - to make him the subject of gossip and rumour, nothing comes close to who he supports.

Does he kid on he loves St Mirren to disguise his actual passion for Rangers? Is he one of those strange types who believe it's somehow possible to have a wee team and a big team?

Or have we all got it wrong and he's secretly a Borussia Moenchengladbach devotee?

Here, at last, I can exclusively reveal the truth.

"IT'S funny, but I was doing something on Eddie Thompson's death the other day and it struck me that his love affair with Dundee

United was a bit like mine with St Mirren.

He had no lifelong connection with them, but when he moved up there from Glasgow, aged 24, he took to them and that was him hooked.

That's pretty much my story too. I've heard a million times that I'm only a kiddy-on supporter, but the truth is that I never once claimed to be born and bred a Buddie.

On Only An Excuse, wee Johnny Watson portrays me as a Rangers fan from Paisley, when the complete opposite's the truth - I'm from Govan, but follow St Mirren.

It was that wee swine who really kicked all this stuff off. After he started taking me off, everybody was asking who I really supported.

I'm long past caring about it, to be honest. I don't get annoyed or laugh about it, it just goes in one ear and out the other.

Though it was funny after that Rangers game. For a start, I was about to interview Walter Smith and he went: 'Take that smile off your smile before you ask me any questions'.

I'd taken my brother Jimmy - he's my stepdad Alex's son - to the game along with his wife Dorothy, my partner Celine and her son Conor. The wee man's a bit torn about who to support - when he's with his dad it's Rangers, but with me he tries to be into St Mirren, bless him.

But there's no hiding it with Jimmy, he's Rangers through and through. So I fixed up for them to go in for a drink after the game and when I was done with Walter and Gus I went down to meet them.

Jimmy must have been getting it in the neck from everyone about what I was really was. So when he saw the look on my face and shouted that to the room, the everyone fell about."

SO, what IS he really?

Fill a flask and settle into your favourite armchair for that one. It takes a fair bit of explaining.

"TO BE honest, I had a pretty wayward existence as a kid. I actually preferred playing football to watching it and it's still my greatest regret that I was denied a professional career by a tragic lack of ability.

I played with Albion Motors, who got to the quarter-finals of the Scottish Amateur Cup in 1973. Ayr United and Partick Thistle gave me trials and I then got an offer from Irvine Meadow, who were Scottish Junior Cup holders at the time.

But by then I was a journalist and decided that was a safer career option. I went to London to work for a magazine instead and never regretted it - even if I am still hoping to get picked up by a senior club one day. I mean, I'm only 57.

But back when I was wee, trying to make it in football was all that mattered. All around me, though, were Rangers fans. I went to school in the shadow of Ibrox. We even had a headmaster, George Brown, who'd been a director at the club.

I guess I rebelled against all of that, particularly the bigotry element. I couldn't get my head round it then and I'm no nearer to understanding it half a century later.

Plus, my mum wouldn't let me go to Ibrox because she was worried about the big crowds. Which makes it strange that when I asked to go with pals who supported Clyde and Third Lanark to see their teams, she said yes, even though it meant two buses across Glasgow.

It's not that I never went to see Rangers - you couldn't live that close to them and not. If I'd lived in Janefield Street or somewhere like that, I'd have been the same with Celtic. If you're lucky enough to be within touching distance of big stars, you want to see them.

During the holidays, we used to walk through Bellahouston Park to go to the Summerton Road baths in Govan and on the way back at lunchtime we'd see players coming out of Ibrox. That was a huge thing for us.

By the time I was ten and 11, Rangers had the great team with Baxter, Caldow, Wilson and the rest and there were plenty Saturdays when I went down to get a lift over or got in for the last 20 minutes when the gates got opened.

But what most people don't know is that by then I was actually a HEARTS fan. At the end of the 50s, they were the big team in Scotland and I suppose I was attracted by the fact that they won things. I was still into them well into the 60s - sounds weird now, but I remember being broken-hearted when they lost the 1968 cup final to Dunfermline.

So where did the St Mirren thing come from? Well, my dad died when I was five and my mum re-married to Alex Rowan. He was steeped in St Mirren, he's watched them through thin and thin, the dark days and the darker days.

He had them like a disease. And it turned out to be infectious."

THERE are plenty who'd say that infection must have messed around with Chick's brain.

As he admits himself, the easiest thing in the world would have been to give in and follow the herd down to Ibrox.

But as long as I've known him, he's always been a guy who's gone his own way, done his own thing and lived with the consequences.

"WHEN I started going to Love Street, people round our way looked at me like I was daft. To them, Paisley was the ends of the earth.

But then I realised that to Paisley people, GLASGOW was the end of the earth. What are we talking about here - seven miles? Yet you try telling a Buddie that they're part of the city and they'll bite your head off.

I've been on a few testimonial committees for Saints players over the years and can't believe the opposition you get when you suggest holding dinners in one of the big hotels in the city. They're like: 'Glasgow? You kidding?'

You know, everybody gets uptight that Rangers and Celtic buses leave Paisley every week. But by the same reckoning, people shouldn't come from outside Paisley to watch the Saints - and that's daft.

Anyway, my career started taking off and I got sent to cover St Mirren games. When that happened, dad started coming with me.

Then, as I got to know people at the club better, they'd get me tickets for him. Every season, my brother Jimmy - Alex's son - would buy dad his season ticket and the club looked after him. I suppose I reckoned getting him into places he hadn't been would impress him. You do that with your dad once you grow up.

The time the St Mirren thing started growing on my personally was around the end of '74 when Fergie arrived from East Stirling. It's a sign of how small news it was that I was sent to cover it, because I was way down the pecking order at the Daily Express back then.

I remember there being about half a dozen reporters in the old boardroom. We got tea and digestives - and not even chocolates ones.

After that, I got to know Fergie quite well. Maybe he saw me as a young guy on the way up, the same as he was, because in his eyes I didn't seem able to do wrong.

We used to play five-a-sides on a Tuesday afternoon at Bellahouston Sports Centre. The rest of us kept that going long after he'd left for Aberdeen.

So with that and with the decency I found in other people around Love Street, the place started to mean a lot to me. Then the whole fairytale thing started, the run to the title and into the Premier League, and dad was loving it.

The other guys I was really close to were Alex Smith and Jimmy Bone. I'd love watching JB playing in the black and white - that solo goal of his against Aberdeen about 1981 was one of the greatest I ever saw. So when he and Alex took over in '86, it was great news for me.

Not long after that, I lost my had. And I guess I've just carried on what he felt for the Saints. Through him, Love Street's become a really special place for me.

Over the past 20-odd years I've been around the place as much as possible, become friendly with other managers, have sponsored players, hosted dinners, helped with videos.

So, dyed-in-the-wool? No. But shot through with affection? Definitely."

AT A time like this, that affection has to be mixed with reflection.

The club's looking forward; the fans can't help looking back.

Fans of Chick's age - says me sounding like a youngster - also can't help thinking that things will never be the same again.

"DON'T get me wrong, Stewart Gilmour and George Campbell have done a fantastic job. Without them there might not be a St Mirren today, so maybe in the long run moving to a new stadium is a small price to pay.

It's just that the older you get, the more you fear change, so it's probably when you get to this vintage that you get more bothered about leaving Love Street behind.

But there's a new generation out there who won't feel that way and generations to follow who'll grow up with the new place and come to think of it the way we do the old one.

I can't say I was thrilled about the stadium as it went up, even though it made perfect financial sense to be building it. It's amazing what a bit of St Mirren-ification does, though. Once you get your stamp on a new home, it feels more comfortable.

Plus, let's be honest. If you analyse it closely, Love Street's a dump. It's had its day, the facilities aren't good enough any more.

Yet for all that, it will always remain one of the most magical places in my life. There's Turnberry, where I love to play golf really badly. There's Millport, a little piece of heaven on earth. And then there's Love Street.

These are places you can set foot in and immediately feel better about life, no matter how it's treating you.

When this season started and you knew the end was coming near, it became any excuse to go down spend time there. Because pretty soon you'd be there for the last time, which didn't bear thinking about.

Like most people, I've spent a lot of time these past few months thinking back, dredging up memories of all the best and worst bits of our time following the Saints.

My favourite game was actually away from home - Christmas Day at Kilbowie in '76. I went with dad and the place was a lock-out. What a game, back from 2-0 down to draw 2-2.

As for Love Street, the memory that will never leave me's the Hammarby game. I'd been over in Sweden and we'd all been overjoyed at Brian Gallagher's hat-trick that gave us a 3-3 draw. So to then be 1-0 up with only a couple of minutes to go at home only to lose 2-1 ... it was just a nightmare.

My favourite player has to be Tony Fitzpatrick. He epitomised everything that's good about the club and about professionalism. The way he buzzed around filled the whole ground with energy, you couldn't help but enjoy watching him.

I loved Jimmy Bone as well. And Ian Ferguson, for far more than just winning us the cup. He was a terrific player, someone who got you out of your seat.

Then there was Guni Torfason, one of our first foreign buys and a really good striker. And Campbell Money, a terrific keeper who could have gone all the way if he'd believed in himself more.

But Campbell and everyone else who played in the '87 cup final is a hero forever. It's the biggest triumph I've seen with St Mirren, yet also a day of such mixed emotions; the feeling of elation coupled with the shudder at having watched the worst game of football in history.

Most of all for me, though, it was about being with dad. He wasn't keeping that well and I knew it'd be his last chance to see us win the cup again. Come to think of it, I knew it was probably my ONLY chance to see us win it.

Alex Smith was brilliant. He got dad a seat right behind the directors' box and I gave him the keys to the car so he could go down and wait for me while I did my interviews for Radio Clyde.

The scenes of joy when we won were incredible. After the presentation, I was interviewing the manager live on air and he said at one point that they couldn't have lost and let my dad down. Well, that was me. I was ready for crying and couldn't wait to get the headphones off and get down to see dad.

But here's a real Paisley man for you. I got to the car, all smiles that he'd seen us win it and he went: 'Won it? Aye, we won it - but that Ferguson and Abercromby won't do for next season'.

I thought he'd be doing cartwheels, but he was miserable as sin. He didn't even want to go for a drink. He was already fretting about the following season.

Eventually I coaxed him into a pint, but he still wasn't happy, so I got him a bottle of Black Label and a bottle of champagne, took him home, told my mum to make him drink them and went out to enjoy myself.

As it turned out, Hampden was his last big day, because he died the following February. On the day of his funeral, Saints had a game at night. Yet in walked Alex and Jimmy, which was a magnificent gesture. It meant everything to me.

I'd been working at the Evening Times back then as well as doing my stuff with Clyde, but my marriage was over and life was feeling pretty messed up, so I decided to quit the paper and try other stuff.

When I told dad he wasn't happy. He was old school, a guy who believed if you had a job you kept it for the security. That was in the January.

I can't tell you how many times since then I've wanted to see him just once and let him know it all worked out for the best..."

A Necessary Evil

Thursday, October 9.

THE moment has come.

Five days after we beat Rangers on a day that made Love Street grin from floodlight to floodlight, it's time to finally set foot inside its replacement.

Welcome To The FeegieDome right enough.

Chairman Stewart Gilmour's meeting general manager Bryan Caldwell down there and asks if I want to have a wander round with them.

I meet Gilmour at Love Street, where he's locked in crunch bonus talks with the players.

Or rather, playing an uproarious game of Deal Or No Deal in the canteen to decide how much the Board should give them for a squad night out in Edinburgh.

He emerges £1200 lighter. The players are laughing, the chairman forcing a smile.

While all this is going on, I've been leaning on the black-painted brick wall at the mouth of the tunnel, gazing through the rain at an empty stadium.

On Sunday, it was buzzing with excitement, electrified by our 1-0 win over the UEFA Cup finalists, the first time we've beaten them here in 22 looooong years.

Now, it's silent again. Its gutters dripping, red blaes track puddle-strewn. Scanning the stands, you can pick out broken seats. The black-and-white striped paintwork on the North Bank roof is long faded to shades of grey.

141

I step out into the downpour, turn and look up at the main stand. The red pie stalls at either top corner look shabby, the floorboards ready to give way, the girders weary of holding up a battered roof.

My eyes come down to the enclosure beneath the stand, with its uncomfy and its rusting grills over the dressing room windows.

The whole place is unutterably beautiful.

As Stewart calls out from the other end of the tunnel that we're ready to go, I feel like shouting back that he couldn't be more wrong.

IT'S STILL a wellies and hard hat job before they'll let you into the FeegieDome, industrial gloves and a hi-viz bib too. The contractors are in charge for another six weeks, St Mirren folk still treated as visitors.

Once the keys are handed over, the office staff will move in, the team will come and train, Tommy the groundsman will get to grips with the sprinkler system and the million other things to deal with daily.

Today, the pitch is being lined for the first time. A symbolic action, one when a piece of grass becomes something different, something special.

It's a perfect surface, huge and spirit-level flat. On three sides of it, the stands are all but ready to rock, only a few rows of brilliant-white seats to be bolted in between rows of matt-black ones behind the far-end goal. On the far side of the track, the stand that runs the length of the touchline has the letters SMFC picked out in white and grey to give a 3-D effect.

It looks pretty good. In fact, I'm actually starting to feel a little guilty for all those negative thoughts over the past eight months. Maybe this is all it needed, a look inside rather than just standing across the road, getting all grumpy and nostalgic.

As we stop and look around, there's a shout from behind us and there's vice-chairman George Campbell, big and balding, rough and ready, a dry wit behind a hangdog expression. Like Gilmour, he hasn't been down here for about three weeks and sees major changes.

They both look happy. They ask if I'd ready for the tour.

Almost.

But before we go anywhere, there's a question I have to ask: Are you happy to move?

The chairman pulls a face, shakes his head and grunts: "Nah."

That'll do for me.

The vice-chairman has more to say on it, just as he tends to have more to say on everything.

"Some fans are still giving us stick for all of this," he barks. "But Love Street's falling to bits. It's time was up, even if we didn't have to move.

"It's little things that let us down, like not having a Players' Lounge, somewhere for their wives and kids to go for a cup of tea at half-time. You try to bring new players in and they see things like that and it might just change the way they feel about signing."

Gilmour chips in: "Yeah, but it's the training facilities that really swing that one - and when we get the new complex up and running at Ralston, it'll be really impressive."

Ralston's in the east end of town, on the road to Glasgow. A posh area, all trim bungalows and gleaming cars. And it's there, come the Spring, that St Mirren will move into a sprawl with grass and artificial pitches and £100,000 of upmarket-Portakabin changing facilities.

We wander through to what will be the main entrance. They're putting down floor tiles, the centrepiece of which will be a club crest.

Standing there, I get a weird feeling about the differences of scale around this place. From outside, it seemed way too small. From trackside, it looked plenty big. But now, inside the glass doors which will be the first port of call for visiting players and directors, it's almost claustrophobic.

Pretty much the way I feared it'd be all these times I'd looked across from the railway station.

And from then on, everything on the main stand's ground floor seems small-scale.

Here's an idea of how tight for space it is in there; they put aside a lump for a club shop, then realised they didn't have anywhere for a gym the players could use.

So they halved the shop and squeezed the gym in behind it.

This is how the staff will have to live in the new stadium, jostling for elbow room. It's hard to tell for sure right now, because none of the dividing walls have gone up yet. But it's fair to say no one's going to be inviting the band of the Royal Marines into their office for a private concert.

The manager has a room right at the top of the tunnel. Compact and bijou, you'd call it - and next door, the coaches have what's basically a large walk-in cupboard to change in, with a shower room off it.

The away dressing room's way better than the one at Love Street. Though as we've seen, that wouldn't be hard. It's a decent size, or at least it seems decent before benches and lockers go in. The shower area's fine and the toilets - as they are throughout the stand, for punters, staff and stars alike - are quite smart, finished with dark wood units.

Then, on the other side of the tunnel, you pass two disabled toilets and come to the home dressing room.

Here, I'm officially shocked.

At first glance, it looks biggish. Until your eyes focus in the unlit late afternoon gloom. And see that at the far end, the rows of the stand are quite clearly visible at ceiling level. The room drops in height dramatically, until there's no way a self-respecting centre-back could stand on his tippy-toes against the furthest wall.

Were I a player, it would dispirit me to walk in there for the first time. I'd feel like a bit of an after-thought.

Now, I know the Board had to cut their cloth to bring it all in within budget and make sure we moved with no debt. But our team should be the first thought on anyone's mind - they need to feel right to play right and it this doesn't strike me as a feelgood dressing room.

Suddenly, I'm feeling bad about the new place again. I ask the two men behind the move what they think.

"We're happy with the scale," says Stewart Gilmour, "though we'd have liked a bigger boardroom."

George Campbell shrugs: "People can want it to be bigger and better and whatever, but plenty clubs will come here and see it and wish they were like us, debt-free and with no overdraft. We've got clubs in the SPL no bigger than us who are £10million in the red."

The stairs to the upper floor are still swathed in scaffolding, so we go outside, up an aisle between the rows of seat - still way too few, the way it looked from the other side of the road - and in to where there IS plenty space.

The bit where they'll coin it in on matchdays.

No cramming corporate punters into every nook and cranny here, no serving meals out of hostess trolleys in the middle of the landing. Now, there's a function area that'll take 200-odd, with a bar and kitchens at the far end and a hospitality box for private parties.

This will be commercial manager Campbell Kennedy's kingdom, full of home and away fans when the Saints are playing and - he hopes - packed out for conferences, weddings and birthday dos the rest of the time.

144

It takes up more than half the length of the stand. The rest lies undeveloped so far, but the Board want to turn it into a pub. If they pull that off, then along with the corporate side and three five-a-side astroturf pitches behind the away stand, they could be quids in.

And, says Gilmour, repaying a debt at the same time.

"People have been so loyal to us," he says, as he shows off the function suite toilets, "maybe too loyal.

"I'm talking about fans at the turnstiles and corporate customers alike. They'd put up with some pretty poor facilities, yet they keep coming back and that means so much to us.

"In fact, I say put up with, when the more accurate term would be 'endured'. Watching St Mirren at Love Street has been a feat of endurance, no doubt about that.

"I mean, look at these toilets. They're pretty good, as are the ones down inside the turnstiles. At Love Street ... well, we've all seen them. We've all used them. The ones at the end of the main stand have been there forever. People walking up the new stairs into the stand can look down and see you pee.

"As for ladies' loos, it's a fact that a lot of men simply won't bring their wives, girlfriends or daughters to games because the facilities are so poor.

"Now, we can say to whole families that it's all there for them. Clean, comfortable, safe."

George Campbell says: "The front entrance at Love Street's a bit embarrassing, eh? The wee white plastic conservatory tacked onto the door, anybody able to walk in and out. At the Rangers game, we had six people who got in with last year's season tickets.

"All these wee things add up to a huge reason why moving's the right thing, whether we actually WANT to move from Love Street or not. And given the choice, no one would want to. It just has to be done."

THE first spade went in the ground here on January 8. But it's been a project a decade in the making.

It started with a phone call from the Clydesdale Bank that, in his own words, made George Campbell shit himself.

"The overdraft had gone over £1m and they were calling it in," he sighed, clearly still stung by the very memory. "It was a disaster.

"Stewart and I were new on the board compared to most of them. The former chairman, Bob Earlie, had convinced us to invest and we'd lumped in most of what we had. Now, we stood to lose it all.

145

"That was when Reg Brealey, who used to be chairman of Sheffield United, came in with an offer of £1 a share to take the club over. For the older directors, it was an appealing offer. It got them off the hook and most would have been glad to walk away with a few bob.

"But he would have spelled disaster for the club and most other people knew it. So we dug around and got as much information on him as we could to show the bank and the Board and try and put doubt in their mind about accepting his deal.

"Then, Stewart and I went to see an accountant and he suggested we try and mount a takeover of our own. We got a hold of Bryan McAusland - who's still on the Board today - and a few other people and we raised £500,000.

"The next problem was with Bill Barr, whose company had built the Caledonia Stand. He was still owed £440,000 and was getting anxious. We told him that with us in charge, he at least had a chance of seeing his money, but with Brealey? No chance.

"Thankfully, he went with us, spoke up for us with the bank and we got the rest of what we needed."

At this point, there's only one question for the pair of them.

Why?

Why put themselves in this deep when any sane men would have run a mile?

Campbell shrugs and admits that his shares were his pension fund and he couldn't afford to risk that. Gilmour taps his heart and says: "Yes, there was a huge financial issue. We had £500,000 invested and we had to protect it.

"But I'm also a St Mirren man. I couldn't let the club go down - and that's where it was going.

"When we got the money we needed and Brealey was out of the picture, we put a deal to the rest of the Board. We'd work to make the club viable and give their shares value. They were glad to get out and be free of all the hassle.

"Which only left the chairman at the time, John Paton. For me, he'd have been happy to welcome Brealey because there was a job waiting for him. Now, he seemed to think the same would happy with George and I running the show.

"When we said there wasn't a place for him, he basically refused to go. So we told him: 'The choice is yours, leave by the door or the window.'

"And suddenly, St Mirren was in our hands."

Almost immediately, it began to burn their fingers.

Barr Construction was taken over and the new owners wanted that £440,000 the old boss had been happy to take a gamble on.

A group of football club directors who'd already shelled out all they had and more were left scrambling around for another small fortune.

Gilmour, Campbell and three others took out personal loans to square off the debt. Campbell transferred the family home into his wife Susan's name in case everything came tumbling down.

Now, they really HAD to dig in and make the club work, or they'd never see that money again. Now, the task loomed over them like the meteor plunging towards Earth in the movie Armageddon.

"There was a tipping point after which St Mirren as a club would never be the same again," said Gilmour. "It was around the 94-95 season, when we'd been out of the Premier League for four years and going nowhere. We'd had the years in the 80s and the turn of the 90s when money was spent like water on players who only took us downwards and now the price had to be paid.

"Previous boards had made the fatal mistake of forgetting who we are, that we're a small-town club with ambitions to punch above our weight now and again.

"Like Hearts and Motherwell and more, they believed they could compete with the Old Firm, when all the notion did was create debt.

"Look at the SPL league table from any season. Look at the order the 12 teams finish in. It's no coincidence that income and support pretty much dictate what position we all finish in. It's not a happy thought, but it's how the game has gone.

"We realised that early on, but the people we inherited the club from hadn't. That's why we're in the position we are today. That's why Love Street had to be sold.

"Every drawer you opened back then, you found another unopened red bill. Sheriff's Officers were turning up demanding money. George and I were constantly writing them personal cheques."

Campbell laughs: "Whenever I said I was going to a Board meeting, Susan would frisk me for the cheque book, because she knew I'd come home having spent more money."

BOTH men learned the value of counting the pennies early in life.

Campbell was brought up in the rough, tough Glasgow housing scheme of Pollok and even after doing well in the stationery business, he still strikes you as someone who'd go round after you turning off lights.

As for Gilmour? He leans on a barrier just behind the press box,

147

looks to his right and sees where it all began for him.

Through a gap between the stands, he points to the one other building still standing on Ferguslie Park Avenue. The little grocery-and-booze shack his dad, Newton, used to run.

"He bought it in '64," he smiled, "and sold it again in '82. It's been closed for years, but I still remember being in there like it was yesterday.

"I had to work behind the counter, or there was no pocket money, simple as that. Dad grafted day and night and he passed that ethic on to me.

"Being around the people of Ferguslie was like a degree from the University of Life. They were fantastic folk, hard grafters, hard drinkers, hard men and women. The whole area gets a bad reputation, but this was as good a community as you'll ever come across.

"If anyone was on their uppers, someone else would always help. On a Friday, when the men got paid, they'd come in for a carry-out and if they saw a wee old woman buying her messages, they'll get her a wee quarter-bottle for in front of the fire that night.

"Dad had a huge tick book, but the debts were always paid off. His customers were proud folk."

Then he laughs and says: "And I'll tell you something else that working there taught me - never drink cheap wine. I remember the first time I smashed a bottle and when I mopped it up, years of grime came with it.

"The floor was back to as clean as the day it went down. So if the stuff's as strong as an industrial cleaner, just think what it does to your insides..."

TODAY, Gilmour runs a successful sportswear firm supplying schools and clubs. It's based in Clark Street, just yards from the stadium. But mostly he's only making flying visits to the job that pays his mortgage, on his way to the one that puts it at risk.

Year after year, his time with St Mirren has a been a constant round of trying to give managers the money they need to put a decent team on the park, negotiating with the bank, schmoozing councillors and supermarket bosses, placating fans fearing their club's going down the toilet.

Thinking about everything but football, in fact.

Until a Saturday, that is. When he and George Campbell and their fellow directors sit and sweat and fret, fidget and curse, turn pale and purple in equal measure. All because they know one tiny human error on the park could have massive consequences on all they've tried to do off it.

That was always the one element out of their control. Where the team's results would leave us if and when a new stadium came along.

In 1998, in the midst of the whole overdraft-and-Brealey crisis, only a scrambled win at Stirling kept us in the First Division. Two years later, we climbed into the SPL. A year later, were down again.

In 2006, with a deal to sell the ground now signed, Gus MacPherson took us back to the top flight. By the dying embers of the following campaign, we were staring down the barrel of another relegation.

Another day nearer Coronary City for Gilmour and Co.

Gilmour shudders and says: "The second last game of that season, away at Motherwell, was something else. We went into it second bottom, a point ahead of Dunfermline, who were on a great run.

"At half-time, we were 1-0 down. They were 1-0 up at Caley Thistle. Four minutes into the second half, we were 2-0 down.

"Right then, George and I were looking at each other and wondering what the future held. We were committed to the new stadium. It's costs couldn't go down if we did - but our crowds would and our income would.

"Then John Sutton scored to make it 2-1 and five minutes later, Billy Mehmet made it 2-2. But we'd still be going into the last day a point behind. It wasn't enough.

"Then, we heard Caley had equalised. A few minutes later, big Sutton scored again for us. And right at the end, news came through that Caley had scored again.

"As the final whistle went, we realised we were four points clear and safe. The relief was just unbelievable. After all the work we'd put in, all we wanted was to stay in the top flight. See, once upon a time the gap between it and the First Division was reasonable, but now it's huge. And becoming unimaginable.

"So yes, staying up was huge, especially as it became obvious from early the following season that Gretna were going to go down and everyone else was safe.

"It meant we'd go into the last few months at Love Street still a top-flight club.

"That meant everything to us."

HERE'S why. Here are the nuts and bolts of how we ended up standing in the drizzle in an almost-finished stadium, a few weeks away from our heritage being swallowed up by a corporate monster.

The new Board, led by Gilmour and Campbell, got Brealey off the club's case. But the bank was a different matter. To keep the club running - and running forward, however falteringly - meant going to the well again and again to top up the overdraft.

Add that to the £400,000-odd the club owed its directors for paying the stand off, plus all the normal business of tax, VAT, wages, transfers - oh, and the small matter of debt piled up over a couple of decades - and it became clearer by the week that the only way out was to sell up and start all over again.

When we first talked about moving, just after the turn of the millennium, it was Morrisons who looked likely to snap up Love Street.

But then Morrisons took over rivals Safeway - who already had suprmarkets in Paisley - and the deal all went colder than a bag of ice in a freezer cabinet turned up too high.

For Gilmour, that turned out to be no bad thing.

"Sometimes it takes what looks like a problem to get you towards a solution," he says. "Take the Brealey thing. When you look back, him trying to take over the club was like a boil on our cheek coming right to the surface so we could burst it.

"And in the same way, Morrisons not fancying Love Street wasn't the worst turn of events. The money they had been talking wouldn't have covered what we needed. We had to think bigger."

STILL, it was just the beginning of years of rumour and counter-rumour, of fears and smears, of political agendas and pernickity pen-pushing.

Of directors swallowing ulcer medicine like the first cool beer on a hot day.

Of fans doing what successive pre-Gilmour boards had done; sticking their fingers in their ears, shouting la-la-la-la and hoping our worst nightmare would disappear in a puff of smoke and a rollover jackpot.

I remember at the time writing a column saying that if my six lottery numbers ever came up, I'd feel it my moral duty as a fan to plough millions into keeping St Mirren afloat.

Yeah, I know. There are times when it pays to think first and be moral later.

Especially when the rest of the country is able to make your words into a handy cut-out-'n-keep reminder of your idiocy.

BY 2003, the council had agreed to sell 12.5 acres on Greenhill Road to the club and surveyors were already drilling soil samples from ten feet below street level. Yet, bizarrely, politicians were still to decide whether or not we could build a stadium on it.

I mean, what the hell else did they think we were going to use it for? A skating rink? A meditation area?

For the first time, Gilmour was using words like "administration" to describe our prospects should the plans be thrown out.

Soon, he was using "catastrophe".

The heat was on.

A full nine months later, local MP Irene Adams and MSP Wendy Alexander got on board, telling the council that the shopping facilities were "much needed" because of the building of 500 new homes in the area.

Adams called the stadium plans "impressive".

Alexander went further and said: "They're brilliant."

You can see how she went on to be leader of Scottish Labour.

AT this point, all the fans really knew of the new stadium was grapevine stuff; we'd heard scare stories of asbestos lurking in the soil, of only two stands going up, of artificial turf instead of grass.

Gilmour did his best to allay fears by inviting questions to be sent in to the club website.

Pay particular attention to his answer on when we'd move home.

Q. **With the SPL criteria being reduced to 6000 seats, will the capacity of the stadium be around this mark rather than the 10,000 seats mark?**

A. *It will be somewhere in between. We certainly need more than 6,000 seats but having said that we definitely don't need 10,000. It will be somewhere between 7000 to 8000 seats.*

Q. **How soon will work start after planning permission is hopefully given?**

A. *Very quickly. I would hope that the work would start within six months of receiving permission.*

Q. **How real is the possibility that we could be ground sharing next season?**

A. *Unlikely for the upcoming season. For the following season I would say possible but highly unlikely. Any agreement to sell Love Street will be on the basis that the buyers take ownership of the stadium where we would stay as tenants until the new ground is ready to be in.*

Q. What are the consequences of planning permission not being given?

A. *Absolutely horrific, as the bank want their money back. St Mirren must have a decision in place by the beginning of next year, we must either have planning permission and are moving on or we will have to look at an alternative disposal of St Mirren Park. I'm convinced that if the bank see we have a cast iron plan in place they will wait and let it see out it's outcome but they wish something positive to get their money back by the beginning of next year. If we can't get planning permission for a supermarket and new stadium then we will have to look at selling to property developers which will help clear the debt but will be nowhere near enough to build a new ground.*

Q. Are there any plans for a special goodbye game?

A. *Yes, I've no doubt that we will arrange something special as it will be a very emotional day when we leave Love Street.*

Q. Will bits of the ground be auctioned off to fans?

A. *Absolutely. There are several possibilities but we'll address them in due course.*

Q. What is the projected cost of the stadium?

A. *We've got a projected cost which is OK but that was for a 10,000 seated stadium. What we are now trying to do is utilise the money in other areas from the savings which would bring us income in the longer term.*

Q. Is there a buyer for Love St on the table?

A. *We haven't got an absolute buyer. We are running the planning application ourselves and if that gets the go ahead from the Council then we won't have a great deal of difficulty in assuring a buyer.*

Q. Is that buyer Morrisons?

A. *No.*

Q. How much will we make by selling Love St?

A. *We have a base price which we expect to get which covers building the new stadium and clearing off the debt.*

Q. How much of the debt will be dealt with by the entire plan?

A. *I would hope that 100 per cent of the debt would be taken care of but worst case scenario would be 90 per cent of it cleared.*

Q. Will any investment be required from outside sources (for example the Council) to make the project work?

A. *No. We may well apply to people like Sport Scotland for assistance with the 5-a-side pitches and community areas but that would have nothing to do with clearing the debt and building the new stadium.*

Q. **Who will have ownership of the stadium when it is all said and done?**

A. *The stadium will solely belong to St Mirren Football Club.*

Q. **Do we have any plans to invite another club, perhaps a junior club, to sell their home, and plough their money into the building of a co-owned ground where running costs can be split?**

A. *I don't think we would want to bring in a co-owner, I don't see that as a way forward for the moment but there's nothing to stop a Junior club playing at our new ground as a tenant.*

Q. **When is the earliest that we could expect to move into the new stadium?**

A. *If all goes well I would expect the move to take place between October 2005 and December 2005.*

Q. **Are the Club being professionally advised or represented in valuing the Love Street stadium and purchasing Greenhill Road? How does SG feel about the advice given so far?**

A. *Yes, we are being fully advised by a top Glasgow company. We are happy with the advice and information that we have been given to date.*

Q. **Is SG satisfied with the expected purchase figure for Love Street being sufficient to pay for the new ground and to clear the debt and if not will he guarantee that no action will be taken on the new ground until an offer is received at that level?**

A. *Absolutely. We haven't got the money to start building a new ground until we are actually able to buy out the secured creditors on our old ground so we couldn't do anything until we actually have a contract in place to buy Love Street.*

Q. **Will the expected Purchase Figure be fixed by St Mirren once the planning consent is obtained for Love Street. I'm assuming based on the level of debt and quote price for the building job and land purchase.**

A. *Obviously we'll try to get as much money as we can for Love Street, the more we can do the better. To be honest on the budgeted figure we had from two years ago the actual new stadium will be,*

153

on the terms of kitting it out internally, pretty basic. I would hope that we can get more money from a good sale and raise the standard of the internal fittings, we could also possibly raise the number of 5-a-side pitches that we could put down which will generate more long-term income.

Q. **Has SG asked Renfrewshire Council if they will support their local club financially in the same way that Highland Council did with Inverness CT for a soft loan?**

A. *At the moment Renfrewshire Council are more interested in getting the money we owe them back from us. I have to say that Renfrewshire Council have been very supportive in most things that St Mirren have done. I don't know how the soft loan is operated with Inverness, I'm not even convinced that will be the case. I'd suggest that you don't always believe what you read in the papers. I know the Scottish Office isn't keen on Councils giving money to football clubs in the way of cash so I'm not convinced that there is a soft loan.*

Q. **Is the new ground being built on Fixed Price contacts?**

A. *It will be. With us looking to change the specification of the new ground we're not in the position to get prices but it will be on a fixed price contract. There's no way that we would go forward with an open ended contract.*

So, in the new place by the end of 2005.

He was in for a major disappointment.

But hey, check out the big brains on some of the punters who sent questions in - never mind stuff about how many pie stalls we'll have, Saints fans want to know about Soft Loans and Fixed Contracts.

Never let it be said that we're not an intellectual bunch.

IN MAY 2004, the Board took a deep breath, drew themselves up to their full height and slapped in the most important document of their lives. The sheaf of paper by which St Mirren Football Club would either stand or fall.

They asked Renfrewshire Council for a 10,000-seat ground at Greenhill Road and a superstore where the old place stood. They simply HAD to get permission for both.

This time, it was vice-chairman Campbell who went public, pointing to Glasgow Airport's 5000 workers and another 1000 about to be relocated by Rolls-Royce to nearby Inchinnan, all of them needing to buy a loaf at two in the morning.

Because let's face it, that's the genius of your Tesco culture. They've taken what used to be a bind and turned it into a leisure activity.

Once, you used to need to go for the messages, as we called shopping round our way. Now, you choose to. Whatever time of day or night you fancy, no matter what you need.

I remember being on holiday in Orlando in 2000 and as my wife Melanie had just found out she was pregnant, she spent most of the fortnight either throwing up or talking about throwing up.

So we're lying in bed about half two one morning when she nudges me and says she's not only ready to vomit, she's got a stinking sore head as well.

Would I be an angel and pop out for some painkillers?

Fifteen minutes later, I'm in this Wal-Mart the size of a small country. Staring in awe not only at the sheer scale, at the sheer amount of stuff for sale, but the incredible number of customers milling around.

You're standing there thinking that they must all be heading for the bit that sells insomnia medicine. But no, they're buying food, toiletries, suitcases, lawnmowers. It's mental.

I spent about half an hour walking round the cheese display alone, counting 117 different kinds including spray, meat-flavoured, fish-flavoured and 100 per cent non-dairy.

When I got back with the pills, she was sleeping. Course she was.

But I lay there for ages, wondering what the hell happened to a country to make so many people spend so much time willingly doing something that back home was generally a case of in, out and home as quickly as humanly possible.

That was then, though. This is now.

Welcome to the 51st State.

Where we too want non-dairy cheese at dead of night, when we too want televisions in the next aisle to crisps which are in the next aisle to nappies.

We're off our nut - and I include myself in this, because I've seen me driving home from a match at near enough midnight or back from the airport at 3am after a foreign trip and thinking: "I could pop into Tesco and get a few things just now. Save time later."

But hey, if we hadn't all been seduced by this retail rohyphnol, St Mirren might be dead by now.

So God bless stupidity.

SEE, the Clydesdale Bank have shown a lot of restraint towards our club over the years.

In fact, had we been any other business, the chances are our doors would have been shut long ago.

The story's the same all over the country - probably all over many other countries, too. Banks have customers who support their local football club, which makes pulling the plug on them one hell of a business risk.

But even that risk starts to seem acceptable after a 20 years or so of baling that club out.

And so it came to pass that on March 8, 2005, we Saints fans got it told to us like it was.

Gilmour and his fellow directors needed a £700,000 overdraft; from the same bank who'd almost pulled the plug on the previous board at the tail end of the 90s.

Fair play to the Clydesdale, they agreed - but on one condition.

No, not that the Board had to spend a night in the ole haunted funfair over by Gallowhill Swamp. That Scooby Doo-stylee punishment would have been the easy way out.

The REAL news that spooked Gilmour was this.

If he didn't get the go-ahead to build a supermarket on Love Street by May 31, the stadium would still have to be sold to pay off their debt.

"Alternative disposal", the bankers called it.

The Beginning of the End, we called it.

With no ground, we'd be what Airdrie, Hamilton and Clyde had been. Stateless, aimless, begging and borrowing a place to play; knowing that place would be visited by fewer and fewer of our fans the longer the arrangement went on.

In fact, let's not kid ourselves here.

For all we knew, we could have ended up like Clydebank. No more than a bunch of players, a bag of balls and a kitbag full of strips the gaffer took home for his missus to wash.

After 128 unbroken years in the town, some of them even successful, this was it.

By April of 2005, just a month before the final decision on the project would be taken, Gilmour admitted he was in the dark over what their chances were.

"If anyone has any information." he said, "please come forward and tell us."

On May 20, Gilmour pleaded with fans to march on Cotton Street and the council planning meeting that would decide whether professional football in Paisley had a future.

Pen-pushers were recommending the stadium project be approved, but without permission for a supermarket in its place because of the possible effect on business at rival shops across the town.

But the politicians were the ones who had to make the final decisions.

They were the ones who'd have their pictures in the Paisley Daily Express if they screwed the club.

They were the ones who needed to keep the voters sweet.

Gilmour said at the time:

IT'S crucial that as many people as possible turn up to show the councillors the depth of feeling for St Mirren there is in the town and that there is a desire for the club to be saved. Councillors have it within their power to vote to overturn this recommendation from planning officials and I'd urge them to do just that.

If Love Street isn't sold to a supermarket operator, the club will not have the money to build this new stadium. In a nutshell, if we don't get approval for a supermarket, St Mirren will not exist in Paisley.

A condition of our overdraft is that if we don't have permission to build a supermarket, we have to sell the ground anyway and that is most likely to be for housing. Unfortunately, the value of land for housing is about half what you get for retail and that's not enough to build a new stadium.

We believe a supermarket at Love Street would have a minimal impact on Paisley town centre. In fact, our consultants believe it would bring shoppers CLOSER to the town centre than they they are at the present.

Love Street is actually closer to the centre of Paisley than the new Morrisons supermarket which councillors have allowed to be built at the back end of the former Anchor Mills site.

Then he really turned on the emotional blackmail.

If councillors vote with us, they would not only be voting to save St Mirren, they would be voting to keep a major part of Paisley's heritage, they would be voting for the tens of thousands of youngsters who attend our football camps and coaching classes in Renfrewshire Council schools and they would be voting to keep something positive and something special for the future.

If they decide to allow a supermarket to serve a large part of the town - North Paisley, which doesn't have such a facility, they will be

157

remembered as the people who helped save St Mirren for Paisley, its people, its heritage and its future.

Over the next three days, more than 3000 Saints fans - and supporters from all over Britain - signed an online petition begging the council to let the plans go through.

And so to May 24. A whirlwind day for Stewart Gilmour in more ways than one.

"I booked to go Portugal on a golfing holiday and decided to go ahead with it," said as we wandered round the track at the new ground. "But I also had to be at the meeting, so while the other guys were heading for the first tee, I was on a plane back to Glasgow.

"I got picked up at the airport, went to the meeting, did what had to be done and got back on a plane back to Portugal again.

"How long was I back? Four or five hours at the most.

"But they were maybe the most important four of five hours of my life..."

BEHIND closed doors at the grey, soul-less HQ of Renfrewshire Council, they were voting on a matter of life and death.

Inside the meeting room, 30 fans had been allowed to join Gilmour, his fellow directors and manager Gus MacPherson.

Outside, another 200 punters wore scarves and waved flags, as if queuing to get into a big game.

They'd jeered the arrival of council leader Jim Harkins for his comments that: "I will not be intimidated by fan power. My conscience will be clear because I will do what is best for the whole area. I have sympathy with the club but we have to weigh up the impact on other stores in the town."

But others in that chamber were on our side. Councillor Terry Kelly had said: "The main three things you associate with the town are the Paisley pattern shawl, Paisley Abbey and St Mirren. Paisley without St Mirren in it is inconceivable."

SNP member Richard Vassie warned: "The cost to Paisley in ending its partnership with St Mirren is inconceivable."

And Nat colleague Ian Taylor added: "I stood with my son at Hampden in 1987 to see St Mirren win the Scottish Cup. They brought pride back to the people of Paisley. They are an asset not only to Paisley but the whole of Renfrewshire."

And so, outside the building in the shadow of the town's magnificent Abbey, they waited. And fretted. With every minute, they began to fear the worst.

Then, after what felt like days, news of the final score filtered out.

Ayes...9

Nays...5

The good guys had won. The Saints were safe, for now.

Gilmour and MacPherson were mobbed as they left the chambers. People sang and hugged like we'd won the cup again.

The chairman was delighted. But he didn't exactly sprinkle a path of rose petals for the politicians to frolic across on their way to the pub.

The official description of his mood on the club website was "philosophical". But judge for yourself.

SOME councillors voted for us, some against and that is their decision. I was a bit disappointed that some based things on our financial position without knowing all the facts. They commented that last year we lost £100,000, but they forgot that we were running these two planning applications which cost about £250,000 and are paying £140,000 a year in interest on our debt which has been absolutely crippling, but that's not going to happen any more.

Then he took a few breaths and got a neck massage and went on:

This now gives St Mirren financial stability but if the vote had gone against us I would probably be sitting with Partick Thistle chairman Brown McMaster tomorrow thrashing out a deal to ground share at Firhill which would have been the start of a slow death for St Mirren.

But we can now look forward to remaining in Paisley and being a part of the community just along the road in Ferguslie Park. I also believe that the supermarket will be good for the people who live in the Shortroods area.

Now, we'll have a modern stadium with modern facilities and 5-a-side pitches which will bring in income streams outwith the football club. I think the whole process will happen between the next 18 to 24 months.

We'll remain at Love Street for now but I've got to admit that it will be a sad day when we finally have to leave it.

Diehard fan Willie Bell, one of those who made it into the room, grinned:

When the vote came, it was like a wave of relief right through the hall and it carried all the way out to the fans outside.

The feeling was fantastic, like a winning goal at Love Street.

But how often does your team score what you think is the winner -

only to see out of the corner of your eye some tight-shorted little traffic warden standing there with his flag up, delighted at the chance to spoil anything from your weekend to the rest of your life?

Now, this traffic warden stood there in the shape of the Scottish Executive; the people who could wave a flag and stop our celebrations in mid Yeehah.

If they reckoned there was reason to dispute what the councillors had decided, they could call the application in for a fresh inquiry.

There was every chance the delay that would cause could push the Clydesdale Bank's patience beyond its credit limit and snooker us forever.

Which is why, come August 16, the sigh of relief from the Boardroom echoed round the housing schemes and pubs of Paisley.

The Scottish Executive decided NOT to call in the planning application. Gilmour called it 'the catalyst for regeneration of the town's North End'.

IT'LL be sad to leave Love Street, but there was no alternative. We would have had to sell the ground no matter what the outcome of our planning applications - the difference now is that we can raise enough cash to pay off the debt and stay in Paisley in a fabulous new stadium less than a mile from St Mirren Park.

Remember that word, sports fans.

Fabulous.

Anyway. Back to the chairman.

WE CAN all recall the fantastic scenes at Paisley Cross and the Town Hall when we brought the Scottish Cup and the League Championship back to Paisley. These were great days not just for our supporters, but also for the whole of Paisley and Renfrewshire.

It gave everyone such a huge lift in morale and there will be a lot more of these wonderful days in the future.

Who can forget the look of excitement on the faces of the youngsters who stood in front of the Town Hall as the open-topped bus arrived when we won cup and the League title?

I am sure these same youngsters will be standing there again - albeit a little older - waiting for the team to arrive for another great St Mirren celebration.

The directors, players and staff at St Mirren can now make sure that the Saints DO go marching in ... and keep on marching for a long time to come.

At which moment I got something in my eye.

And as far as anything public went, that was pretty much that until April 25, 2007, when Gilmour waved a piece of paper like Neville Chamberlain coming back from Munich.

Except with a Tesco logo on it.

The supermarket chain were buying Love Street for £15m. The money would build the new stadium and leave £2m over to pay off our debts. Gilmour said at the time:

THIS is an historic day for St Mirren. It is the day the club has been saved.

We said from the start that the only way the Club could survive in its present form and remain in Paisley would be to sell our ground for enough money to pay off our debts and build a new Premier League-standard stadium.

Thankfully, for the fans, the players and the whole of Paisley and Renfrewshire, this has now been achieved. We can look forward to a new era of financial stability and hopefully, the success on the park that stability can bring us.

We will have a modern stadium with more opportunities for commercial off-field activities which are crucial for any modern-day football club.

Then, on December 3, he told the club's AGM:

St Mirren Football Club are delighted to announce that construction of our new 8000-seater stadium at Greenhill Road will commence on January 7, showing completion for November 28.

On permission from the SPL, SFL and SFA, this would allow the first match to take place in January 2009 once every team has been played at home and away.

After which he added:

The future's bright, the future's black and white!

Oooh. And he was doing so well and all...

On January 7, workies moved in. Thirteen days later, the chairman and Gus MacPherson put the hard hats on and went through the traditional building site ceremony of sticking the first spades in the ground.

On February 18, the first bits of steel went up.

Forty weeks from completion. Pretty much the same as a pregnancy.

Which makes me think there must be something really clever and poignant to be written here.

But I'm damned if I can think of it.

GEORGE CAMPBELL'S had to go back to work. Bryan Caldwell, the general manager, is away discussing big-match segregation with the police.

So now it's just me and the chairman, up at the back of the main stand again, me waiting for him to speak and him lost in thought.

He's thinking about Love Street. About being a wee boy on the terraces, a young businessman fancying a piece of the club, a middle-aged man risking his home and his health by taking over the reins.

Eventually, he breaks the silence.

"We've had some fantastic times there, eh? Some brilliant days to remember it by.

"We've won two titles in my time as chairman, under Tom Hendrie in 2000 and Gus in 2006. That season we also won the Challenge Cup.

"Beating Rangers the other day, that was huge for everyone. We really needed a result like that as the games ticked away before the move.

"There's nothing like the feeling of a win against one of the Old Firm and it hasn't happened that often these last few years, so you milk the enjoyments when one comes along.

"When I think of Love Street, though, I go back nearly 50 years. The first team I really remember was about 61-62, with Cockles Wilson, Jim Clunie, Tommy Bryceland and Totty Beck. They got to the cup final. Then we had guys like Cammy Murray and Jimmy Robertson, some of my earliest heroes.

"I used to go with my grandad, who had a company called Sim's Sweets. He took me to the 1959 cup final, when we beat Aberdeen 3-1.

"When we came back to Paisley, we went to a barber's shop in County Square called Reid's where grandad used to go for a shave every morning. We went up to a balcony above the shop and watched the team coming back on the bus with the cup.

"His seats were L59 and 60 in the main stand. I used to go there with him when I was a wee boy, until I got big enough to go on the North Bank with my pals.

"When it comes to the last game, I'll look at where we sat and it'll all come flooding back."

He puffs out his cheeks hard, like he's already preparing for that day.

Which, in some ways, he has been since the day and hour he took over the Boardroom.

"It'll be tough," he says, quietly. "But you have to keep telling yourself that it has to happen, that there was no other way out. The main stand's not good enough, we've no decent car parking, there's those toilets and the corporate punters all being squashed in and ... well, too many little things to mention.

"But that doesn't mean I'm any happier to go than anyone else is. Than you are or any other fan is."

SO, as we stand here in the rain, 114 days before the new stadium opens, only one question remains.

What's he going to be doing as the old one closes?

"Hiding," he smiles. "Hiding and crying.

"God knows how everyone will keep the emotions in check. It'll be a nightmare. You just hope we get a result and go away with one last happy memory.

"One thing's for sure, though - when the game's over and we've all toasted the old place, I won't be the last one out of Love Street.

"I just couldn't face that, the loneliness of it all.

"At some point, I'd love to slip away quietly, say my goodbyes in my own way and go for a right few pints in the town.

"Then, when the hangover's gone, we'll get on with the rest of our lives..."

WE shake hands, he heads off.

I stay for another look around. Still haven't seen the main stand from the other side, so I wander round the track to take a look from just above the 3-D SMFC lettering.

On the way, I'm thinking that, yes, I've been unfair on this new home. Pre-judged it from a distance, tried to balance the worth of an empty shell against what a lived-in, seasoned temple of football has given me and so many others like me.

I walk up the aisle of the far-side stand, still feeling the same way.

Then turn. And realise I should have trusted my judgement all along.

Because the main stand lets the stadium down. It is, as feared the first time I saw the steps go in, too small.

It's high enough to get another six or seven rows of seats in, to have those seats rising more steeply all the way to the roof. But instead, those seats end halfway up. And then there's just a huge expanse of grey panelling, with the windows of the executive box and the police control room set into it.

It wouldn't matter so much if the telly cameras were going to be on that side. But they're not, the gantry they'll stand on is just to my right.

Which means the view everyone will get forever and a day is of a half-hearted effort where the impressive core of our stadium should be.

Look at Falkirk's place. Now, for me, they overdid it on the main stand. If they'd taken even a third of the size and therefore the cost out of it, they might not be sitting with a half-finished ground today.

But boy, is it gorgeous. Soaring. A real statement that says: This club means business.

Ours, I'm afraid, sort of whimpers: We'd love to mean business, but we didn't have the cash.

From the Board's point of view, that was the way to go. Keep the costs in check. Given a straight choice of the stadium or the balance sheets being pretty on the eye, there WAS no choice.

With the sizes they were working to, they needed to have room upstairs in that main stand for the function suite and the bar. That meant trimming the seating back.

And anyway, there's no point whining now, because it's a done deal. All of it is.

One hundred and fourteen years at Love Street.

One hundred and fourteen days from it closing.

One million tears already beginning to well.

Decca Knocked Back The Beatles. We Sacked Fergie.

WHEN I close my eyes and think of Love Street on matchday, it's always the same match.

I'm looking down on the old place as if from a sponsored blimp, players like Subbuteo men and fans like ants. Thousands upon thousands of ants.

Sixteen thousand three hundred and eighty-seven, to be precise.

It's January 29, 1977. We're humping Dundee United in the sunshine and on the frost.

Fergie's Furies are wearing Sambas. And it really IS just like watching Brazil.

That day, that Scottish Cup Third Round tie, will for me forever be our club and our stadium at the joint peak of their powers.

Sure, there have been bigger games and way bigger gates.

But more excitement?

Greater belief?

More downright gallusness?

Surely not.

I'd been watching St Mirren pretty much since I could walk and the short version is that it had been pretty much a struggle all the way, bar the blip of a 1968 Second Division title triumph.

Now, we had a season that would imprint itself indelibly on all our psyches.

Since coming down from the top flight in '71, we'd gone down and down, slowly but surely. By the time the first couple of months of '74-'75 had gone and there were few signs of real improvement, it was time for massive change, to come out swinging or stay crumpled in a heap.

165

Out in the big world, a lot of people were saying something similar about music. Everything was bland, all Billy Don't Be A Hero and Sugar Baby Love, satin flares and cheesy grins.

We were at rock'n'roll bottom. It would take punk to blow all the cobwebs away, get people thinking again, lay the foundations for decades to come.

Alex Ferguson was our Johnny Rotten.

When he took over at Love Street, in October '74, the UK number one was John Denver with Annie's Song.

When he was bumped, in May 1978, it was Boney M doing Rivers of Babylon; so maybe the musical analogy doesn't stack up too well after all.

But the one about Fergie does, no problem.

He WAS punk. Just as Sid Vicious was the only one who actually DID do My Way his own way, so this young, pig-headed manager battered every obstacle out of his way to get what he wanted.

Without doubt, that was ultimately fame, fortune and power. But why not? Who wouldn't want what he's earned himself in a magnificent 34-year, 30-odd-trophy career?

The means to his end, though, began with proving he could take a failing, wheezing, shambolic mess of a club and turn it into one to be feared and respected.

Whatever the reasons behind his downfall, no one can argue that he did exactly what he said on the tin.

Our average gate in 1974 had been 1908. Within four years, it was 11,230.

He got us there by getting off his backside, by hitting the streets and yelling at us to get off our backsides and get down to Love Street. The motormouth with the megaphone, leaning out of a mate's car and giving us no option but to do what he said.

That was him then. That's still him now, irresistible.

Sir Alex has spent the past 30 years making it his sworn ambition to say as little about his time at Love Street as possible. To someone like me, it's a time of never-to-be-repeated magic; to him, it now seems a time in his life that was soured beyond repair and which is best forgotten.

But in an interview with Robert Philp in the Sunday Herald in August 2008, he gave a rare, brief glimpse into what he was thinking at the time.

"*I PHONED Jock Stein to ask what he thought I should do when St Mirren wanted me to move from East Stirling. He told me: 'Go and sit in the stand at Love Street and look around. Then do the same at Firs Park and you'll have your answer'.*

There was no money available, so we used to bring in kids from all over the place on Monday, Tuesday and Thursday nights. St Mirren already had a terrific scouting system - led by an incredible guy called Baldy Lindsay who was a taxi driver in Kinning Park - but I increased the network so we had guys working their socks off running round here, there and everywhere prospecting for nuggets.

I had more scouts than Baden-Powell.

We had so little money that when I wanted to sign Jackie Copland from Dundee United I had to approach the supporters' association for their financial help. The fee was £17,000 and the fans generously put up a loan of £14,000.

But the only real way forward was by giving youth a chance. When it came to selling St Mirren to young players or their parents, my assistant and old Rangers team-mate Davie Provan and I promised them two things; that they'd be given the opportunity to express themselves and that no matter their age, if they were good enough then they'd be given the chance of playing in the first team.

It was also important to me that St Mirren played with a certain style and flair and I was fortunate that so many of them were very receptive to that ideal. Lads like Frank McGarvey, Billy Stark and - later - Peter Weir had great skills and an even greater desire to play the game as it should be played.

Then there was Tony Fitzpatrick, who I made club captain when he was still only 18 because of his drive and hunger for information to improve himself. Perhaps the greatest satisfaction I derived from my time at Love Street was in providing four players - Fitzpatrick, Stark, McGarvey and Bobby Reid - for the Scotland Under-21 team in 1977.

That was an incredible achievement for a club outside the Premier Division.

Mind you, I didn't always have success. One of the lads I used to ferry back and forth between East Kilbride - where we both lived - and Love Street was a small, skilful midfielder who I doubted would grow sufficiently to make the grade.

You can take it as read that Alistair McCoist never tires of reminding me of my lack of judgement..."

FERGIE saw talent in players others had discarded. He had faith in groundstaff kids. And he plucked some from obscurity to turn them into household names.

For me, none was better than Billy Stark, the lanky, curly-headed midfielder who ran like he was on castors and who had the ability to frustrate and delight almost in the same movement.

We've discovered some pretty good players down the years. Iain Munro, Ally McLeod, Gordon McQueen, Bobby McKean, Stevie Clarke, Paul Lambert and more have gone on to fame, fortune, caps and medals.

But in this fan's eyes, none touch Starky for sheer quality.

Alongside the scurrying Tony Fitzpatrick and the dynamic Lex Richardson, he formed as balanced and talented a midfield as you could ever wish to see. When they clicked as a trio - which was pretty much every week - it was the first sure sign that Alex Ferguson had what it took to be a top, top manager.

Starky had eight years at Love Street, five in a terrific Aberdeen side after re-uniting with the Great Man and then an outstanding spell at Celtic that included a starring role in the 1988 league and cup double.

By his own admission, though, nothing compares to '77...

"I CAME to St Mirren straight from playing juvenile with Anniesland Waverley, so all I knew of the really bad days were what other people told me. Maybe I was one of the lucky ones.

When I arrived, we'd just sneaked into the new First Division after the leagues were reorganised. The top six went in with the bottom six from the old top flight and St Mirren were sixth.

You have to wonder what might have happened to the club - and to Fergie's career - had they not made it. But they did and that was the start of everything.

In the summer of '75, Fergie made his mind up where St Mirren had to go and cleared out the old guard. He went with the likes of me, Frank McGarvey, Tony Fitzpatrick and Bobby Reid alongside a few experienced men in John Young, Walter Borthwick, Billy Johnston and Donny McDowall.

I never played reserve football, he threw me straight in. I was really lucky. That first season I played in almost every game and it was a crash course in senior football. It was a shorter league season, just 26 games and then into a one-off called the Spring Cup.

We finished sixth, then won our Spring Cup group and went to the quarter-finals before going out over two legs to Morton. That was a huge disappointment, but it felt like we were going somewhere.

The next season, we really took off.

168

I was lucky enough to go on and win all the domestic honours. I played with and against some real stars and got to travel across Europe. But I never enjoyed a season the way I did 1976-77 with St Mirren.

Not long ago, I was out with Ricky McFarlane - who was the physio then, but went on to manage the team - and as usual, the conversation went back to us winning the First Division. You can't help it, that achievement will never leave any of us.

When anyone asks me about it, I still call it the greatest season of all time. There was just something special going on at Love Street back then and it was amazing to be part of. The crowds went up and up, the confidence grew, the headlines got bigger - and at the heart of it all was Fergie.

He ran the show, top to bottom. No one was in any doubt about that, from the dressing room to the boardroom. He had a drive and a conviction that left you in no doubt that he was going places. He laid the foundations for things that St Mirren would achieve long after he'd gone.

I've seen a lot of managers since then who have some of his qualities, maybe even some who are better at this or that than he was. But no one else has had EVERYTHING.

Fergie has everything. He's unique.

The other thing about him was that he didn't get done the same way twice - and I'm convinced that trait helped us win that game against Dundee United in the cup.

The year before, we'd gone to Cowdenbeath in the first round on a really frosty day. Fergie didn't want to play, but their manager, Frank Connor, was older and wilier and won the battle.

Next thing, we're all scurrying around the High Street trying to find a shop that sold training shoes - and if you know Cowdenbeath, you'll know that it's not exactly crawling with superstores.

We lost 3-0. Fergie was raging. And when he was in a mood like that, you just knew someone would pay for it sometime.

Sure enough, throughout the title-winning season he made damn sure games went ahead no matter the weather. He made sure the opposition knew we WANTED to play when we didn't.

Early on, we went up to Montrose when it was blowing a gale and the rain was going sideways. They wanted it called off. He fought to make sure it went ahead. Then he sent us out a minute before kick-off in short-sleeved shirts and we hammered them 4-2.

That was him, always thinking."

WHICH brings us back to January 29, 1977.

That morning, I was due to play for the 16th Paisley in a BB league game at the Racecourse, but as soon as you woke up you had that horrible feeling in the pit of your stomach that it wasn't happening.

Postponed. The most depressing word in football's vocabulary, with the possible exception of Lawrenson.

Even if there's six inches of water on the pitch and you'd need to swim through the town to the stadium, the final confirmation that It's Aff has always felt like a boot in the stones.

I remember being freezing on the walk down to Morar Drive to meet the boys for the bus into town. The ground being rock-hard. But still refusing to believe that there wasn't a council groundsman who felt the same desperation to get the games on.

As we walked round to the pitches, the sun was blinding, but breath came in clouds. Even as we were going up the tarmac-ed side road to the pavilion, boys and cars were coming the other way.

Still, you had to go right to the door, to check the list on the wire gates. To find out for yourself, not second hand.

And then we turned round and trudged back again.

Usually, we'd have gone across the dual carriageway and back into town on the train from St James's. But there was no rush today, so some of us walked down, on to Caledonia Street and round by Love Street. The STV truck was outside, cameras all set up to make us the main highlights game on Third Round day.

If it went ahead.

If?

The word didn't exist for Fergie.

A year on from the humiliation of Central Park, he was ready. Adidas Sambas bought in and laid out so the boys would grip the flinty surface.

What drove him on more was who we were taking on - not just United, but the Premier League leaders. And not just that, but a team managed by Jim McLean; a man already obsessed with turning a provincial club into serious challengers to the Old Firm.

They would become firm friends and sworn enemies in one, firebrand bosses of the New Firm who, for the glorious first half of the 80s, ruled the roost.

But today, Wee Jum was the big name. Fergie was the upstart.

Ninety minutes later, as Billy Stark remembers with huge pride, the world was only talking about one of them...

"THAT game will always be THE game for me from that era. Just unforgettable.

The huge crowd, the frosty pitch, the fact that they were top of the Premier and we were top of the First Division.

All week we got huge publicity, most of it generated by the manager's reputation. It was him against Jim McLean, a real battle of wits between two fiery characters.

In the end, the result made it look like we'd won easily, but some big dumpling in a No8 shirt did his best to make it harder by missing a penalty early on. You've no idea how that made me feel - and it was even worse when they went into the lead.

But we kept playing our football, Bobby Torrance got a couple of goals, I managed one and Frank got another. In the end we were playing with them - you just don't get a feeling like that from football all that often.

It all just clicked. We put it all together that day and the fans loved it. The atmosphere was amazing, something I for one had never experienced. As that season went on, the crowds had just got bigger and bigger and for a young lad out of the juveniles, that was something really special.

The papers loved it, too, and gave us massive headlines. We felt like we'd arrived. Then we drew Motherwell away.

There were nearly 27,000 there that day and when you looked round it seemed like nearly everyone was a Saints fans. It was an incredible atmosphere.

What a doing we took at Fir Park, though. They were a big, hard team full of big, hard men and they set about us. We held on for a long time and it was 1-1 well into the second half after wee Frank scored, but they got a winner and we were out.

It was the first time we'd lost since September.

Fergie was furious about the treatment we took that day, but there was nothing anyone could do about it. We were out and that was that."

THE Hampden dream was over, the innocent wonder kicked right out of us. I don't remember ever feeling as depressed about a game as that Motherwell defeat left me. They had stood against - and on - everything Fergie was all about.

And so, the league it was.

We would score 92 goals in that championship season, but the first was put in for us by Dave Clarke of East Fife in a 1-1 home draw. There were just under 2500 there.

By the time of our next home game, a Tuesday night against Hamilton on my 14th birthday, we'd lost 2-0 at Falkirk and 300 had decided to stay away.

They missed the birth of a legend.

I'd come home from school that day, got my birthday money together, jumped on the bus into town and walked round to Alexander's sport shop.

Two minutes later, I was walking back to Smithhills Street, clutching a plastic bag with my new home strip in it.

Plain black and white stripes, black inset collar. No trimmings, no badge, no sponsor's name.

As simple as it was beautiful.

Later, when I'd grown out of it, tucking the sleeves inside the body allowed it to become a rather fetching pillow case. It stayed on my bed until I bought my first flat at 22.

Not a great turn-on for the laydees, being laid gently down on an eight-year-old St Mirren shirt.

Anyway, back to September 14, 1976.

Donnie McDowall got the first goal, Walter Borthwick made it two and by half-time we were 3-1 up. It finished 5-2. All but Frank McGarvey of our scorers had moustaches.

We'll maybe discuss another time why the modern game needs more moustaches. What matters here now is that we did not lose again for 193 glorious days, until THAT Saturday at Motherwell.

Twenty-six games, 18 wins, 67 goals. Crowds up to 3000, then to 4000, to fives and sixes. More than 10,000 against Clydebank, Morton, Dundee and Clydebank.

And almost uniquely in St Mirren's history, when those big games dawned and the big numbers rolled up, we did the business. We were 100 per cent at home to our three nearest title rivals.

We were the best, no argument.

The best in that division that season by a mile - and maybe the best the club had ever had.

Billy Stark still recalls it all like it was yesterday...

"WAS IT a unique time? Maybe that's too strong a word. But it was very, very special, that's for sure.

At the time, when you're a kid, you kind of take things for granted. You just turn up and train and play, you take the praise and you take the doings and you get on with it.

172

It's only when you look back that you realise just what you were part of. We were all in at the very start with a man who's gone on to be the greatest British manager of all time, maybe even THE greatest, full stop.

Week by week in that First Division title season he strove for perfection. If you were looking for pats on the back, you had a long wait - a well done was rare and when it came, you treasured it, it was a kind of Utopia. More often he'd look for faults in what you thought was a really good performance, because he never wanted you to be comfortable. He always believed you could do better and he wanted you to believe it as well.

It was hard sometimes, but I for one couldn't possibly have had the career I enjoyed without what he did for me back then.

Was it fun? That's not the word - when you take the leap from juvenile to professional, the stakes change. I mean, you always want to win, but suddenly you HAVE to win. You're not playing with your mates for fun any more, you're playing for wages and for your place, maybe for the manager's job.

So when it goes right, when you win, there's real satisfaction. And when you play football the way St Mirren played it then, there's a pride in entertaining people.

But fun? I don't know. It certainly wasn't at the start of the season, when we were really shaky, but once that run got going we really hit our stride. There was a spell when we had Dundee, Clydebank and Morton at home within a few weeks. We beat Dundee 4-0, had a tough 0-0 with Clydebank then put five past Morton.

That was us established as contenders and we never looked back. Fergie had brought in Jackie Copland to add a bit of experience and it all come together. We had a fantastic Christmas Day game at Clydebank when we came from 2-0 down to draw 2-2, then won 6-3 at Morton on New Year's Day.

And while I still believe the United cup-tie was the highlight under Fergie for me, the night we went to Dundee and clinched the league was really special as well.

They were men. We were boys. But we hammered them 4-0. To become champions in itself was an amazing feeling, but doing it that way meant even more.

I scored one and Frank got a hat-trick, but it's a fantastic performance by big Peter Leonard I'll always remember. He was a striker who was in and out of the team, someone the fans either loved or hated. That night they loved him, because everything he tried came off. He was brilliant.

173

The mood that night was just wonderful - even Fergie let his guard down, because as we pulled out of Dundee, he ordered the driver to stop at the Swallow Hotel. And never was a place better named, because we had a right kick at it that night.

Now and again I go up to the loft, pull out a box full of memorabilia and look through it for a magazine called The Saints that the club published at the time. It had great pictures from that night and they still mean everything to me."

THAT SUMMER, Ally MacLeod left Aberdeen to take over the Scotland job and the Pittodrie board made a move for Fergie. He turned them down to see his boys through their first season in the big time.

Life among the top boys started well, too. We won 3-0 at Fir Park early on, backing up Starky's claim that Fergie rarely got done twice in the same place.

When Rangers came calling in September, their fans hurled bottles and tried to get on the park - Blue Devils, the front page of the Sunday Mail called them - but we kept our nerve and drew 3-3.

A few weeks later, Starky waltzed in for the most gorgeous goal you ever saw and we beat Celtic 2-1 at Parkhead.

We were doing fine. If you were a fan.

As the season went on, Fergie made two massive signings - old head Jimmy Bone, to help the McGarveys and Starks through it; and Iain Munro, who'd started as a winger with us at the turn of the 70s, gone on to Hibs and Rangers and returned as a left-back of genuine quality.

But for all that we were progressing, when you look back there was one game that must have made Fergie wonder. One painful afternoon that must have had him thinking if there was maybe more out there for him, a quicker way to turn his ambitions into reality.

Saturday, October 8.
St Mirren 0, Aberdeen 4.
WE got picked off that day. Bullied. It was boys again men - and men with pedal-bin haircuts too, wee Drew Jarvie notching a hat-trick and pulling us up mighty sharp.

In the dugout, you wondered if the manager was having second thoughts.

BY then, Fergie was imposing himself on everything. He was like a dog spraying its territory, marking out lines that those he stood between him and his ambitions daren't cross.

It's a trait that today sees him lampooned as much as he's feared, but back then ... as Billy Stark admits, shock and awe didn't begin to describe it.

"I REMEMBER we went to Alloa in the Spring Cup in '76 and won 4-1. We'd already beaten them 3-0 at home and were cruising into the last eight.

But at time-up, Fergie went storming in to referee Brian McGinlay's room and gave him dog's abuse. He left him without a name, you could hear him shouting from right down the corridor.

Brian hadn't done anything wrong in the game. I don't remember there being a big decision to make. That's not what it was about, though - this was Fergie putting down a marker with one of the biggest-name officials in the country. He was telling him to remember the name.

That became one of his strongest weapons, his ability to intimidate, to use mind-games to gain an advantage. He took it up a notch at Aberdeen when they were going to Ibrox and Parkhead and up again with Man United.

People criticise him for it, but it worked then and it still works now. He strikes fear into people without having to say a word, his reputation does the job for him.

It's all psychology. Some of the stick he dished out in the dressing room was vicious, but it wasn't personal. It was about finding out who had the guts for the fight and who hadn't. He didn't have the time to mollycoddle us and he didn't have the money to replace us, so he verbally booted us into shape.

He used to go mental. I mean, lose it.

There was a legendary time in that Premier League season when we'd lost at Hibs and went back into Glasgow to a pub called the Waterloo. It was a fairly normal thing to do, have a few pints on a Saturday night to unwind from the game, but when Fergie found out he lost the plot.

Worse than that, though, he went all week without saying anything even though we knew he was raging. The following Saturday we were at home to Partick Thistle, managed by wee Bertie Auld, who Fergie hated. When we beat them 2-1, we reckoned all would be forgiven, that he'd be ecstatic. Not so.

He told us to get in the dressing room and wait for us. So we waited.

175

And waited. Someone joked that he must have been waiting for our medals to get engraved. But after about an hour we'd had enough, so big Jackie Copland got sent upstairs to see where he was. When he came back, he said the gaffer was just coming.

Just coming? He nearly took the door off its hinges. He was blazing, I never saw him so angry.

He picked up a Solripe lemonade bottle and hurled it in the general direction of the showers. We ducked. It smashed. Glass and ginger went everywhere. The stain it left on the wall's the one they ending up just varnishing over, like it was a memorial to his time at the club."

In that Sunday Herald piece, Fergie himself said of the Waterloo incident: "I made them sign an agreement they'd never enter that pub again because I was determined to end the drinking culture that has always been a curse in British football."

Starky smiles at that one.

"I DON'T remember him making me sign anything. But then again, my mind might just have blanked out the whole business...

But I'll tell you this - the effect on the dressing room right then and on the boys from then on was incredible. He had made his point, just as he had that day with Brian McGinlay and just as he has done so often since."

ON A WET Wednesday night in mid-December, we played Liverpool.

Us. Against the European Champions. King Kenny, the lot.

It was our Centenary Game and the place was packed. Wee Billy Abercromby scored, we drew 1-1 then lost on penalties. What a night, what a memory.

Three days later, we were at home to Celtic. Another full house, another thriller.

We were 3-1 up with time ticking away, loving it. Then, another lesson.

Andy Lynch makes it 3-2. Joe Craig sticks away a penalty with 90 seconds left. It feels like a defeat.

It is, in fact, a lesson. That the really good teams play to the final whistle and beyond.

It's one that Fergie would store away and which, one magical night 21 years later, would make him a European champion.

After that blow, wins became hard to find.

We beat Clydebank at home on Christmas Eve, then didn't get another victory until - ironically - we went to Parkhead and Jimmy

Bone and Frank McGarvey sent us home smiling.

By mid-March, the Bankies looked pretty much doomed and the other relegation place was between us, Thistle and Ayr United.

The crunch game at Somerset Park on the 18th. Mud, that's what I remember about that day. A claggy pitch, battleship-grey clouds, rain tumbling.

It was the kind of game when no one had to say what was at stake, you could just feel it in the air, in the mood of the car on the way down the A77, in the turnstile queue, at the pie stall. The banter was muted, the football just the same.

As Starky confirms, the players felt it just as much as the punters did...

"WE ALL knew how big that game was. It was huge for us - lose it and a lot of people wondered if this team who wanted to play all the football had it in them to come back.

Honestly, I don't know if we would have. But we had no intention of finding out.

When we came into the Premier League, the manager never sat us down and told us we'd win it, but at the same time we never felt any fear. We knew we were good, that we could play football and that we could win games.

But by the time we got to Ayr, it was tight at the bottom. There were only maybe three points in it, so this was a real tightrope.

Ayr had solid players, journeymen like Walker McCall and Gordon Cramond. They'd beaten Celtic twice at home and we'd lost there in the November, so it wasn't going to be easy.

It wasn't a day for football. It was a day for digging in, something maybe we weren't known for. But we proved something to ourselves and to everyone else that day..."

Jimmy Bone was brilliant at Ayr, everything Fergie had signed him to be. Just as we'd been bullied against Aberdeen, now he was intimidating opponents, rag-dolling defenders and bringing us up the park when the pressure was on.

We hung in a bit that afternoon, always just one slip - quite literally, on that pitch - away from disaster. Lose and you wondered if we'd have it in us to recover.

There were just three minutes left when McGarvey slid in at the far post and poked home the only goal.

I'll be honest, he was never my favourite Saint. But in that relief-charged moment, he WAS a Saint.

177

On Wednesday, April 26, we got humped 5-0 away to Thistle; but the misery lifted when we heard Ayr had been beaten 3-1 at Tannadice and were now six behind us with one game left.

I missed that last game, away on a weekend down south with the BB. No texts back then, of course, no websites, no Soccer Saturday. So it was after five before someone got a call that we'd beaten Celtic 3-1.

Fitz scored, McGarvey scored, another Fergie find called Dougie Bell wrapped it all up with a goal on his debut.

Our first season in the Premier League had been a narrow escape from the drop, but it ended on a high.

Well, the fixture list did, at least.

Read here the words of Mr Willie Todd...

From The Guardian, May 31, 2008.

I WAS the chairman who brought Alex to St Mirren in 1974 and people forget that we actually struggled for the first two years he was in charge. He had a very bad start.

But Alex gradually got things together, basically because he brought so many good, young players to the club. The likes of Frank McGarvey, Bobby Reid and Billy Stark meant we had a young team but a successful one which got us out of the old First Division and into the Premier League.

We stayed in the Premier League in season 1977-78 and that was a big achievement. Crowds had been as low as 1000 when Alex took over; in his last season we sometimes had gates of 20,000 plus.

Alex did a great job for St Mirren. Nobody at the club worked harder than he did during the time he was there and everyone was very grateful for what he achieved. I got on well with Alex at the time, we were good friends and I have seen him a few times since. We have still been on good terms and I have been delighted at how well he has done. But in 1978 it was a simple case of myself, as chairman, doing what was best for the football club. I had no option but to sack him in the end.

Four days before he eventually left I knew perfectly well that he had told all the staff that he was moving to Aberdeen. A famous reporter of the time, Jim Rodger of the Daily Mirror, told us that Alex had asked at least one member of the squad to go to Aberdeen with him.

It was a clear breach of contract on his part; he was still under contract to St Mirren and Aberdeen had not contacted us to discuss compensation. There were various other stories at the time, such as one about Alex wanting players to receive tax-free expenses, but that was

178

not the real issue. The issue was St Mirren being destabilised because the manager wanted to leave.

In the end the case went to an industrial tribunal because Alex thought he had been sacked unfairly and St Mirren won hands down, on every count relating to his breach of contract; the minutes of that meeting show you that.

I do regret it. As I said we got on very well. It was just a pity Aberdeen had not come out and said they wanted our manager because we could then have spoken about compensation and done things amicably.

TODD is football's equivalent of the man at Decca Records who said no to The Beatles.

The man who, on May 31 1978, sacked Alex Ferguson.

Thirty years on, after keeping his head permanently beneath the parapet, he finally went into print with his reasons and they seem pretty clear-cut.

But at the time, all was confusion. Rumour. Innuendo. No one knew what the hell was going in, except for the bare fact that we'd just got rid of the best manager we'd ever had.

Or were ever likely to have.

I'd just finished my O Levels that week, so the swanning around had begun. It was lunchtime when the news got to us. We were across the road from Camphill High, playing football in Durrockstock Park.

At first, you were just like: "Aye, right."

It was a wind-up, had to be.

Then, someone else was shouting the same thing through the fence. Someone else was running back from their house, all breathless and eyes popping.

Even then, though, it was like that morning at the Racecourse when you knew the game would be off, but you needed someone to actually say it to your face. I refused point blank to believe Fergie had gone on the basis of schoolboy chatter alone.

So as the bell went, I was walking up Waverley Road, up the grass by the library, along past the Ivanhoe Road shops, past the top of the 59 Steps and into No25.

No rolling news in '77. Not even teletext. So on went the telly and radio at the same time, waiting for the next bulletin.

When it came, at two o'clock on Radio Clyde, my heart sank.

I cried. I shouted in anger at no one in particular. Then I just sat down and stared at nothing for a long time.

Within two years, we'd be third in the league and through to the UEFA Cup. We'd qualify again in '83 and '85, win the Scottish Cup in '87. Good times, good trips, good knees-ups.

But all of us - from a fan like myself to a man in Billy Stark who gave eight years to the cause - you were always left wondering: What if...

"THE sacking came right out of the blue. The season was over, we'd stayed up and we were looking forward to another crack at the big teams. The last thing we thought was that the manager would leave.

I think the first time I spoke to him after it all happened was when he was on the way up to Aberdeen to sign his deal there. He worked his way round all his main players, just saying his piece to us.

How was I feeling then? Devastated.

His credentials had soared over the previous couple of years and so had ours. He was the man. To lose him was ... well, it was distressing, to be honest.

But it was a lesson as well. For the first time, I experienced this side of a footballer's life, of knowing that you couldn't get too comfortable with a gaffer, because there could be another one along when you least expected it.

When the club brought Jim Clunie from Southampton as Fergie's replacement, I remember Willie Todd giving him the big build-up to all of us, but none of us knowing the guy from Adam.

All we could think was that it had been constantly onwards and upwards with Fergie and that we didn't want ANYBODY else. It felt like we'd come so far, but now we had to go back and start all over again.

Ricky McFarlane was brilliant for us at the time. He'd been physio under Fergie and now stepped up to be assistant manager. He did a lot for Jim and was a real players' man as well. When he became manager after Jim left, he deserved his chance.

We did well for a few years after that, but the truth is that the standards had been set by one man - Alex Ferguson. And when the momentum he left behind slowed up, it was hard to get it going again, because no one else could quite put their finger on what it was he had that made it all happen.

Years later, Aberdeen would find exactly the same thing when he left for Old Trafford and manager after manager tried to re-create what Fergie had achieved.

When I was with him at Pittodrie and we'd be going to Ibrox or

Parkhead or playing in cup finals, I never once remember going into the game even with the slightest fear that we'd lose. Fergie instilled that confidence in you, a belief in yourself that maybe you didn't know you had.

He dedicated every minute of every hour to making himself and everyone around him better. He never stopped and he never has. "

AND we gave it all away.

It's easy to look back now and say Todd and his board should have moved heaven and earth to keep Fergie, that we should have given him the keys to the whole town if that's what it took to have him pushing our football club towards places it could never have dreamed of being.

But in 1974, St Mirren were an old, faded club with an old, faded attitude. With memories to cling to and little else. This young guy who came their way hit them like a tornado, blasted the cobwebs off them.

Personally, I'm not sure if these accountants and shopkeepers and painter-decorators ever quite learned how to handle it. I'm not sure they ever really accepted being pushed around by a man who had no time for protocol or forelock-touching.

Alex Ferguson wanted results, he wanted them yesterday and if that meant bending the rules, pulling a few strokes or even blatantly ignoring his directors, then tough.

We got into that Top Six, didn't we?

We won the First Division, didn't we?

We stayed in the Premier, didn't we?

We got the turnstiles whizzing round like a cabbie's meter after midnight, didn't we?

What more do you want?

Respect, probably. Their place. To be asked now and again instead of told. To at least indulge themselves in the pretence that they were the ones running the show.

All these years on, I still can't believe we sacked him because he was talking about going to another club. Willie Todd says he had no choice, but that's surely not the case.

If he really was that miffed about Aberdeen sniffing around, all he had to do was refuse permission for them to talk to Fergie and make him either resign or get the Pittodrie board to stump up compensation.

Or better still, shrug and admit he'd outgrown us, shake his hand and thank the Lord we ever had him.

Call me cynical, though, but I've always had the feeling that it was a handy excuse to get rid of a man who was more bother than he was worth - just like the next chairman then sacked Jim Clunie after a 2-1 win at Parkhead, because he'd sworn in front of ladies.

Decisions like those have always seemed to sum up my club. More concerned with doing things right than getting things done; with keeping up appearance rather than hiking up attendances.

Yes, we may have gone on to Europe after Fergie left, but Starky's bang on; we did it with his wind in our sails.

Big picture? There's no doubt in my mind that we have never been the same since the day and hour he was punted.

Today, he could have been Kindly Uncle Alex, patting his old club on the head and passing us on the best of the rest from Man U.

Instead, a guy who gave us back our pride and our belief doesn't much fancy giving us the time of day.

He'd have gone soon enough, of course. Probably that summer, in fact.

Our mistake was in not letting him go with our blessing.

It doesn't take a genius to work out that Fergie knew from early on that he'd been wrong to turn Aberdeen down.

He'd done it for the right reasons, to try and push on the job he'd started at Love Street. But what is it they say about the road to hell and all those good intentions?

One final quote from the man himself speaks volumes:

"Just as East Stirlingshire cannot be a St Mirren, so St Mirren cannot be an Aberdeen and Aberdeen cannot be a Manchester United," he says. "Had I recognised that fact when Aberdeen first spoke to me, I would have saved myself a great deal of heartache."

Perhaps.

But for all that hanging on made his heart sore, every minute he stayed simply made ours soar.

Let's hope that one day he can remember us as fondly.

Twice In A Lifetime

I set the video on rewind then went to do my important thing; I told Kenny all about it. Five months old he was, all snug and content, blissfully unaware of all the excitement as he rushed through the hours until morning. So I sat by his cot and told him the story of How We Won The Cup. Then I placed a kiss on his cheek and whispered that one day it would be his turn to be there when we won it. The perfect end to a perfect day.

Once In A Lifetime,
Penthouse & Pavement, 1999

WHEN I was growing up, the Scottish Cup Final always fell on my dad's birthday.

Or at least it seemed to, until I looked back through the record books.

Then it turned out that since I was born it'd only actually been held on May 6 twice - in 1972 when Celtic beat Hibs 6-1 and when Rangers beat Aberdeen 2-1 six years later.

So how come whenever I think of the Scottish Cup Final I think of that one special date on the household calendar? Maybe because the first time it DID fall on May 6 it struck me just how much I wanted St Mirren to be there one day on that day as an extra-special present for him.

It never happened.

When we finally made it, in 1987, we played Dundee United on May

16, ten days after dad turned 59. He didn't go. He and my mum stayed home and watched Kenny. The quote at the top is from the chapter about that day in my first book.

It was the one downer of the whole occasion, dad not being there. He should have been, it was in the rules. He'd been there when we won it in '59 and he'd told me so much about the game and the bus ride home and the victory parade through the streets and all I'd ever wanted was for us to relive it all together. But by the time we got there, he'd fallen out of love with it all.

Looking back, I should have dragged him out the house that day. Maybe he thought I didn't want him to be with me. Maybe at the time I just didn't show him what it meant to me.

That's why I'm now glad that I not only made my promise to Kenny that night in '87, but that I was able to keep it. If and when we ever won something again, I wanted more than anything for us to celebrate it together. And we did.

On May 6, 2000.

It was a blazing hot day, a week after we'd wrapped up the First Division title with a 3-0 win over Raith Rovers at Love Street. That night, April 29, Kenny's little sister was conceived.

Don't ever say I don't know how to party.

The last game of the season was away at Inverness Caley Thistle, the game Matt Kerr mentioned earlier. There must have been 3000 Saints fans up there, half of whom had been there since the Friday, giving it yeehah. The whole weekend was one long carnival.

Even when we ended up doing things the stupid way.

The St Mirren way.

After nine years in the First Division, this was our time to step back in among the big boys. Whether actually being there made us happier or otherwise is an argument for another time; but getting there was a real blast.

Tom Hendrie's team were irresistible at their best; wing-backs Iain Nicolson and Ian Ross storming down the sides and firing in endless diagonal crosses, big Mark Yardley leaping and knocking them down, Junior Mendes and Steven McGarry always there to pounce on the bouncing ball.

We had some memorable performances - the 6-0 at Kirkcaldy that kick-started the whole thing; a flowing 4-1 win at Cappielow, capped by stopper Scott Walker running 80 yards from a cleared corner to meet a cross with a wonderful diving header; an 8-0 home romp over Clydebank.

But the real joy for me came when my sports editor, the Geordie genius who was Steve Wolstencroft, called and said: "Why don't you follow your team on the run-in..?"

Oh all right then, if I must...

So I phoned Kenny and said: "I'm doing the last five games. Want to come with me?"

And he went: "Well, if you insist..."

SO this became our time. Just as 1976-77 was the peak for my dad and me, the season when we saw the Saints win a title together, now my son and I would go side-by-side down the finishing straight.

To say we watched Hendrie's men stumble as the finish line came into view was like saying Alex Ferguson has finally overcome his battle with chronic shyness.

It began like this...

ST MIRREN 1 FALKIRK 0

FALKIRK came with a chip on their shoulder. And left wearing the whole fish supper.

By next Saturday's grudge match with Raith they'll have chucked on a single haggis, two pickled onions and a portion of curry sauce.

Salt and vinegar? No thanks, there's enough in their stinging wounds already.

If they thought the world was against them after the EssPeeEll snubbed their promotion bid, what happened at Love Street convinced them.

This was like watching an Old Firm game at Parkhead, except with the away team as Celtic. They battered on the door, threw the kitchen sink, looked like they HAD to score sometime.

You know the script. Right at the death they're hit on the break by a team out on their feet and it's goodnight and drive safely.

The fact that they got the square root of sod all off ref Cammy Melville didn't help.

He got up their noses from the fourth minute, when Tommy Turner was too casual and too short with a passback, Kevin McAllister scampered in, knocked the ball past Ludo Roy and went down.

As Melville raced over, hand in back pocket, you thought Roy was walking. Instead, McAllister was booked for diving.

I'm writing this before I've seen a TV replay, but I'd swear in court McAllister is NOT a cheat.

The wee man was close to tears as he said: "I never dived. No way. Roy caught me and he even said so - so did Tommy Turner. But the ref had two options, give a penalty and send off the home keeper in the first few minutes or book me.

"He chose the wrong one and that was it started. We should've had at least one other penalty when Roy flattened Gareth Hutchinson in the second half, but we got nothing.

"I'm going home now to shut the doors and not go out again."

It's a crying shame Melville had such influence, because this was a terrific game. It was raw emotion, all-out attack, two teams with everything to gain. Saints had to open their new Love Street end stand to cope with the crowd and the constant noise made it a thrilling occasion.

Falkirk deserved better from it. But what can you say about a St Mirren team who started without four regulars, lost top scorer Mark Yardley seven minutes in and ended up subbing a sub as injuries piled up?

Jammy? Probably. Courageous? Definitely.

They played the last three minutes of normal time and EIGHT added on with ten men when Tom Brown elbowed Andy Lawrie just after Paul McKnight's heart-stopping winner.

Actually, it was nine and a half men if you count giant German striker Jens Paesleck limping on a damaged calf after Kevin Christie hauled him down at 0-0 as he raced clear. Christie wasn't last man, but it was as professional a foul as you'll see.

It was also as awesome a scrap between two honest men as you'll see and it's another crying shame it was spoiled by a weedy ref blowing for every bit of contact.

Christie needed treatment three times after running into the brick wall that is Paesleck, but each time he got up as if to say: "Is that your best shot?"

He might even have won the game just before Saints scored, but his towering header from a Davie Nicholls corner was brilliantly tipped round the right hand post by Roy.

Christie sighed: "I thought it was going in - yet from the next corner St Mirren broke away and scored. It's hard to take.

"I had some battle with the big German. His game's all about winning flick-ons and he's very physical. I just can't believe it was all for nothing.

"From where I was standing, I thought their keeper was going off for bringing down Crunchie. The boys reckon we could have had another three penalties.

"But what can you do? We had all the pressure and never scored. Now the title's looking difficult and we've got to beat Raith next week or they'll go above us.

"We'll certainly be up for it, because some things they said about us when we were trying to get promoted weren't called for."

Huge, shaven-headed, with taped-up ear-rings, Paesleck's already a cult hero. And if he's not the most stylish, when three more one-nils mean the title he might prove priceless.

He said: "I like Scottish football, it's played the way I play. I enjoyed facing their No5, but I think maybe he should have had a red card for fouling me, yes? After that tackle I could not run and my fingers feel broken from another clash.

"But I had to play on, we had no more subs. So I was just trying to keep our fans shouting. They were wonderful - it was a great noise. If they keep supporting us and we keep winning it will be a great achievement."

Paesleck might have scored with a couple of headers and a shot before the deadlock was broken. But what must Falkirk be thinking about the chances they lost?

Minutes in, Roy dropped a cross and Hutchinson fired over an empty net. Nicholls was one-on-one on 76 minutes and poked wide. Christie's header looked a goal all the way until the Frenchman's heroics.

Then in came the corner, Saints cleared it wide left and suddenly had men over. The whole ground was on its feet. The tireless Steven McGarry was galloping down the left, seeing a black and white shirt inside and lobbing a pass.

The shirt belonged to Paul McKnight, on for injured sub Robinson who'd replaced the hobbling Sergei Baltacha. He got the pass then also got lucky when Jamie McQuilken slipped.

What a moment for a boy just minutes into his home debut.

He shot, a mishit that put Myles Hogarth off balance. It seemed to take forever, rolling and bobbling and seemingly going wide. But then it bobbled one last time, hit the inside of the keeper's left post and trickled over the line.

The noise, the joy, most of all the relief, were incredible.

Yet then came even greater tension.

Brown walked, Falkirk piled forward and left holes, Junior Mendes and Paesleck wasted chances. Melville added on EIGHT minutes.

When it finally ended, Falkirk looked drained. Saints went wild linking arms to salute their delirious fans. It was a stunning victory plucked from absolutely nothing.

Manager Tom Hendrie said: "We were without Ian Nicholson, Ian Ross, Barry Lavety, Scott Walker and lost Mark Yardley early on. Baltacha went off right after half-time, then young Ryan was caught across the knee by Nicholls.

"Jens was hobbling, Tom Brown stupidly got sent off and we were down to the bones. So that goal and this win might be the most important of the season. It was also our fifth clean sheet in a row and despite all our goals that's what wins titles.

"You have to feel sorry for Falkirk. We were maybe a bit lucky at times, but it was a great game which both teams went all out to win.

"The ref got it right with the McAllister incident. He dived. Their second penalty claim, when Ludo came out for a bouncing ball and Hutchinson went down, was tighter. But we'd have been angry had it been given."

In one final drama, Tommy Turner needed a police escort to his car after threats made by Falkirk fans. Nonsense like that does their club's cause no good.

Everyone at Brockville has taken the crippling knocks of the past few weeks with dignity. Neds wanting to fill in opposition players have no place there.

ONE down, four to go.

Livi away, Ayr away, Raith at home, Caley away.

Two wins would almost certainly take us up. Three and we'd be champions.

Dunfermline were the only fly in the ointment, the team we'd swapped top slot with for months. Their next game was a nailed-on win, at home to doomed, dismal Clydebank; ours was at Almondvale.

Kenny and I sat in the yellow seats and prayed the boys wouldn't turn the same colour when the chips were down.

LIVINGSTON 1 ST MIRREN 2

NEARLY there now. For the first time, the winning post's in sight.

We can't finish outside the top three after Raith's defeat on Saturday and barring a total collapse by Falkirk we're virtually promoted.

You'd think I'd be relieved. But forget it. Saturday was a day for the best brown suit and next week at Ayr will be no different.

This being successful business is bad for your health.

It started with a minute's silence in memory of the Hillsborough dead and the rest was 90 minutes mayhem with no respect for the living.

188

We did it the hard way again, coming off the ropes when our legs were going and sticking the perfect counter-punch on the oppo's chin.

Livvy were suckered and shattered. They'd put us through it in that second half, hammered us 1-1, but we're deadly on the break. You can see our goals coming from 80 yards away.

One minute they were swarming down our left, the next big Scott Walker had slid in and won it and Tommy Turner had burst clear and he was playing Hugh Murray away.

Suddenly it was last week against Falkirk all over again. Them caught up the park, us exploding like a black and white thundercloud.

Steven McGarry had it on the D, but couldn't get a shot off. Pushed it into Mark Yardley on the penalty spot. Tries to turn, defender blocks. Back to McGarry. Blocked again. Bodies all over the shop.

Then - don't ask me how - it's at Yards's feet and big Ian McCaldon's away to one side like Gourock and Yards pokes it and it's in. IT'S IN! Right in front of our lot. They were dancing on the track. Our bench turned into one big 12-legged tracksuited trampolining beast.

I turned to my wee fella and we gave it a major hug. His face was beaming, hopefully with happiness and not embarrassment at his old boy hugging him in public. In the car home, we'd cheer when the result came on as if we didn't already know it.

This is the best thing of all about seeing us edge ever-nearer to the championship, seeing it all unfold with your son at your side. Me and dad did it in 1977 and this is every bit as perfect.

Of course, you can think these things after it's over. At it the time it's: "Does anyone have a number for Pullar's of Perth?"

After leaving it late to beat Morton and Falkirk and riding our luck against Airdrie, we agreed an early goal would be the very dab to settle things down. And 24 minutes was early enough.

What was McGarry's strike like? It was like watching Sevvy hit a beautiful 9 iron, like the arc of a perfectly-cast fishing line, like ... OK, let the scorer himself tell you:

"Their defence were pushing up to halfway and I was going with them when the boy Rowson played a ball back, but it went beyond them and they were caught square.

"I was onto it first and could have run in on goal. But I was about 30 yards out and decided to take a chance. Even though their keeper looks about 12 foot tall, I thought I could chip him, so I went for it.

"It was some feeling when it went in - I was thinking about my family and friends in the stand, them and all the other friends I've

189

made among our support since I got into the team. I'm a local boy and a fan, so I'd be up there if I wasn't playing. They mean everything to me and goals like that are for them."

I think I'll ask my missus if we can adopt him.

So that was us in the box seat. Raith were 0-0 at Brokeville and by 3.30 there was still no goal news from East End Park. Then we found out that was because Clydebank weren't there yet. As soon as the radio said the game had finally started, so did the avalanche.

The nine goals we were better off than Dunfermline were worth an extra point if it went to the wire, so every one the Bankies let in hurt us. Another eight like we took off them and we'd be back to square one.

Still, just into the second half I got four separate calls from Falkirk to say they were one up and things looked cosy. For a few minutes.

Then Livvy turned it on.

They threw three men up, made us go four at the back, Brian McPhee started playing and we wobbled. McPhee whipped one front post and David Bingham flicked in sweet as you like.

McPhee was on his knees in ecstasy. I felt like falling to mine in despair as they came at us like demons and the season hung in the balance. Barry McLaughlin and Walker held us together at the back and in midfield Ricky Gillies came off the bench for a triumphant prodigal's return.

Tom Hendrie said later: "Ricky was on such a low when he came back from Aberdeen, short on confidence and on fitness. That wasn't the same man out there. That was someone who can contribute to any side."

Slowly, we sucked Livi's enthusiasm dry. And then we hit them. Yet again we'd dug in, shown incredible character and come out the other end intact. Tom Hendrie must be so proud of the unit he's created at St Mirren, because I sure as hell know I am.

After all the doubts about our bottle, the guts this team has shown welded to their ability and the craving for a party among our success-starved fans surely makes us worthy winners now.

Only one downer on Saturday. Some lads at the back of the Saints end wouldn't sit down and after McGarry's goal one of them took a header over the seats. Ambulance folk went in to help him, but he was blotto and gave them dog's abuse.

As he was led towards the first aid room, blood smeared on his face, Paisley's finest screamed and blinded at the families in the Livvy bit. And I thought: "Hey - that's my home town!"

Hopefully missing a win as thrilling as this will make him realise what a berk he was.

WHEN I look back, it strikes me how biased that report is, how much the fan came through in every line. Couldn't help it, though - and hey, that was why the gaffer asked me to follow us down the finishing straight.

In this job, you're neutral 99 games out of 100, no matter what some paranoid punters believe. You watch the game for what it is, start with a blank sheet of paper and fill it with whatever unfolds in front of you.

Yes, you put feeling into it - or, at least, you should; whether enough journalists do is an argument for another day. But no matter how wrapped up you get in any match, it's never quite the same as covering your own team.

That's when you put real feeling into the words. That's when the joy and pain of winning and losing are etched in every keystroke.

That's what the gaffer wanted, the agonies of being so near to glory chronicled by someone who'd have been on the terraces had he not been in the press box.

As Michael Parkinson once said of the football reporter on the his local paper: "He was a Barnsley man writing for Barnsley men about Barnsley. So sod impartiality."

In these final five weeks, I was a St Mirren man writing for St Mirren men. If anyone else had a problem with that, they were confusing me with someone who gave a monkey's.

Anyway, as we were winning that Livi game, Dunfermline were beating the poor old Bankies 6-0. Next, they'd go to Inverness.

Us? We'd invade Somerset Park in our thousands for a day that would begin with nerves and end in ecstasy.

And for me, in a marquee on the pitch at Brockville, crumbling old home of Falkirk. Fulfilling a promise to a Bairns-daft mate to help with a fundraising do, but wishing I could be teleported to where the greatest fans in the world were having the biggest party in 13 years.

AYR UNITED 1 ST MIRREN 2

SOME moments will stay with you for the rest of your life. This was one of them.

It was 4.50pm and I'd just come off the phone from Caley Thistle, who'd confirmed they'd lost 2-1 to Dunfermline. Once again, the title was in the balance.

Our five-point lead was shrinking to three with two to play. The Fifers would have their tails up now. That old devil called doubt was sticking its fork up our backsides again.

When Junior Mendes put us ahead just after half-time against ten men we'd looked home and hosed. But then David Craig scrambled in from a corner with our defence frozen and we hadn't looked like scoring since.

Ayr had beaten us a man short at Love Street and now they could do it again. We were wobbling. From dreaming of actually clinching the title, we could see it slipping away again.

There were 93 minutes gone when we slung over one last cross. It was bread and butter for a keeper as confident as Marius Rovde, but he dropped it. Barry McLaughlin tried to shoot and booted the keeper's hand. It was pinball in there.

And suddenly it was at Paul McKnight's feet. Again. Just like the Falkirk game. And again, the little Belfast boy steadied himself and buried it.

After years in the shadows at Rangers, he's become a legend with two kicks of the ball.

I cannot even begin to describe the feeling, but if you support Queen's Park or Alloa or Ross County or Dunfermline or Queen of the South you'll have had it too on Saturday.

There's disbelief and relief and ecstasy and your heart's racing and you're trying to speak but only actually making noises; but it doesn't matter, because the people you're leaping around with understand perfectly.

Some of our players were in a big pile and about 70 yards away Iain Nicolson was flat on his back and Ludo Roy was going out of his box in his box and the bench were going tonto.

There were a lot of people on the pitch who thought it was all over. Scores of fans had come over the wall and you started to click they didn't know the real score from Inverness.

Mark Yardley said later: "The punters thought we'd won the league and so did we. They were all signalling to us from behind the goal with two fingers up on each hand. They'd heard it was 2-2 and Paul's goal would have made us champions.

"It was only when we came off we heard the right result. But it was still fantastic. We pulled it right out of the fire again and to be promoted is incredible."

Tell me about it. I was in a daze when it all finished a few blurry seconds later and I guess I still am. We've done it. We're up. We're back.

As I came down from the stand, I met an old school pal called Davy Davidson. We almost broke each other's ribs hugging. Then I went down the tunnel and out onto the track and watched our 3000-plus fans file out, all wearing the same look I must have had.

What else in life but football makes ordinary people feel as good as we did then?

I mean, all you Alloa fans and Ross County fans and Dunfermline fans and Queen's Park fans - did you know what to do with yourselves when you'd made it? Could Queen of the South supporters get their heads round their unlikeliest of Houdini jobs?

Even Rangers fans, spoiled by success and handed the league by default, must have felt at least a fraction of the innocent wonder I did at 4.50pm that Saturday. If they didn't, theirs is a very different football planet from mine and I don't want to go there.

Kenny looked like he was going to burst with it all. When it was 1-1 and we were up against it he'd put his head against my shoulder at one point as if to say ... well, I don't know what it was as if to say, but it was cool.

And when we scored, when we won, when we were promoted? If only I could have photographed his expression and kept it to look at whenever life goes wrong.

He'd brought his Lavety 9 away strip in the hope of hanging around and getting some of his heroes to sign it. He wanted to frame it as a memento of the day.

He'd got a couple of signatures when one of the young lads who hadn't been playing asked him if he'd like it taken into the dressing room and two minutes later the big white No 9 had the entire squad on it.

I mean the entire squad, too. Saints had brought every player on the books to Somerset Park and every one went back to Love Street for beer and champagne, equal shares of the glory even if they'd only carried the kit hampers.

Here's hoping we're all celebrating again next Saturday night after the win over Raith that would guarantee the title. If not, we can do it at Inverness. Just as long as we do it.

But even if the wheels came off now, we're there after eight long years.

My night ended on the pitch at Brockville, under a giant tent that made the stadium look far more impressive.

It was a Back The Bairns do to help Alex Totten keep his Bosman players for next season. It was a superb night, but then again after what happened at 4.50 I'd have had fun buried in the desert with jam on my head while Sydney Devine sang The Best of Steps.

Past midnight, their keeper Myles Hogarth went in the Hope Street End goal in his white tux and faced penalty kicks for a fiver a go. There was a fantastic spirit despite everything that has happened to them.

Best of all, though, was that despite it all everyone was warm in their congratulations for my team and what we've done. These people genuinely want us to win the title now.

Or at least, they don't want those b****** Fifers to get their hands on it…

AND now, we were ready for a party that would make last Saturday night's look like a wake.

Beat the Rovers and the title was ours. For Fergie, read Hendrie. For Fitzy and Starky, read Ricky and McGarry.

Beat the Rovers and the title was ours.

Sounds simple when you say it quick. But this was St Mirren, this was a club with a masters degree in snatching disaster from the jaws of triumph.

Not today, though. Surely not today.

Not when the new stand we'd built as our entrance fee to Club EssPeeEll was being opened pre-match. Not when every kid in the town seemed to have a new scarf round his neck and a fluttering flag in his hand.

Not when my boy was there, watching his dad fidget and bounce in his seat like Jack Douglas with piles.

No, this would be the day when it all went according to the script.

Eventually…

ST MIRREN 3 RAITH ROVERS 0

AND so, I finally got to keep that promise.

Thirteen years ago, when the team came home to Paisley Town Hall, I got my trembling hands on the trophy and kissed it. On Saturday, I watched my boy hold the league championship trophy and do the same.

We were standing in the tunnel when our chairman Stewart Gilmour came in holding our Holy Grail. He gave it to me. I passed it to Kenny. He planted a smacker on it and life was wonderful.

He'd watched most of the game in his usual season ticket seat, but after Barry McLaughlin headed the third goal and all the fears and nerves were finally swept away, I went down and caught his attention and got him to come and join me up beside the injured players.

We couldn't get this close and not be together.

And so we'd seen out time, my arm round his shoulder and a lump in my throat the size of Yards's backside, willing the moment to come.

That last half hour was like lying awake at three on Christmas morning, knowing all the pressies were under the tree downstairs.

Shug Murray told me later the players hadn't been sure what to do in those dragged-out closing minutes. Chase another goal? What if they lost one? Because if they lost one, they could lose two and then..? So they just passed it and passed it and passed it and kept asking the ref for time checks.

It'd been a strange game, a strange day. Turning up at half past one to see stalls selling Champions 2000 flags, T-shirts and scarves was unsettling - what if it was all premature exhilaration? What if Raith did us and Dunfermline scored a bucketload and we had to go to Caley next week needing not to lose?

Our fears seemed justified in a first half when Raith could have been home and hosed. Ludo Roy had two brilliant stops, the bleach-blond Craig Dargo might have had a penalty instead of a booking for diving and Tommy Turner booted Javary's header off the line. We rode our luck like drunk men on buckled unicycles and half-time was a blessing.

Now, I don't know what was said in the dressing room - maybe Tom Hendrie was taking the paint off the walls. But out in the stands, it was eerie. No one was saying much, there was no buzz. Everyone was on edge.

Yet just to prove how strange it all was, before an hour had gone we were 3-0 up and wondering what the fuss had been about.

And when George Clyde finally blew for time and the title was ours at last, it was like a dam of emotion bursting. Grown men wept. And so did big weans like me.

I'd been welling up in me from the moment Yards smacked the first in the top corner. When Steven McGarry's header glanced in like Dalglish's at Anfield in '77, my lip was going. After the third it was like watching football through a jelly.

My one worry in those final minutes was the fans. Would they come on the pitch? Would the presentation be called off? Would it be like Maine Road on Friday night [where a pitch invasion caused chaos as home fans mistakenly thought their team had won the Championship], scared players riding a wave of misplaced euphoria?

No one need have fretted.

Not a soul came over the side, not one, not even during the scarf-laden lap of honour after Lord MacFarlane had handed Tommy Turner the famous old Scottish Football League Championship trophy.

I told the wee fella to remember it wasn't the First Division trophy. It was the real thing, the one Celtic and Rangers won nine times in a row and Fergie won for Aberdeen and which dated all the way back to 1891. It was history.

But let's face it, they could have glued a tin can onto a half-brick and given us it and it would have still looked as beautiful.

Round the corner at Caledonia Bowling Club come half six, that trophy once handled by Billy McNeill and Jock Stein, by Bill Struth and Alex Ferguson and even Doug Rougvie - for it's important to remember that when you get close up to the beautiful game, you realise it has the odd blackhead - was filled with champagne and passed round from players to management to punters and back.

Everyone looked at it with utter awe.

Then the tears came again.

When we won the cup, I'd thought that was it, that this would be my one return for all that investment in gloom.

I never thought I'd be as happy again. But I was wrong. Seeing my son kiss that trophy at Love Street beat everything.

If we'd never won another match, never mind another title, I'd have died a happy fan.

AND then, like the week before, I walked away from the knees-up.

It was Gordy's stag weekend in Dublin. The rest had gone out the night before and I'd promised to be there after the game.

What a diddy.

Sure, we had a fantastic night. But you can get married any time. You might only get to be there with your kid when your team wins the league once in a lifetime.

Still. We'd be there for the final chapter, the lap of honour masquerading as an away game against Caley Thistle. The last 90 minutes of 3240 in a gruelling campaign, our chance to sign off in style.

Eight years on, it's still hard to write that with a straight face...

CALEY THISTLE 5 ST MIRREN 0

AND SO to the bit the Old Firm will never get to enjoy.

No matter how big and powerful they are, even if they win

196

everything in sight, they'll never get to parade their trophies through the street.

It's the greatest sadness of Scottish football. But do I care? No, I don't.

Celebrations like these don't come around often enough to be sidetracked by life's little problems. Ask any Saints fan who sat through a bizarre Saturday at Caley Stadium.

They watched their title-winning heroes ship five goals - which might have been ten - and yet they danced in the sunshine and sang We Don't Give A Monkey's.

When it was over, when the season was over, 2000 came on the pitch and crowded around the tunnel until the team appeared in the directors' box and Tom Hendrie made a speech.

Twenty-four hours later, as the Holy Grail was held aloft on an open-topped bus, it seemed the only people in Paisley not lining the route were still lying drunk in the Highlands. Well, them and the burglars having a field day.

Not everyone's off on a Sunday, you know.

From Love Street, down past the Sheriff Court, round the Sneddon, under the railway arches to the Town Hall and an emotional bow on the balcony, every man who helped turn my club around were feted like kings and they deserved every cheer from every fan. Nope, the Old Firm don't know what they're missing.

They win their latest pot, do a quick half-lap of honour, then it's back to their respective corners of Glasgow with police in between keeping them apart.

One man's enjoyment becomes another family's grief as stomachs are knifed, faces cut, ribs booted in. The songs of hate ring out in the night and the fans join in.

But, like I said, I'm confusing myself with someone who cares.

Yesterday was for simple football lovers, the kind who really suffer - no, not the halfwits losing it because their team's only second in the EssPeeEll - and who wait half their lives for just one glimpse of silverware.

Last time Paisley saw scenes like these was on Saturday May 16, 1987, when Alex Smith's boys brought home the Scottish Cup. The streets were chocca.

Next day, before the team went off to Singapore for a four-team tournament (which we also won, by the way), there were 12,000 at Love Street to see the silverware paraded again.

Now a town had its party hats out again, even if the team had worn theirs a day early.

It was maybe fitting that we went out with heads hung low, because all this success makes you forget what being a St Mirren fan's all about. We were starting to get cocky.

Caley soon kicked that out of us.

When David Xausa scored the first, a boy along from where me and the wee fella were sitting said we'd have to win it the hard way. When Mark McCulloch made it two, he said: "Ah well, it'll be 3-2."

Then Paul Rudden cocked up a passback, Ludo hesitated, Barry Wilson slid it out of his hands for 3-0 and the boy said: "Four-three? Hell of a comeback."

It might have happened, too, had Barry Lavety's header not hit the post and Hugh Murray's lob past Les Fridge not gone wide and ... ah, forget it. We were minging. I'm conveniently ignoring Caley's missed one-on-ones and Ludo's saves and Scott Walker heading off the line.

Let's face it, this was a rout.

By the time sub Martin Bavidge hit the fourth even Tom Hendrie had stopped shouting. Our fans started singing We Want Five and the Caley support gave us a standing ovation for it.

McCulloch then obliged and I can honestly say I'd never been in a more surreal atmosphere.

The worse the result got, the more the party rocked. No one was for leaving - in the end Hendrie had to spell it out: "Go away and have fun in the town."

And so they did. Saints fans in grass skirts, in black and white top hats, with face-paint running in the heat and flags everywhere went for it like there was no tomorrow and when tomorrow proved them wrong their hangovers made them wish they'd been right.

There were so many families up in Inverness and I only hope come next season it's not back to just dad and the occasional kid. I'd love it if mum and grandpa and the whole damn lot of them stayed behind the Saints.

Your local team's for life, not just for days when you've already won the title.

But that's for July. This is now and right now an entire town is ecstatic. That's the power of football, the power to unite - it can do more for a population's feelgood factor in 90 minutes than politicians will in a lifetime.

In the car coming home from Inverness, the wee fella was talking about how the season had started for us. We were in the airport, coming home from holiday in Orlando, when he went on an Internet machine and found out we'd beaten Rangers in a friendly.

He came running up to tell me and said: "D'you think if we keep winning and go top of the league the new sponsors might build us a stand so we can get promoted?"

I told him not to get too carried away, but who was kidding who? I was already dreaming. And now our dreams have come true.

Isn't football a special game?

Most special of all that Saturday was that it was my dad's birthday. I knew for sure he was watching from way up in the best seats.

And that he'd have watched the goals flying past us and rested easy in the knowledge that supporting St Mirren will never change.

WHICH is probably the thing I love us for most of all.

Saint Shug

SO, by now we know only too well that Love Street's been sold to save St Mirren.

But if it wasn't for a shy wee fella from Coatbridge, there might not have been a St Mirren left to save.

Shug Murray.

His real name's Hugh, but no one who knows and loves him calls him that. Except maybe his mammy.

Though after what he did for the club on May 2 1998, we could have called him Sir, Highness or Supreme Ruler of the Universe and it might not have done him justice.

Which might sound a tad over the top for a kid who'd only scored the winner in a league game away to Stirling Albion. Unless you know what that game meant.

His old coach Matt Kerr's already told how he cried when the final whistle blew. The chairman admits how relieved he was when it was over.

That day at Forthbank really was crunch time for St Mirren Football Club.

Defeat meant almost certain relegation and an end to full-time football. Yet that, as the doctor said as he examined the lettuce stuck up Graeme Norton's bottom, was only the tip of the iceberg.

We were talking meltdown at the bank, hostile takeovers, the ground being sold off. Maybe even the end.

Instead, we got victory. The feelgood factor from which propelled us halfway up the First Division the following season and all the way to the top the one after.

Winning that title in 2000 made a whole town believe again. It also gave Stewart Gilmour and his Board reason to think they hadn't invested in a pup.

So when young master Shug smacked his 56th-minute shot high past keeper Mark McGeown, he did more than just keep us up.

He knocked over the first domino in a chain that led us to where we are today.

HE WAS 14 when he first walked through the front door, an excited boy who'd only ever been to Love Street once before.

Today, 16 years on, he's as much a part of the furniture as the treatment bench in the home dressing room.

He signed his first professional contract on January 21 1997. At the time of writing, he's started 329 games in all competition plus 27 as a sub and scored 15 goals.

Vastly experienced, but still fairly young - turning 30 five days after Love Street's last game - he's irreversibly intertwined with this club's recent history.

The only Saints player ever to win three medals in national competitions, the 2000 and 2006 First Division titles and the 2005 League Challenge Cup. Probably the last player we'll ever have who's around long enough to be awarded a testimonial.

I was lucky enough to be asked onto his committee. It was an honour to help raise a few bob for a guy who's sweated blood for the black and white shirt for the whole of his adult life so far.

Talk to him about it all now and you hear someone full of joy and pride to have spent half his life as an adopted Buddie.

Yet as he speaks, he wears a look that suggests he's not quite sure how he got here from the night he was first plucked out of a crowd by a talent-spotter with good taste...

"I WAS playing with Wolves Boys Club when scout Joe Hughes came and saw me and I got invited into train. I think I'd only been at Love Street to see Celtic.

I remember they were just seating the North Bank when we got shown round, then we went over to train at the Pitz five-a-side complex on the other side of the town.

After a year, I signed as a S-Form. Joe had come to the house to talk to my mum and dad, Louisa and Tommy, and promised that St Mirren was a club where youth would get its chance. Jimmy Bone was the manager and without much money around, it was the only way for him to go.

The likes of Ricky Gilles and Brian Heatherston were already in and around the first team and that finally sold me. Plus, Joe had been in school with my dad's brother, so we trusted him.

He was as good as his word and there was never a chance I'd regret my decision to go to Love Street.

When I was 16, I left St Ambrose High in Coatbridge in the January and signed full-time straight away. It was a two-year YTS deal, at £75 a week - £80 once they paid my expenses. Sounds pennies now, but it was a fortune to me. And I was getting it for playing football.

I'd be up sharp every morning, down to Blairhill Station, into Queen Street, walk round to Central, another train to Gilmour Street, then run up to Love Street for nine o'clock. If you were late, you got fined. You soon learned discipline.

They made me one of the two kids in charge of the kit. It was our job to make sure all the training gear was out for the first team every morning and to pack the hampers for games on a Saturday.

But Friday was the day we hated. Some Fridays, we didn't even get to train, because we'd get taken away to clean pigeon shit off the seats in the main stand and the North Bank. Not a lot of fun.

If it wasn't that, then Jimmy's assistant Kenny McDowall would have us on our knees in the dressing room, cleaning the grout between the tiles in the big old bath with a toothbrush and a bottle of Jif. Or out in the car park, washing cars for the directors and the management.

When my two years were up, I got taken on full-time. I don't actually remember how long it was for or how much I got, just that it felt good.

Tony Fitzpatrick was the manager by then and on the opening day of the '97-'98 season he gave me my debut against Airdrie at Broadwood. We were 1-0 down at half-time, but Junior Mendes got a hat-trick and we won 3-1. I got the full 90 minutes. It was a great feeling just to be picked, but to win was magic.

I went on to play about 30 games that season, had my first experience of derbies with Morton - and then experienced that amazing day at Stirling, of course.

All these years later, the boys joke that I never stop talking about it, but the truth is it's always other people who bring it up. It means a lot to St Mirren people.

It was a huge game. Like I'm sure everyone else says, had we gone down we might not have come back. We were talking part-time football, so boys like me might have been let go.

We simply had to win.

It's amazing to think that today we're about to move to a new stadium, we're in our third season in a row in the top division and we're one of the most financially-sound clubs in the country.

But if we're lost at Stirling ... well, who knows?

We'd had a meeting with Tony and he'd drummed in how big it was. The club had been going through so much money trouble, plus all the takeover talk with the guy Brealey. What we probably didn't need to hear was that we'd never won at Forthbank!"

The team that day was: **Alan Combe, Brian Smith, Barry McLaughlin, Norrie McWhirter, Paul Fenwick, David Winnie, Steven McGarry, Tommy Turner, Tom Brown, Junior Mendes, Hugh Murray. Subs (not used): Mark Yardley, Andy Roddie.**

"ON the day, Tony decided for some reason to take my usual No7 shirt off me and give it to Steven McGarry. I don't know if he thought it would be a lucky charm for him, that it'd help him get a goal. But I wore the No11 - and it was me who scored.

It was just before the hour. I remember Tom Brown coming in off the right and pushing a pass to me, then me taking a touch and just ... well, hitting it, then watching it float into the top corner.

It was an amazing feeling.

We still had half an hour to go, but I don't think we were ever under that much pressure. We just wanted it to be over and when it was, everyone went daft. The fans all wanted to party. It was like a huge weight had been lifted off of everyone."

Nine years and three days later, he did it again. Popped up with a goal when his team, his club, his town needed one most.

It was the opener in a 2-0 win away at Dundee United that kept alive our hopes of staying in the EssPeeEll for one than one season this time.

It was his only goal of that campaign. In fact, it was the first goal he'd ever scored in the top flight.

He knows how to pick his moments, this boy.

"YEAH, that was big as well, the game at Tannadice.

We'd played Dunfermline at home on the Monday night, live on the telly, and a win would just about have put us safe at the bottom. But they were on a great run under Stephen Kenny and beat us 1-0.

Next day, the papers were full of how that was us, how Dunfermline were going to stay up. They were only a point behind us now and it wasn't looking good.

We sat in the dressing room last night, listening to their fans singing in the Caledonia Stand. We could hear their players messing around with beach balls they'd got from the crowd.

The gaffer told us to take it all in, to remember them celebrating like they'd stayed up when there was still a lot of work to do. It made us all the more determined to finish the season on a high.

It would really have hurt to go straight back down after winning the First Division, because the same thing had happened when we went up in 2000. I didn't want to go through all that again.

That year, we'd been pretty much down and out, then started getting results. When we beat Dundee United in another Monday night game, it gave us a chance. On the Saturday, we had Aberdeen at home and it was 1-1 at half-time, while United were losing 2-0 to St Johnstone.

We ended up winning 2-1, but then we heard United had come back to win 3-2 and we were down. When you saw the goals on the telly later, it was fair to say the St Johnstone keeper Alan Main chucked a couple in. It wasn't pretty.

Our fans still let him know what they think about that to this day.

Anyway, next time round we went to Tannadice desperate to get a result and we did brilliantly to get it. I got a goal halfway through the first half and then big Kirk Broadfoot sealed it right at the end. It was just as well, too, because Dunfermline then hammered Motherwell on the Monday night."

Which took us to Motherwell. And, as he recalls with a huge smile, probably the greatest game of the 350-odd Shug has played in.

"IT was the most enthralling experience you could have as a player. We went through every possible emotion that afternoon, ending in absolute joy.

But for a long time ... I tell you, it really felt like we were going down again. It felt like there was no way back.

We went in 1-0 down at half-time and heard Dunfermline were one up at Inverness. In the dressing room, there were riots going on, the place was going bonkers about our situation.

Then out we went and lost a second goal from a penalty right away. Ross McCormack, I think it was. Hard to remember clearly, I only know I walked back to the centre circle in a daze, thinking we were a goner.

The gaffer decided to change it and brought on John Sutton and Billy Mehmet for Andy Millen and Alex Burke. Almost right away, their keeper Colin Meldrum let Sutty's header slip through his legs and it all changed.

From that moment, we were never going to lose. They just folded. Billy equalised, then we heard Caley had done the same up there, then Sutty got another one for us, then we heard Caley had scored again.

When our game ended, we thought we'd stayed up, but heard they were still playing at Inverness. Then we heard it was over up there and we were going mental, us and the fans together. But then someone else said there was still five minutes to go up there and we were left hanging on again.

Eventually, the news came through that it was definitely finished and we had definitely stayed up. To stay up with pretty much the team who'd won the First Division was some achievement, a real tribute to the gaffer and his staff and all the players. It gave us confidence to try and kick on the following season, which we did.

That day has to go down as the highlight of my career, despite the medals I've been lucky enough to win.

The league in 2000 was tremendous, because we'd been tipped for relegation at the start of the season and instead we produced some fantastic football and loads of goals. To win the title again in 2006 was magic and I think this time I maybe appreciated it more with the time that had passed.

And in the same season, we beat Hamilton 2-1 to win the Challenge Cup in front of 10,000 at Airdrie. That was a brilliant day.

The great thing about the two league titles is that we clinched them both at Love Street, the first time against Raith Rovers and then against Dundee.

It was only right that the fans got to see days like that, because they've been tremendous through some really hard times.

Leaving the place is going to be really sad. I mean, it's become my second home. I've seen those seats go into the North Bank and watched the two new stands go up behind the goals. It's changed so much as I've grown up.

I spent my first two years in the away dressing room, then graduated to across the corridor. I pretty much know every inch of the place. And I love the pitch, Tommy Doc's always kept it in beautiful nick.

We've had some great games there in my time. Like when we beat Clydebank 8-0 in the 2000 championship season and I scored the goal of my life.

The ball bounced up in front of me, I went to header it and somehow ended up juggling it on my forehead between a couple of defenders. Then I got it down, drifted past three or four more and stuck it in the corner.

People ask how I did it. I tell them honestly: Not a clue!

We just seemed to open up and play football like that all season, right from when we went to Raith and beat them 6-0 in about our third or fourth game. And then it was Raith again we played when we had to win to clinch the title."

The game was on April 29, 2000. The team: *Ludovic Roy, Tommy Turner, Barry McLaughlin, Scott Walker, Iain Nicolson (Ryan Robinson, 79),Sir Shug Murray, Ricky Gillies, Junior Mendes (Barry Lavety, 81), Paul Rudden (Ian Ross, 29), Steven McGarry, Mark Yardley.*

"THAT day was something else. It was the first time I'd ever seen Love Street full and it blew me away, but the nerves got to us and we were lucky to go in 0-0 at half-time. Tom Hendrie went mental at us, told us to get it sorted. Wee Junior Mendes really got it in the neck.

We did sort it out, though. We got three goals in six or seven minutes and after that the only decision was whether to go for more goals or sit back and make sure we didn't lose one. We couldn't wait for it to be over so we could celebrate.

When all the presentations and the lap of honour were over, we went to the bar under the Caledonia Stand, then to the Caledonia Bowling Club round the corner and then out into the town. It was an unforgettable night.

We couldn't wait to get into the SPL, but that season was hard, really hard. If I'm honest, the quality of the opposition was far better than it is now - Celtic had the likes of Larsson, Lambert and Sutton, Rangers had van Bronckhorst, Numan and Ronald de Boer. Even Motherwell had Don Goodman, John Spencer, Ged Brannan, really good operators.

Since then, a lot of clubs have run out of money and the standard's dropped. But that season? Tough going.

Anyway, I played the next season back in the First Division, before the club offered me a new contract which was ... well, let's say it disappointed me. So, in the summer of 2002, I made the biggest decision of my life and decided to move on.

Looking back, it was a gamble that backfired, a big mistake. But sometimes you have to do what you think's right at the time. So I went to Livingston for a bit, but nothing came of it. Then I heard Mansfield wanted to sign me, so I went for a week's trial, but they mucked me about.

After that, I was fed up and came home. No club, the season already started. It was a rotten time.

Then, thankfully, St Mirren came and offered me the chance to come back and I went for it. I ended up signing on for less than they'd put on the table in the first place, but it got me back playing again.

It's my one regret of all my time here, walking away. It set me back career-wise and in terms of wages.

The one positive from it was that the fans were great with me. They could easily have seen me walk out then come back and told the club to get me to you-know-where, but they didn't and I can only thank them for that.

In fact, I just want to thank them for everything over all these years. They've always given me a fair crack of the whip and were really supportive when I had my testimonial in 2007.

I got a game against Derby County, as well as an indoor tournament at the Braehead Arena and a cracking dinner, but the supporters had other fundraising dos for me and that meant a lot.

People say I'll probably be the last player who hangs around long enough to get a testimonial - and that's a bit sad. But at the time, it's maybe quite an honour for me."

AND now, like everyone else at this time of upheaval, Shug gets in the mood for reflection. Not so much about what's gone, but what still might be to come.

As the third EssPeeEll season under Gus dawned, he was outstanding in the luckless 1-0 opening day defeat at Parkhead. But that day, he was used as a holding player in a five-man midfield - and once we went back to a 4-4-2, he spent most of his time warming the bench.

After a couple of second half run-outs away to Hearts and at home to Dumbarton, he got his next start away to Dunfermline in the CIS Cup. I was up behind the goals with my son and cringed at the abuse the team took as we slumped to a 2-0 defeat.

Yes, we were really poor. But the torrent that poured down on Gus was awful - and what Shug himself took wasn't far behind. It was one of those nights when every time he touched the ball he seemed to get worse. It just wasn't happening and, five minutes before we lost the first goal, he got the hook.

There can be few more dispiriting sounds than sarcastic cheers as one of your own trudges off.

Shug didn't deserve that, poor night at the office or not. But he's smart enough to know that what he's done in the past has nothing to do with might happen to him in the future...

"GUS has been great with me, even though I've not always been in his team. He's a great man for fitness and he makes sure we all live our lives the right way, because the days of sneaking a few pies and not getting around the pitch as well as you might are long gone. The heart monitors and the body fat machines don't lie.

We've got a fitness coach, a sports scientist and a video analyst. We get our body fat taken every six weeks and the test results pinned up on the dressing room notice board. There's no hiding place if you've not met the gaffer's targets.

For me, behaving myself's not a big problem, though. I might still think like a young boy, but I'm not. I'm nearly 30 and it's time to settle down. I got married to Janine last year and we'd like to have kids soon.

They gave me a two-year contract last time round and at the time when that happens you're delighted, but it's gone before you know it. I'll be a free agent at the end of the season and if they offered me a new deal I'd be delighted to sign.

If they don't? Well, that's just part of being a footballer. There's no real security, not long-term anyway. They don't owe you anything, no matter how many games you play for them.

I don't have a clue what I'd have done if football hadn't worked out. My dad had a scrap metal business - he's retired now - but I didn't fancy going into that. As for when my career's over, I still don't know what to do. Probably I'll do my coaching badges, that'd be a start.

But there's still a good few years in me yet, I'm fit and willing and can still do a job. I still love going into my work every day - and that's what it is, your work. You're no better than anyone else.

Anyway, whatever happens to me, I wouldn't change a single thing about my time with St Mirren. Even that time I left, I ended up back here, so it was obviously meant to be. I've played in good teams and with good players. I've been lucky,

The best I've played with? I'd have to say Brian Hetherston. What a talent he was - and the pity was, no one ever saw the best of it.

His brother Peter had been a really good player with Falkirk, Raith and Aberdeen, but if he doesn't mind me saying so, Bubbles was better. Some of the things he did in training were frightening; the ball would be falling out of the sky and he'd just pull it down with his foot, almost without looking.

He was another Coatbridge boy and once I turned pro, I used to travel with him and Jim Dick. They were some pair of characters.

Brian didn't have an easy life and no one ever really got the full potential out of him at Saints, so he went on to Raith and actually played against us the day we won the league.

But he suffered from epilepsy and had a really bad attack in 2001 that did him a lot of damage. Then, in 2006, we heard he'd died. It shattered all of us who knew him.

That day, I thought back to a bounce game we'd played against Rangers at the Kibble playing fields round the corner from Love Street. Our first team were away in Ireland, but for some reason Bubbles had been left behind and played for the reserves.

He was directly up against Barry Ferguson that day, but totally dominated him and we won 2-0. That's how I'll always remember him. What a loss to the game he was."

THAT'S typical of Shug, a boy with a heart in an era when many only have an ego.

He loves his football, loves his club, would do anything for his mates.

For me, he's the last great Saint of the Love Street era. A guy who's always there, always ready, always desperate to be all he can be.

The day we beat Rangers, he was left out again. I watched him jog out to warm up, again and again, without ever getting the nod.

Then, with about five minutes left, Gus finally told him to get stripped. With four minutes to go, he sprinted on to replace Garry Brady.

With two minutes to go, 12 yards from our goal, he threw everything he had in front of Kenny Miller to prevent a certain equaliser.

With one minute to go, he was one of the four black and white heroes who climbed together on the line to stop Kirk Broadfoot's header.

That's Shug.

Play him for five minutes, play him for five seconds. But however long he's out there, you can be sure he'll leave absolutely nothing of himself behind.

"WHEN I came here as pretty much a wee boy, I couldn't have imagined becoming the first player ever to win three medals with the club. But it's happened to me, which is amazing.

It makes me feel so proud to have helped bring that kind of success to St Mirren. But as much as that, I'm proud to have played a small part in the bigger picture of the club going from the dark days when we could have gone under to the situation we're in now.

If 20 years from now, people remember me as the guy who won three trophies and helped us out of trouble, that'll do for me."

YOUR Highness, that's the least we'll remember you as.

To me, you'll always be one of the most honest men ever to wear the shirt.

To every one of us, you'll always be the man who saved the Saints.

Oh, and the application to have you elected Supreme Ruler of the Universe is in the post.

Goodbye My Friend,
It's Hard To Die...

Hampden Park, May 15, 2002.
ROBERTO CARLOS shoves the pass off to Santi Solari and hares down the line. The return ball's weighted perfectly into the left-back's path.

He meets it on the bounce, hooks it over the first defender's head.

It falls out of the sky towards Zinedine Zidane.

Time seems to stand still as he steadies himself to strike.

In that split-second of anticipation, you get the feeling something special's about to unfold before your eyes. You just didn't imagine it'd be THAT special.

I'm in the Hampden press box, right in line with the great man as he turns his shoulders, uses his arms to get his balance perfect. Anchors with his right leg, swings his left.

It's almost at right angles to his body when he meets the ball and sends it soaring in an arc, beyond the windmilling arms of Bayer Leverkeusen keeper Joerg Butt, right into the roof of the net.

You don't decide to leap out of your seat. You're up before you know it.

You applaud and you never want to stop.

Gelsenkirchen, June 16, 2006.
ARGENTINA are popping the ball about for fun. One, two, three passes. Four, five six. All in their own half. It's eight before they cross into enemy territory.

But even then, Serbia and Montenegro aren't freaking out. As it goes five yards, ten yards, from Riquelme to Mascherano to Ayala, into Cambiasso and back to Riquelme and out wide left to Sorin, they're not making a dent.

It's not until pass No21 that you realise they've only been lulling the AufSchalke Arena into thinking they were going nowhere.

Then, boom. It's Saviola into Rodriguez, back to Saviola, square across the edge of the box to Cambiasso.

In to Crespo, just inside the box.

Cambiasso runs.

Crespo back-heels.

Cambiasso hits it first time, scooping the shot left-footed, hard and high to the keeper's right.

Back in the BBC's World Cup 2006 studio, Alan Hansen gushes: "That was a masterclass. If there's a better goal in this tournament, I'm going home."

And you know what?

No matter how attractive that proposition sounded, none of us who were there could have wished for anything to top that moment.

Saitama, June 21, 2002.
WE'RE at foothills of Mount Fuji, where they come to worship their Gods.

But in a stadium on the outskirts of town, tens of thousands are singing hymns to the Big Yin's representative on earth.

Later, plenty will claim it was a fluke. Watch the eyes, though. Check the body shape. When Ronaldinho lined up THAT free-kick from 42 yards, out near the right touchline, he knew exactly what he was doing.

It was one of those moments that made you gasp. Made you gawp. And, yes, made you laugh a little.

David Seaman? He wept publicly and it was hard to blame him; the anguish and humiliation, must have been overwhelming.

Ronaldinho had started to take over the game the moment he drove at Sol Campbell and slipped a pass into Rivaldo's path to equalise Michael Owen's opener. Now, he was in total charge.

From high over his left shoulder, I watched him line up as if to dink into the mixer. But then, at the last second, he adjusted his stance, turned himself in just a touch towards the left. Gave himself a better angle to put the ball towards the far post.

No, not towards it.

Inside it.

Right between the angle of post and bar. Centimetres above Seaman's waving glove.

The level of the guy's cheek was right off the scale. Ditto the ability to place a ball into that small a gap from what far a distance.

Within ten minutes, Ronaldinho's joy would turn to fury as he saw a straight red for a nothing-y challenge on full-back Danny Mills.

But he'd get over it. One look at the replay of his golden winner would make sure of that.

Paisley, October 2008.
THREE massive occasions. Three of the best goals in footballing history.

Three more reasons I'm a lucky boy to do the job I do.

Whenever I have a look back through the cuttings, the programmes, the souvenirs from 27 years of reporting on football, the number of huge moments I've seen first hand home right between the eyes.

Your pals have to settle for seeing it all on the box. I'm there in the flesh.

It's a joy, it's a privilege.

But here's the truth.

None of it will ever compare to a two-yard deflection in off a backside in front of the Love Street end.

For me, that's TRUE football beauty.

Because it's OUR beauty.

You can gasp at ZZ's volley, find yourself hugging strangers at the mesmerising mastery of those Argentinian artistes, grin at the bucky-toothed Brazilian's gallusness and the pony-tailed Englishman's pain.

Yet you will never truly connect with them, or with any great goal you're privileged to witness.

Not unless it's of YOUR boys scoring it. And especially when he scores it at YOUR park.

And even more especially when it's not a two-yard deflection, but something a ZZ or a Ronaldinho would have been proud of...

St Mirren 1 Rangers 0
TWENTY-TWO years and 200 days they'd waited for this result.

This was their last chance.

What a wonderful way to take it.

Young Stephen McGinn had just come on as a sub to give his team fresh legs as they prepared for the final Rangers onslaught.

Instead, he used them to stride forward, pick his spot and curl the most glorious shot beyond Allan McGregor's despairing right hand and into the far corner of the net.

In that moment, he became the first Saint to score a home winner against Rangers since Billy Abercromby on April 19, 1986.

And on the Ibrox club's final league visit to Love Street, too.

It was a goal that lifted Gus MacPherson's men off the foot of the table - and surely to goodness silenced the halfwits who'd been calling for his head after a couple of dodgy results.

It was also one that condemned Rangers to a result that was nothing more than they deserved for a performance that simply never got going.

When they looked at the fixture list back in July, this must have been one of their banker away victories - and yesterday, it would have taken them three points clear of Celtic once more.

That's the beauty of football, though, even in a land where the status quo rules more often than in a 70s rock music club.

Though let's be honest here. But for McGinn's magic moment, this would have been the one of the most forgettable games in the old stadium's history.

Its gutters are leaking, its girders are creaking and its stonework's crumbling. And for 70-odd minutes here, its very foundations were groaning. From sheer boredrom.

The goal was St Mirren's only shot on target as MacPherson tried to heal the wounds of a rotten week.

As for Rangers?

Long before the end, they'd run out of ways to get through MacPherson's re-shaped 3-5-2 formation and were reduced to hitting and hoping from long range or lumping in meat and drink crosses.

Yes, they laid siege in the dying minutes. Yes, that bit made nail-biting viewing.

But it was too little, too late - and their faces at time up told you they knew it, shirts pulled over heads and eyes screwed right shut.

They'd been poor in a first half without a single clear-cut chance, but with the constant, crystal-clear soundtrack of tedious anthems about Derry's Walls, Bobby Sands, The Sash and a famine that - and as a local, I can confirm this - never reached Paisley.

Eight minutes in, Pedro Mendes went in the book for downing the charging Dennis Wyness 35 yards out. Steven Robb's curling free-kick wasn't dealt with, Garry Brady bobbled the rebound wide.

Soon after, the first Rangers opening, Kenny Miller feeding Jean

Claude Darcheville down the right of the box and Will Haining lunging into an immaculate blocking tackle.

On 25, Gary Mason played a square ball to no one and Kevin Thomson strode forward to hammer a shot that Mark Howard parried before John Potter hoofed clear.

Then it was Thomson again, slipping three half-hearted challenges before unleashing a drive that Howard tipped over.

Then, right on the break, the kind of moment that makes you unsure whether to rant or laugh about refereeing standards.

Charlie Adam met a Steven Davis corner near post, Mark Howard didn't appear to touch the ball before it went wide low at his near post, but Willie Collum gave a corner.

The Saints players and fans went mad. A goal now and Collum would be under huge TV scrutiny.

So while Davis's second centre was still in the air, he blew for a foul. Whether there was one or not.

If Rangers were going to score, you fancied them to do it off a set-piece and four minutes after the break they should have, Madjid Bougherra heading over from Adam's pinpoint right-wing corner.

Inside the next 90 seconds, both Miller and Kirk Broadfoot blazed over from inside the box, before Darcheville tested Howard from distance.

They looked visibly stung by the flea Walter Smith must surely have put in their ear.

But it didn't last.

Just before the hour, Thomson went off - carried old style by Pedro Mendes and Charlie Adam - after coming off second best in a 50-50 with Brady. On loped Kyle Lafferty.

Miller darted near post for a low cross and saw his shot deflected for a corner that led to another. As it was about to be taken, on came Kris Boyd for Darcheville, his fate sealed minutes earlier when he made to shoot from 16 yards, kicked his standing foot and fell over. The away fans had what they wanted now. Apart from a goal.

Boyd gave them a half-chance of it on 72 when he nodded a long ball deftly into Miller's path, but out telescoped Potter's right leg to save the day.

Saints threw on Craig Dargo and McGinn for Wyness and Andy Dorman, fresh legs for the final push.

McGinn - grandson of ex-Celtic chairman Jack - was there to do his running back the way, staying with midfielders as Rangers laid siege to Howard's goal.

The kid had other ideas.

The tireless Billy Mehmet did really well to keep the ball in play in front of the main stand and it found its way to the youngster.

For a moment as he let fly from 22 yards, the shot seemed to be bending wide.

But just as it got beyond the flailing McGregor, it came back like a golfer's fade, nestling just inside the post and sending the home support utterly nuts.

Fourteen minutes left now, plus VAT.

All hands, feet and heads to the pump.

Boyd headed Sasa Papac's cross flush against Howard's right-hand post. Fellow-sub Kyle Lafferty's nod from Charlie's Adam corner was kicked off line by Steven Robb and as Miller made to bury the loose ball, Shug Murray made a magnificent sliding block.

Howard turned Davis's cutback behind with his legs. When the corner came in, Kirk Broadfoot met it with a header that was heading for just under the bar.

As it looped in, FOUR black and white shirts leapt as one under the bar to clear.

That said it all about the effort St Mirren put in to winning this historic game.

The roar from the home support when Bougherra then nodded one last chance high and wide came from way down in their toes.

It said everything about what it all meant to them.

But more than for them or for the players, this was a victory for Love Street.

If it never sees another, it can clang its gate shuts with a smile.

NO bobble in off a backside, this one.

What young McGinn produced just about 3.32pm on Sunday, October 5 was absolutely stunning; both in the sense that a gorgeous woman is stunning and in the sense that it literally hit you like a frying pan in the face.

Had a Rangers player scored it at the other end, their lot would have celebrated, course they would. But after a minute or two, they'd have composed themselves and got back down to the more important business of singing about 17th century history.

Why? Because going ahead was what they believed was their right, an inevitability. For us?

Well, for 22 years and 200 days it had felt like an impossibility.

When your team does something so special this rarely, you don't cheer and then settle back into whatever mood you'd been in before the shot left the foot. You don't harumph that it's about time too.

Watching the game again later on telly, the main camera angle - on a gantry under the roof of the North Bank - didn't do McGinn's goal full justice. It was at the wrong side to capture the bend of the ball, the boy's body language as he watched it slew away from goal then back in again.

From up in the very back row of the main stand, though, it was art. It was poetry.

It was f*****g brilliant.

Jack Ross down the right touchline. Billy Mehmet, with that no-job-too-small attitude of his, craning to keep the pass in play and nod the ball into McGinn's path.

The sub striding forward, looking up, aiming for McGregor's right-hand post. Taking a split-second to realise where the ball had ended up.

After that, the biggest job was not joining in with the madness erupting all around. I had seen us beat one half of the Old Firm or other plenty times, but never from the press box. By now, I was pretty sure Love Street would close without the duck being broken.

In fact, it is to my eternal shame that I'd arrived at Love Street fully expecting us to get humped.

Yet now, out of absolutely nothing, we were leading. And it hit home. Hard.

This was it, it really was our last chance. If we threw it away now. If Rangers scrambled an equaliser. Or, worse, if...

No, hang tough. Keep the faith.

Easy to type those words now, eh? But then, on that crispy-sunny afternoon, those final 13 minutes plus three on the fourth official's board and a little dab on top of that just ... well, just because it's what the Bigot Brothers always seem to get ...

They seemed to last forever.

When you're chasing a goal, time rushes by like water over stones. When you're defending the narrowest of leads, stop all the clocks.

Anyway, it's all there in the paper. We hung on like heroes and we celebrated like cup-winners.

It was Love Street's last truly great day.

BUT if that game drove another fact of St Mirren-supporting life home, it was that as special as a goal might be, sometimes it's not the moment you remember most.

In the case of that Rangers game, that moment happened at the other end of the park. Deep in added time, Mark Howard punched a corner straight into Kirk Broadfoot's head. His effort was looping just under the bar. We held our breath.

And then FOUR - count 'em, FOUR - guys in black and white leapt under the bar to get the ball to safety.

Will Haining got his shaven head on it. But any one of Jack Ross, Shug Murray or Steven Robb would have done the business had their mate had missed.

Steve Welsh's photograph of them rising as one is one of the greatest sporting snaps I've ever seen. My paper used it across most of page 62 the next day and within hours, I'd been inundated with requests from players and punters wanting to know how they get a copy to blow up for their walls.

Yes, the goal had been unforgettable, one that would make McGinn welcome back through the doors no matter where his career took him.

That togetherness, though. That desire. That all-for-one moment of playing for the jersey ... wow, that was the one. That's what made our day.

That's what said it all for me about St Mirren and about Love Street.

Haining landing in the back of the net, cramp kicking in. The other three peeling each other off the turf. The rest running to them, back-patting and high-fiving.

Thousands of us clenching our fists and gritting our teeth and yelling with defiance. Even if, up in the press box, some of us were doing the yelling under our breath.

As all of this went on, it struck you that this was what our club was all about. This was why we allowed it to choose us, why we kept coming back no matter how crap things got.

This was why we cared.

The theme of Hope v Expectation has kept coming up in my ramblings over the years. Those who support really big teams - the Bigot Brothers, Man U, that level - don't get what it means. To them, anything but victory will always be unacceptable.

But to those who support St Mirren - and dozens of clubs like us - victory will always be a bonus.

All we ask is that if we're not going to win, we see in our players a reflection of our own passion. By which I don't mean chasing lost causes, running after through balls you know fine well are going for a bye-kick just to earn some cheap applause.

No, the real passion is making sure no cause is EVER lost.

That's what those four guys leaping to our rescue represented. Desire. In that instant, they made flesh what I've felt every time I've ever been to watch my team.

NOW, I don't claim to be the world's most devoted supporter. There are hundreds of Saints diehards who have seen five times the games I have.

Dad started taking me in '64, when I was just a toddler, but my first solid memories aren't for another four years. By 1981, I'd started as a trainee reporter on the Clydebank Press and was covering the Bankies every Saturday, so getting to Love Street turned into a midweeks-only treat.

Which means that at 46, I've really only had maybe 13 years when I was there week in, week out, home and away.

When I sat down to finish this book off with some favourite Love Street moments, it struck me that a lot of you reading it - presuming a lot of you do read it - will have been at a whole lot of games that I missed because of work.

Some of you will read about goals scored in the dark days of the early 70s and go: "Who the hell's that old tube talking about?"

Others will get to the bit about something that happened in the 80s and go: "Yeah, but this game or that goal was way better."

Others again will notice that I was out the game Saints-wise for most of the 90s and sneer: "And he calls himself a fan..."

But there are no grades of being a true fan, no shades where the black and white in your veins fade to grey like the paint on the North Bank roof.

Once you have the club in your heart, once the stadium becomes your second home, it never leaves you.

NINETEEN SIXTY-SEVEN. The year Scotland decided it was possible to become world champions without having played in the World Cup.

And when a five-year-old Foxbar boy realised his favourite team were allowed to win regularly.

After years of abortive attempts to get out of the old First Division, we'd finally got it right and were relegated. Second bottom, just four wins from 34 games, 15 measly points.

Best thing that ever happened to a kid like me, to be honest.

Because just at the age where football started to mean something,

St Mirren started playing it. We took seven off Forfar and Stenny at Love Street, six off Alloa and won the league by a street with exactly 100 goals in the tank.

What helped make Alex Wright's team even more magical for me was the fact that our centre-half Andy McFadden lived in Foxbar Road, just along from my Uncle Sam Mathers. When you're wee, that really matters. Come to think of it, if a Saints player lived round the corner from me now it'd really matter.

A year or so ago, I was hosting a club dinner when Andy was inducted into the Hall of Fame. Just seeing him there, shaking his hand, talking to him ... well, it just reminded me that stars don't need to wear bling and have a Barbie-thin WAG in tow.

Then we had Tony Connell, the left-back with the Acker Bilk goatee. Cammy Murray, the right-back who seemed to play for ever. Bobby Adamson, Bobby Pinkerton and Peter Kane scoring the bulk of the goals. Jim Blair, tall and clever, building a reputation that would take him to a Wembley final with Norwich City.

These were my first heroes. Old-looking men, some of them bald men. No coloured boots or Alice bands or armfuls of Maori tattoo. Just proper footballers.

Their flair carried us into the top flight, where we didn't lose for our first 11 games and we started to believe we never would. Everyone talks about the day Hughie Gilshan scored the winner against Rangers in the fog. In fact, if all of them were there, Love Street would have held more than the Maracana.

Me? I wasn't there. Dad never took me to see us play Rangers or Celtic, he hated the baggage the pair of them brought, so whenever we played them it was a rush to get the Evening Times Pink on a Saturday night to read the reports.

That teatime when Gilshan was written into history made me sprint back round from the Spey Avenue shops, waving the paper like Neville Chamberlain coming back from Berlin. Just like two seasons later, when the front page headline roared STONEWALL SAINTS after a battling 0-0 with the Ibrox men.

There's never been anything like seeing them and Celtic beaten on our turf. No, not even the privilege of seeing Platini, Cruyff and Gullit face Abercromby, Richardson and Copland in European ties.

To beat the Old Firm - particularly when we were doing it regularly in the 80s - was just wonderful; I mean, the day in '83 when we were 2-0 down to Celtic and came back to win 4-2 with Ian Scanlon scoring from what felt like somewhere beyond the Town Hall? It just blew you away.

Between '79-80 and '85-'86, we played Rangers 14 times at home in the league, won eight and drew four. We beat them 4-1, we beat them 3-0. We OWNED them, baby.

That's what made the day of McGinn and the four-man goal-line clearance so important. One more punch landed on their snooty chins before we moved out.

OF COURSE, that unbeaten run in '68 had to end. And once it did, the normality of fighting relegation kicked back in. We lasted until the end of '70-'71, when only taking one point out of four from Dunfermline was enough to let them stay up on goal average and send us down with Cowdenbeath instead.

Along the way, a couple of games stand out more than any others.

In the winter of '69, we fought out a fantastic floodlit 3-3 draw with that Hibs team starring Peter Marinello, Alex Cropley, Alex Edwards and more.

For some reason, dad and I watched it from the enclosure under the stand. Thinking back, it feels like the place was mobbed. I can still see every detail, down to the little green hoop around the white collars on the Hibs shirts.

Weird what football does to the mind.

The other game? January 71, a second replay with East Fife in the Third Round of the Scottish Cup. We'd drawn 1-1 at Bayview, then the replay had ended with the same score. No penalty shootouts back then, so the captains tossed a coin and the second replay was back at ours.

By the time it came around, we knew the winner would play Rangers at Love Street, a fact that added a real extra edge to your day as your mind wandered away from schoolwork, as you counted the minutes till dad got in from work and had his tea, as you got your first glimpse of the lights, clicked through the gates, heard the crackling tannoy.

I knew that, as ever, we wouldn't be at the Rangers game if we got through. If anything, that made winning this one all the more important.

It went to extra-time that night, Archie Knox got a hat-trick and we won 3-1.

A lot of younger fans probably don't even realise Knox played for us, have only seen him in the dugout with Fergie at Aberdeen and Man U and with Walter Smith at Rangers. But he was a great signing for us, a qualified quantity surveyor who came from Forfar and hit some thunderous goals from midfield.

221

I couldn't tell you what his goals were like that night. But in my mind, they were all magnificent.

Was there ever a St Mirren goal that wasn't?

BACK to the Second Division, this time for the long haul.

Until Fergie turned up, it was a spell that saw us drop from fourth to fifth to - whisper it - 11th over three increasingly desperate seasons.

Love Street in those days always looms in the mind as wet, dank, chilly. Shouts and groans echoing around terraces that once held 47,000, but where now 4000 would have the treasurer doing cartwheels.

To me, not yet out of primary school, there was always optimism. I'd always believe we were just one goal, just one win away from turning the corner.

That first campaign after relegation will always remain one of my favourites of all time, even if it ended in the disappointment of missing promotion by a couple of points.

There were just so many goals at Love Street, so many thrilling games. Plus, we'd unearthed talents like Gordon McQueen, Ally McLeod and Bobby McKean, guys who made us a few bob when they moved on - £30,000 from Leeds for McQueen, £40,000 from Hibs for McLeod, £50,000 from Rangers for McKean - but who'd have been worth fortunes had they come through ten years later.

I remember us being 3-1 down to Arbroath, who'd eventually go up, until the brilliant, unpredictable McLeod stepped in with a hat-trick and we won 4-3.

And then there was McQueen's goal against Albion Rovers.

We beat them 4-0 and I'm pretty sure it was the fourth. We were defending at the Caledonia Street end when this gawky, puppet-looking teenage centre-half dribbled out of his own box, got those big Bambi legs shifting. And simply kept going.

On. And on. And on. All the way up the park, me and dad and the rest with widening eyes as he came towards us. Then he hesitated and you wondered if he'd realised where he was and his bottle had gone.

No chance.

The big fella was only sizing his options up, before absolutely hammering a shot from 18 yards that went through the bottom of the net and trickled out onto the grass behind the goals.

But there was just so much going on that season.

When we lost 1-0 to Stenny, everybody seemed to be in their box for about the last half hour and our captain, Willie Fulton, hit the bar with an overhead kick. When we beat Queen's Park 6-2, they had a right-winger called Alf Stamp who was 6ft 7in.

We only drew two games out of 36, both at home and both within days of each other over Christmas, against Clydebank and Dumbarton. With the best goal average in the division, those results were enough to keep us down when it was all over.

The following season, we still couldn't stop scoring at home - five fours, two fives, a six and seven. The seven always sticks with me, on a day when Hamilton Accies only managed one in return and Gus McLeod scored five of ours.

I won the first goal sweep on him that day, 2p each from our seven-strong gaggle. Felt like a millionaire.

In '73-'74, we sunk to the lowest point in our history, the bottom half of the bottom level. But there was the odd bright spot; like Bobby McKean writing a piece of history that remains intact today.

Last man in Scotland to score a hat-trick of penalties.

Now, here's a strange one. Can't remember who we were playing, but one day in September dad and I couldn't make it to an away match, so we went to Cappielow to watch Morton play Hearts. It finished 3-2 to the Jambos, with Donald Ford scoring all three from the spot.

It was such a rarity we wondered if we'd ever see the like again. Yet just a few months later, after we'd been held 0-0 at half-time by Brechin, our terrific little right-winger matched it.

Right in line with us at the Love Street end, too.

That was also the season we played Stranraer in a Scottish Cup replay on a midweek afternoon because it was the middle of the Miners' Strike and the three-day week. And when we were 3-0 down to Clyde in the League Cup and ending up losing 5-4.

In August '74, I started secondary school. My present from the Buds was a 6-0 humping in the first home game of the season, a League Cup group tie against Airdrie. If memory serves, they even missed a penalty.

That was the campaign when we played Meadowbank for the first time, rattling four past them, and the one when Fergie took over. The next season, we staggered over the line in sixth place, two points ahead of Clydebank and just good enough to make it into the revamped First Division.

On January 17, 1976, we pulled in our first 10,000 crowd under Fergie as we lost 3-2 to Thistle. Pretty soon, gates like that would be the norm, but I've already bored you to death about those days earlier in the book.

So I'll only mention the game against Montrose when we celebrated winning the title in '77, when Bonnie Barr's Majorettes formed a guard of honour for Fergie and the team, when the trophy was handed over and when big Bobby Reid, our own Hen Broon of a centre-half, leapt what seemed 20 feet in the air at the Love Street end to bullet home an overhead kick.

He scored ten times that season, astonishing for a defender. Within another year, his career would have been ruined by a knee wrecked playing for the Scottish League.

What a waste of a fantastic talent, a guy who'd have gone south and been bigger than Alan Hansen.

THE last season of the 70s, the first of the 80s. The start of what we thought was our new life.

Unbeaten at home in the league to the Bigot Brothers and eventual champions Aberdeen - Fergie and all. Third top, our highest-ever finish

Into the UEFA Cup, our first-ever adventure.

All that and the Anglo-Scottish Cup on the table, too. That was one of the great nights, when we ran all over the top of Bristol City to win 3-1 and 5-1 on aggregate. We had 13,000-odd in, the new squared-off Love Street End terrace chocca.

Then it was September and Love Street was seeing European football - even if it would be five years before it saw us score a European goal, Brian Gallagher against Slavia Prague.

Nil-nil against Elfsborg. Nil-nil against St Etienne. One-nil to Feyenoord. All we are saying is...

Still, what amazing occasions. Paisley St Mirren, from losing six at home to Airdrie to taking on Johann Cruyff in six whirlwind years.

In '80-'81, we'd have been in Europe again but for Rangers pipping us on goal difference. We were watching Jimmy Bone go on a mazy from halfway against Aberdeen that won him Goal of the Season from BBC Scotland and still has us talking today.

Me? I was enjoying my last season as a full-time supporter. Well, until they pension me off.

It was only three years later when I went to the Paisley & Renfrewshire Gazette that I got down to Love Street anything like regularly again, though by then I was doing a bit of freelance work that took me around the country to earn a few extra bob.

Calls from the Daily Telegraph were always particularly welcome.

See, they'd seen somewhere that part of our group of papers was called The Johnstone Gazette. So they took me on to cover the local team.

You know, St Johnstone.

Well, it would have been rude for me to contradict the sports desk of such a massive national paper, wouldn't it?

After that, the only spell where I got my fix was while working as a news reporter for the Paisley Daily Express from the end of '84 until the summer of '88. Most weeks I went as a punter, but when our sportswriter Stan Park was off, I filled in.

Sadly for him, but luckily for me, he was ill throughout most of the '87 run to Hampden. Lucky for him, but crap for me, he was back for the final.

Saturday, May 16 1987 was a golden day in the life of a magnificent club.

Sunday, May 17 was the day the stadium got to join in the celebrations.

It's all still a bit of a blur to me, the homecoming. Too much writing to do off the back of too much bevvy the night before.

Plus, I spent most of the day seething with anger.

Some kind of strange loyalty has always stopped me having a go about this for 21 years, but bollocks to it. No more.

The Paisley Daily Express coverage of the final in Monday's edition was scandalous.

See, we printed in Irvine back then, so the deal was that Monday's paper had to be done and dusted on a Friday. Why? Dunno, probably so the top of the tree could get the weekend off. The only hole they left was for the match report from the Saturday game.

But this ... well, this was a one-off. A once in a generation event, maybe even once in a lifetime. We'd done an eight-page pull-out for the semi against Hearts and a 24-pager on the morning of the final. Surely they had to change the rules and start from scratch if we won the thing?

Forget it.

We got Stan's report on the back - **SAINTS SHOOT BACK ON THE MAP!** - a centre-page picture of the open-topped bus and a snap on the front page of Ian Ferguson in his club blazer with the lid of the cup on his head.

The big story on page one that day?

BEWARE OF THE SUMMER THIEVES: Police warn householders to lock all doors and windows.

I was furious. Embarrassed. Still am to this day when I think about it. This should have been a paper to keep forever, one that they had to reprint to keep up with demand.

Instead, it was a waste of ink and trees. A paper I loved had been disrespectful to the club I love, the whole organisation behind the decision to all but ignore the Scottish Cup Final lazy and complacent as hell.

Never felt the same about working there after that.

And I'm glad the whole thing's off my chest at last.

THROUGH the nineties, it was back to midweek visits and the odd Saturday when I wasn't covering a game somewhere else until the Sunday.

Not the worst time to go missing, to be honest.

Relegated from the Premier in '91, treading water in the First for too many years. The whole Reg Brealey business, nearly dropping into the Second.

All that and an array of strips that would have given Barry Venison a migraine.

Not a decade Love Street will remember with much fondness. Not until its final year, at least.

By then, though, it didn't really matter what division we were in, what results we got, whether the crowds flocked in or voted with their feet.

The home of football, the town's other cathedral, the venue of legends and dog-ends, was living on borrowed time. The chairman's said it a few chapters back - it wasn't a case of if we'd eventually have to flit, only of when.

That when is now.

And all the reminiscing, all the moaning, all the tears and souvenirs in the world can't change that.

When I was a teenager with more scarves tied round my person than hairs on my chin, we used to sing a version of the old Terry Jacks song, Seasons In The Sun.

"We had joy, we fun, we had Morton on the run..."

Don't know why, but that came back into my head when I was thinking about this final chapter. Especially the line that's become its title.

Goodbye my friend, it's hard to die...

Real mood-killer, that one. But so many of its lines seem to fit right now.

This morning, the last before the book went to the printer, the front door went. It was a courier, delivering a big, rectangular cardboard parcel that made my heart race the way no cardboard should.

Inside it, swathed in bubble wrap, a moment in time had been captured forever.

A giant canvas blow-up of Will Haining, Ross Jack, Hugh Murray and Steven Robb, leaping under the crossbar to head Broadfoot's effort to safety in the dying seconds of the win over Rangers.

It's awe-inspiringly lovely.

The straining neck veins, the toes pointing for extra lift. You can almost hear their hearts pound in unison.

And in the background, the main stand. Tommy the groundsman's Tardis, the bit where the posh punters went when I was wee, but where I work now on matchdays.

You can see fans standing up in the enclosure. The press box right at the back of all the seats. The announcer's box where Fred Douglas once announced that Clydebank were losing and inspired Fergie's team to snatch a last-gasp winner over Hamilton that eased us towards the title.

On the advertising boards, names like the Clydesdale Bank, such a huge player in the stadium's demise. The Argyll Bar, that would rock with Saints songs all that night.

Decades from now, that photograph will be a time capsule of Love Street's final days.

Think of me and I'll be there, Terry Jacks sang.

Didn't realise he was one of us.

LOVE STREET. Where we learned of love and ABCs, skinned our hearts and skinned our knees.

What was it wee Chick said? A magical place that always makes you feel better, no matter how life's treating you?

And every time when I was down,

You would always come around.

And get my feet back on the ground...

We've all felt the place do that to us when we've caught sight of those glowing lights, clicked through those turnstiles, climbed those steps.

When we've stood at the top of the old terrace behind the goal, peering down on Subbuteo-size players warming up. When we've made our way down and round to our usual spot and settled in beside all the usual faces.

When we're reading the programme, from black-and-white, 6d-a-go photocopied job with the old stick-insect Saint on the front through to £2 worth of glossy magazine.

When we used to hear old Peter - or Big Jim Blair as we all knew him back in the 70s - lolloping over the brow of the terraces with his sombrero on, no teeth in and yodelling: "Olee-olee-olee-olee!"

When a goal out of nothing's lit up the grimmest afternoon. When we've won against all odds.

When McAvennie was teasing markers, Peter Weir was skinning full-backs. When Jim Thorburn or Danny Stevenson, Campbell Money or Billy Thomson were flying to keep shots out.

When one Fergie was being sacked, when another was sitting in the stand sulking until he got his move to Rangers.

When we drooled over our heroes and groaned that the ones we couldn't stand were in the team again.

When we bonded with our dad in a way no other part of our week allowed us. When he put a hand on our shoulder and told us to never mind, we'd win next week.

When he was no longer around to make everything better and we kidded on it didn't matter.

When he told our kids the very same thing and knew they believed us.

When we sneaked a half-bottle of El Dorado in down our flares and passed it round our bum-fluffed mates, then bawled our lungs out for another 90 minutes that took the same again off our life expectancy.

Oh yes, my friends, we had joy, we had fun. We had seasons in the sun.

But the wine and the songs, like the seasons, have all gone...

The End.
Of It All...

Thanks

To Tommy Docherty, Matt Kerr, Stewart Gilmour, George Campbell, Sir Shug Murray, Chick Young, Gordy Waddell and Iain Macfarlane for their time and their words.

To Norman Macdonald for his patience in waiting for all this to come to pass. Not to mention the most valuable four years training I ever had; take his word for it, would-be journalists - if you're not smart enough that they can send you out to interview Prince Charles, don't bother turning up for work.

To Kenny and Georgia for putting up with this taking up so much of their dad's time when he could have been spending it with them. And for never getting annoyed that when he does turn up, he's always late.

To my beloved dad for taking me to Love Street in the first place and to mum for letting her life be dominated by football.

To every player who ever wore a St Mirren shirt at Love Street, even the duff ones. I envy the lot of you.

And to Love Street itself. For everything.